# My Name is Bridget

# My Name is Bridget

## THE UNTOLD STORY OF BRIDGET DOLAN
## AND THE TUAM MOTHER AND BABY HOME

**Alison O'Reilly**

*Gill Books*

Gill Books
Hume Avenue
Park West
Dublin 12
www.gillbooks.ie

Gill Books is an imprint of M.H. Gill & Co.

978 07171 8042 4

Print origination by O'K Graphic Design, Dublin
Copy-edited by Rachel Pierce
Proofread by Emma Dunne
Printed by CPI Group (UK) Ltd, Croydon CR0 4YY

All family photos courtesy of Anna Corrigan

This book is typeset in 11.5/17 pt Adobe Garamond with chapter heads in Formata Light.

The paper used in this book comes from the wood pulp of managed forests. For every tree felled, at least one tree is planted, thereby renewing natural resources.

A CIP catalogue record for this book is available from the British Library.

5 4 3 2 1

**Alison O'Reilly** is an award-winning documentary-maker, broadcaster and journalist from Drogheda, Co. Louth. In 2014 Alison broke the story of the Tuam Babies burial scandal which made international headlines and led to the setting up of a Commission of Inquiry into the Mother and Baby Homes in Ireland. Since then, Alison has written extensively about the Tuam Babies and has spoken to survivors and the families of the children who died there.

Alison began her career in 1994 and has worked with several broadcasting companies including MTV Europe, Sky News, TV3 and 98FM. Her specialised areas of interest include Children's Rights, Mother and Baby Homes, adoptions and crime. In 2007 she won Best Human Rights Director at the San Francisco Women's Film Festival for her documentary *Midnight's Lost Child.* The same year she directed the critically acclaimed documentary series *My Heroin Hell, Rachael's Story* about former heroin addict and bestselling author Rachael Keogh. In 2015 Alison won a Justice Media Award for her work on Irish adoptions and also produced the hard-hitting documentary *Born Addicted.* She has been nominated for Journalist of the Year and Crime Journalist of the Year in the National Newspapers of Ireland Journalism Awards. Alison has worked for a number of national newspapers and is currently a reporter with the *Irish Daily Mail.*

## Notes

All *Irish Mail on Sunday* articles and interviews referenced in this book were researched, conducted and written by Alison O'Reilly.

All *Irish Daily Mail* articles and interviews referenced in this book, as well as all new interviews, including Chapter 13's 'Snapshots of Stolen Lives', were researched, conducted and written by Alison O'Reilly, apart from articles written and referenced by her *Irish Daily Mail* colleague Neil Michael.

Anna Corrigan was not paid for her story; she wanted to tell it in the name of truth and justice. Alison O'Reilly has made a donation to the post-adoption unit of Barnardos Children's Charity.

*This book is dedicated to the memory of the Tuam Babies and their mothers, and to all children who died while in the care of the Irish state and religious orders.*

*I would also like to dedicate this book to my late grandmother, Mai Giggins. My nanny was an inspirational and multi-talented woman who worked exceptionally hard all her life while raising her 13 children alone. She went on to be a proud grandmother, great-grandmother and great-great-grandmother to more than 80 children. As a young teenager, Nanny helped rescue two girls from a Magdalene Laundry with my great-grandmother Margaret Doyle. No matter what came her way, my nanny never stopped getting up and getting on with it. I will always miss you, Nan. Wherever I am, you'll always be.*

# Acknowledgements

With heartfelt thanks to Anna Corrigan for opening her heart and home to me over the past four years. It is Anna's hope that Bridget's story will shine a light on the struggle of thousands of women and children who spent time in Ireland's Mother and Baby Homes.

With special thanks to Catherine Corless and the Tuam Babies Family Group, including Annette McKay, Professor Thomas Garavan and Teresa Waldron, for sharing their stories with me. To the Tuam Survivors Network and the survivors who shared their stories in this book, John Paul Rodgers, Peter Mulryan, Loraine Jackson, Michael O'Flaherty, Margaret Norton, Eileen Macken, Michael Byrne, Pat Duffy, Finbarr O'Regan, Desmond Lally, Breda Tuite, Sharon McGuigan, Terri Harrison, David Kinsella, Sheila O'Byrne, Diane Croghan, Kevin Sharkey, Niall Boylan, Clodagh Malone, Helena Madden Feeney and Mannix Flynn. And for all those affected by the story and who took the time to speak to me.

I would also like to sincerely thank Niall Donald for all his help and support in the writing of this book, and Niall Meehan for his vital checks on my Irish history.

With love and thanks to my beautiful children and to all the children I've been blessed to have in my care. To my parents, Mary and Patrick O'Reilly, thank you for all your support.

To Lennon, Patrick, Claude, Pippa, Sophia, Aubrey, Katie, Sheldon, Aaron, Abi, Remi Rose, Kito, Duglan, Tiernan, Kathryn, Ciara and Conor.

To Teena Gates, Edel Smith, Emma Keegan, Lisa Gernon, Rachel Keogh, Karen Morgan and Shaneda Daly for their patience and kindness.

With special thanks to my Head of News at the *Irish Daily Mail*, Aiden Corkery, who gave me the time and support to produce the 2014 Tuam Babies story and for his continuing kindness. And with thanks to all of the journalists and bloggers who helped keep this story in the media.

Thank you to Noelle Dowling at the Dublin Archdiocese Archives, Grainne O'Carroll and everyone at the GRO Research Room in Dublin, the National Library, Dame Professor Sue Black, Archaeologist Toni Maguire, the National Archives and Patria McWalter at Galway County Council Archives.

With thanks to Professor Geoffrey Shannon and Patricia Carey in the Adoption Authority of Ireland.

To everyone at Gill Books, including Catherine Gough, Sarah Liddy, Teresa Daly, and to Rachel Pierce and Emma Dunne for their editorial work.

# Contents

# Introduction:
# The Moment of Truth

*'Significant quantities of human remains have been discovered.'*

When those eight words were spoken by Minister Katherine Zappone on 3 March 2017, they still had the power to shock, even for those who already knew they were inevitable. The minister was announcing the findings of the initial excavations at the Mother and Baby Home in Tuam, County Galway, which had been ordered by the Commission of Investigation into Mother and Baby Homes. The following day, those eight hard-hitting words would appear in the headlines of hundreds of newspapers and websites in every corner of the globe. It was a very chilling and a very public indictment of both the Church and the Irish state – and, if truth be told, of the Irish people.

The stark facts presented by the team that had conducted the geophysical survey – effectively confirming that the bodies of hundreds of dead children had been buried in a mass, unmarked grave – struck a fresh and horrified chord with people who had become apathetic and desensitised to the crimes of the past associated with the Catholic Church. Even in a world where hundreds of thousands of children are killed every day in various brutal and casual ways, the idea of the remains of innocent children being disposed of in a septic tank was deeply disturbing. The idea that both the Church and the Irish government could have treated children as less than fully human because of a so-called accident of birth, especially in the aftermath of the horrors of the Second World War, was an extremely difficult fact to accept. But there was no denying it now.

What had once been whispered as rumour and gossip was now a proven fact, and Irish people were going to have to come to terms with it.

In the course of her speech describing the findings, Minister Zappone didn't give a body count, but the world was told that the bodies of the children, who were aged between 35 foetal weeks and two to three years old, had been identified as residents of St Mary's Mother and Baby Home in Tuam, all dating to its years of operation, between 1925 and 1961. Through no fault of their own, these innocent children were condemned from birth by Church, state and society, and when their tiny bodies gave up, they were put down in the ground with no dignity and their unmarked, unconsecrated burial place was covered up, never to be mentioned again.

The archaeological team who excavated the site found children's remains in 17 of the 20 chambers of a disused septic tank buried underground in the middle of what is now a housing estate on the Dublin Road in Tuam. The remains were exhumed and taken away for analysis in a laboratory, where experts used dating techniques to determine their exact age. Those findings demolished a theory that had been put forward by Catholic commentators, who had insisted that any bones discovered on the site would date to the Famine era, more than 150 years ago. That wasn't the case.

It fell to Minister Katherine Zappone to tell the world the truth about the Tuam Mother and Baby Home. The press conference was not pre-planned. It was called at the very last minute and reporters rushed to Government Buildings in Dublin to find out what this was all about. This particular press conference had that rare quality in modern politics – the unexpected. In an era where everything seems to get leaked in advance, the excavation's findings had remained a well-kept secret. There had been some odd claims on social media, but no one had confirmed anything.

As the minister stood in front of the microphone in a packed press room, her face said it all – she knew she was delivering news that would reverberate around the world and change many lives forever.

There was a long history leading to this moment. Ninety-two years earlier, the Tuam Mother and Baby Home had opened its doors to young women abandoned by their families and their communities. Five years earlier, an amateur historian called Catherine Corless had begun asking questions about the babies who had not survived the Home – where were they? Three years earlier the *Irish Mail on Sunday* had broken a story no one had wanted to believe – that the babies were buried in a septic tank, dumped and forgotten. Two years earlier the Irish government had established the Commission of Investigation, directing it to examine the records and practices of 14 Mother and Baby Homes and four county homes. The Commission was the response to the exposé carried on the front page of the *Irish Mail on Sunday*, which was headlined: 'A Mass Grave of 800 Babies'. And over all those long years, women and their surviving children had spoken and accused and asked and demanded to know what had happened and, crucially, why it had happened. Catherine Corless had been their tireless advocate, saying over and over again:

> The children are there, I know they are there. We just have to find them, find which area they are in because I believe, and my research shows me, that the children are buried all over the site, not just in the grave we know. They are there absolutely.

This moment of truth had been a long time coming.

It was time for Minister Zappone to speak. Indeed, her willingness to speak out so quickly was striking. Another TD might have held off for a while, might have postponed opening the floodgates. Minister Zappone was herself an outsider in many ways, but she had won the trust of some of the groups representing the survivors of Mother and Baby Homes. Along with adoption groups, they had been campaigning for years, writing to successive Ministers for Children about the tragic circumstances surrounding how they came to be separated from their mothers. She had won their trust by proving to have an appetite for confronting the past unflinchingly, without keeping an eye on the potential for future costs for the government – and she wasn't going to let them down now. Earlier that morning she had telephoned Catherine Corless, who had uncovered the names of the children, to say this news simply could not wait.

*'Significant quantities of human remains have been discovered ...'*

There was a shocked silence in the room. Journalists, photographers and cameramen exchanged glances, knowing they were the first people to hear a story that was going to sweep over the country like a tsunami. The minister continued to read her notes and press release calmly, but with an air of sorrow in her voice:

> This is very sad and disturbing news. It was not unexpected as there were claims about human remains on the site over the last number of years.
>
> Up to now we had rumours. Now we have confirmation that the remains are there, and that they date back to the time of the Mother and Baby Home, which operated in Tuam from 1925 to 1961.

Her words were backed up by a statement released by the Commission of Investigation itself. The Commission had received its Terms of Reference in February 2015, described by then Minister for Children James Reilly as an 'independent commission, which has a three-year deadline and which will cost approximately €21 million', following the signing by then Taoiseach Enda Kenny. Since then, an interdepartmental scoping exercise had been carried out, along with an invitation to survivors of the homes to give their testimony to the Commission. A second interim report had been published on 11 April 2017, but today's announcement was very different. The Commission stated:

The stratigraphic survey, which was conducted in October 2015, identified a particular area of interest and identified a number of sub-surface anomalies that were considered worthy of further investigation.

These were further investigated by a test excavation in November/December 2016 and in January/February 2017. Test trenches were dug, revealing two large structures. One structure appears to be a large sewage containment system or septic tank that had been decommissioned and filled with rubble and debris and then covered with top soil.

The second structure is a long structure which is divided into 20 chambers. [The Commission had not determined what the purpose of the structure was, but it appeared to be a sewage tank.] In this second structure, significant quantities of human remains have been discovered in at least 17 of the 20 underground chambers which were examined.

A small number of remains were recovered for the purpose of analysis. These remains involved a number of individuals with age-at-death ranges from approximately 35 foetal weeks to two to three years.

Radiocarbon dating of the samples recovered suggest that the remains date from the timeframe relevant to the operation of the Mother and Baby Home. (The Mother and Baby Home operated from 1925 to 1961; a number of the samples are likely to date from the 1950s.) Further scientific tests are being conducted.

Minister Zappone finished her speech by saying she was 'here for the survivors', then she opened the discussion to the floor. One by one, the microphone carried by one of the Government Press Officers was passed to each journalist. They asked question after question: who were these children? Who were their families? How many children were there in the grave? Will the area be sealed off? Were the Gardaí involved? Will the children's remains be exhumed? How do we explain this to the families who have been affected? These seasoned reporters were stunned by what they had heard, and the air of shock and horror in the room that day was unforgettable.

The Minister confirmed that a helpline had been set up to support anyone affected by the revelations, but to every question she replied that she didn't have any more information, that she did not know how many children were in the grave. She could only go on what information the Commission had given her, and its work was not yet finished. In spite of this, she had felt the news was not something that could wait.

The news emanating from the press conference spread like wildfire. Within an hour of the announcement, news of the children's remains was all across America as the international press scrabbled to find out what exactly had happened. Their first port of call was Catherine Corless, the woman who had uncovered the children's names. Her response that day was that while she was 'shocked', she 'knew they were there, the Minister knew she could not sit on this information and that it had to come out now. I appreciate that.'

—

The shocking moment of revelation about the Tuam Mother and Baby Home was preceded by a long and dedicated search by Catherine Corless, aided and urged on by adoption groups and survivors, and by one particularly dedicated woman, Anna Corrigan. Anna was the daughter of Bridget Dolan, a woman who had survived the Tuam Mother and Baby Home and delivered two babies there. The question of what had happened to her brothers drove Anna to find an answer. Anna is an ordinary public sector worker and mother of two from an estate in West Dublin, but she is an unsung hero of the Tuam story.

After Minister Zappone's announcement about the findings at the Home, Catherine Corless fielded press inquiries for the next few weeks, talking to reporters all over the world from her home in Tuam, County Galway. She spoke again and again about how she had researched the

Home and the fate of its youngest, most vulnerable residents. She had done all this in 2013, but back then not everyone had believed her research.

Catherine's interest in the Mother and Baby Home stretched back to her own childhood. Some of the Home's residents had attended her school, and she remembered well how no one would speak to them, and how she herself had once mocked a girl from the Home, pretending to give her a sweet but instead giving her a stone to eat and then laughing at her. In later years, she started to ask around about the Home and the children who had died there, and especially about the children's graves. They were located in the centre of a housing estate and were tended to by the Dooley family for a long time. Catherine wrote an article about it in 2012 for the *Journal of the Old Tuam Society* (she didn't have evidence of any kind at that point), but it had been largely ignored. At that time, she had not uncovered the names of the children, but she knew a grave existed.

Driven by a need to know who the children were, Catherine went to the Births and Deaths Registry in Galway and was lucky to meet there a woman called Ann Glennon, who was exceptionally helpful. With no idea where this story was going to end up, Ann Glennon began compiling a list of names of children whose death certs listed 'Tuam Mother and Baby Home' as the place of death. Night after night she worked in the Registry, putting together the list on foot of Catherine's request for information. Speaking to this author on 26 February 2018 at her place of work, the shy and modest civil servant said, 'It took time, but it's a privilege to help out'.

Once she received the full list, Catherine cross-checked the names with Galway County Council Archivist Patria McWalter to ensure they had not been claimed by families and buried elsewhere. She then searched for the burials in surrounding counties, but there were no burial records for any of the children. They had to be in Tuam.

There was local evidence to support her findings. The grave on the housing estate had been discovered in the 1970s by 10-year-old Barry

Sweeney and his friend, 12-year-old Francis Hopkins. Mr Sweeney described it as follows:

> It was a concrete slab and we used to play there, but there was always something hollow underneath it so we decided to bust it open, and it was full to the brim of skeletons. The priest came over and blessed it. I don't know what they did with it after that. You could see all the skulls.

Barry Sweeney's brother knew Anna Corrigan, and she put him in touch with Catherine Corless so he could tell her his story, giving her another piece of the puzzle. And there was another local who had also chanced upon the forgotten grave. Mary Moriarty recalled how finding an unsuspecting child playing with a baby's skull led her to the grisly discovery in 1975. Mary thought she'd found a crypt:

> I crawled over the wall to the child and I asked him if I could look at the skull and he said, 'It's plastic, it's from Halloween,' but when I looked at it I knew it wasn't because it had teeth. So I said, 'Put it back where you got it because that's a proper skull, it must be from the Home.' I went out with my neighbour and there was two other women and we went down to have a look and it took ages to get through the rubble and the bushes but eventually we got in there, the three of us, we could see a hole in the ground and we were looking down and next thing my feet went down from under me and I slid down part of it.

According to Catherine's research, the oldest child who died at the Home was Sheila Tuohy, aged nine, in 1934. One of the youngest was Thomas Duffy, aged just two days old. Most of the children were buried in shrouds, and according to Mary Moriarty, they weren't in coffins. They had been buried and forgotten. Until now.

The caretaking family, the Dooleys, contacted the local councillor, the late Joe Burke, in the 1970s and he in turn organised for the county council to close the entrance to the burial site, level the ground and re-seed the area. Over the years Mr and Mrs Dooley tended the site, cutting the grass, planting shrubs and roses, and they also laid a small cross.

Catherine set up the Children's Home Graveyard Committee, with the aim of erecting a memorial to commemorate the 796 infants buried at Tuam. The committee had a target of raising €50,000 to complete its project. It contacted local media in Galway for help, and that got the fundraising campaign rolling. The committee's focus was that the buried children would at least be remembered. The memorial plaques soon became the central issue, however, obscuring the fact that hundreds of babies and children were lying in a septic tank in a mass grave in the West of Ireland.

The fate of the Tuam Babies had been spoken at last by Catherine Corless and the Children's Home Graveyard Committee, but no one heard them properly. No one except Anna Corrigan, who was busy in the background, gathering a broader picture of the Home that her two brothers had been born in. Initially, Anna thought the memorial plaque to record the names of the dead children was a great idea, when she believed it was a graveyard. But once she'd found out it was a septic tank, it troubled her and gave her sleepless nights. What struck her most was how no one had picked up on the significance of the burial site. It was a septic tank, not a recognised graveyard. Anna couldn't believe the reaction, or rather, the lack of reaction:

Everyone wanted a plaque for the children. It was like old Ireland again, people finding a children's grave, a priest comes and blesses it and it's covered up. No investigation, nothing. And that's the end of it. Cover it all up and leave it at that.

Martin Sixsmith, who had written the book on Philomena Lee's tragic story about her late son Anthony, had visited the Tuam grave with the

BBC in February 2014, after Anna put him in contact with Catherine Corless. But again, the story failed to make the waves it should have made. So, Anna decided to bring the story to the national media.

Three months later, on 25 May 2014, the *Irish Mail on Sunday* exposed the story of the mass grave and a large black-and-white photo of Anna's mother, Bridget Dolan, was placed at the heart of the feature. But it wasn't until the following Monday, 2 June, when the article appeared on the Mailonline website, that the international media sat up and took notice. The story poured out all over social media in an explosion of disbelief. No one could quite believe that this horror story was coming from a small town in Co. Galway.

The foundation of the story was Catherine's meticulous, careful research, which was backed up with documentation and first-person accounts at every point. But once the story broke, there was a backlash against Catherine's research and conclusions, led by commentators who poured cold water all over the story, dismissing it as the work of an over-eager housewife, even though they hadn't unearthed any facts to disprove her findings. Nonetheless, it left many people with the impression that the Tuam Babies story was an exaggeration, a bit of anti-Catholic hype. It took three years for those unfounded views to be comprehensively disproved and dismissed – in the moment that Minister Zappone told the world that it was all true.

—

When Anna Corrigan got a call ahead of Minister Zappone's announcement, 25 minutes before the news broke, she stopped making the dinner, grabbed her house keys and got a lift into town. While her mother's story had featured in the first article in the *Irish Mail on Sunday*, Anna had kept her anonymity for three years, due to ill health, despite playing a key role alongside Catherine Corless in bringing the story of the Tuam Babies to the world.

Ahead of the announcement, Anna was not given any official details and neither were any other families who had relatives buried there. They were never told of the find or of the imminent press release. The warning phone call came from Catherine Corless, who told Anna that an announcement was being made at Government Buildings after 11.00 a.m. that morning, and that remains of children had been found in the grave – and the world was about to find out.

Anna later described that hugely significant day as one of the most troubling days of her life, saying she was in complete shock when the news came out of the blue. Anna later said her two brothers, John and William Dolan, were the only thing on her mind when she heard the news. It took her less than a minute to decide what to do next. As she ran from her house in West Dublin and threw on her jacket, she remembered to notify all members of her recently established Tuam Babies Family Group. She frantically sent text messages to everyone affected, in the hope of letting them know what was about to happen before they heard it from anyone else.

In the meantime, Catherine was also trying to inform everyone who needed to know first.

Anna arrived at Government Buildings and made her way into the packed press room just as Minister Zappone was finishing her speech. Anna would say later: 'People had told me this day would never happen, that the grave would never be excavated. But I always knew it would, and that it had to happen.'

Even so, the news came as a complete shock to her. The 796 names of all the children who died from 1925 to 1961 had been made available by the Department of Social Protection in 2014 while under the leadership of Labour's Joan Burton, then a minister. Burton was herself adopted, and she was vocal about the laws surrounding adoptees in Ireland. Anna's brother John was on the death list, but her other brother, William, was not. Catherine Corless had all of the children's names, but she had not planned to make them public. She had been unable to find any burial records for the children to corroborate her findings. As she said herself at the time, 'if these women had been banished by their families and communities for having a baby out of wedlock, they sure as hell weren't going to take the baby home and bury it. If they didn't want them in life, they would hardly want them in death.'

Then Minister Zappone said what she had to say and the world shifted on its axis. It was plain to everyone present that nothing would be the same again.

Anna was in a daze as she left Government Buildings, trying to process what had just happened. She stared at a group of journalists, who were also making their exit to file their breaking news stories, when she suddenly made a decision to say something. RTÉ cameraman Michael Lee was walking by her and she reached out and said, 'Can I tell you about my two brothers who were born in the Tuam Home?'

The cameraman was on his way to send footage to RTÉ for the *News at One* slot, but he realised this was something he couldn't miss. Before now, no one had come forward in this way, publicly and openly, to say they had two siblings in the Tuam grave.

As Anna described how she had only learned about her brothers in 2012, the reporters who had been heading back to their offices began to eavesdrop on her speech to the camera. One by one, their microphones and Dictaphones began to appear in front of her. Gavin Reilly, formerly of Today FM, asked her, 'Do you mind if I use your name?' Anna nodded and that was it: her story had been made public.

Not wanting to interrupt her flow, Michael began rolling and Anna did not stop. She poured out the story of her research, which she knew inside-out without having to refer to her notes. Having lived and breathed her research for the past three years, Anna was a natural in front of the camera. She recalled how she had written to every relevant Minister and every Garda Superintendent and Garda Commissioner in the hope of getting answers – but that she was still at a loss as to where her brothers were. She had dates, times and background of everything her mother had gone through, and how John and William Dolan had vanished off the face of the Earth.

By the end of that day Anna had been on *The Last Word* with Matt Cooper on Today FM, on RTÉ, and on Al Jazeera. It was no longer a local news story, far from it. The story of the Tuam Babies was all over Sky News, CNN, the *Washington Post* and *The New York Times*. Anna's phone number, which she had handed out to a number of reporters, was now with almost every newsroom in the country, and they all wanted to hear about her search to find her missing brothers.

> I want to know where my brothers are. William is a missing person. I have an open Garda investigation into his disappearance since September 2013 – where is he? The gardaí have told me that they cannot confirm that he is dead. And John's death is also the subject of an investigation since June 2014.
>
> William's date of birth was changed, he's marked as dead on the Bon Secours ledgers, but there is no medical certification of death, no reason for his death and no death cert for him. I'm sick asking about him. I've gone everywhere and no one will answer me.
>
> I've even written to the Pope about this. Has he answered me? No.

There was a look of shock and horror on the reporters' faces as they listened intently to Anna's story.

For the rest of the weekend, Anna and Catherine were interviewed at their kitchen tables in Galway and Dublin. Anna was suffering from PTSD and severe depression and feeling unwell, but she pushed through because she saw this as her one chance to maybe, finally, get some answers.

Anna had relentlessly pursued different arms of the state for details of her two brothers, but she had always chosen to work away quietly on her own. She had refused from the beginning to engage with the Commission of Investigation because she believes her brothers' cases are a matter for the gardaí only. The investigation into William's disappearance and the death of John, due to what she believes was neglect and ill-treatment, pre-dates the setting up of the Commission. Anna had uncovered inspection reports from Tuam that identified John as a very sick little boy, and she firmly believes these are criminal matters.

Once the media got hold of the story and began to explore its various angles, attention turned to the organisation that ran the Tuam Mother and Baby Home: the Congregation of the Sisters of Bon Secours. While the Irish state failed to regulate, monitor and inspect the Home correctly, it was the Bon Secours nuns who had actually buried the dead children in the cesspit. But in spite of the full glare of publicity and the loud demands for answers, the order remained tight-lipped.

In 2014, when the *Irish Mail on Sunday* ran the front-page story about the Tuam Babies, the order had initially made no public statement on the substance of the allegations. Their first statement on the matter came from Sister Marie Ryan, the head of the Bon Secours order in Ireland, who emailed a reply confirming the order had been involved in the running of the Home, but stating its involvement had now ended:

> Unfortunately, I am not in a position to assist you any further as unfortunately all the records and documentation were handed over in 1961 to Galway County Council and through the passage of time the Sisters who would have served at the Home are now deceased. Unfortunately, I cannot put the matter any further.

Significantly, the letter expressed no sense of horror about the existence of a mass grave. Furthermore, Sister Marie Ryan had previously written to Anna Corrigan, on 9 April 2013, stating that a grave existed at the back of the Home.

But now, as the story was picked up around the world, the order did eventually break its silence. Just two weeks later, questions put to the order by the *Irish Daily Mail* were responded to by a representative of top PR firm The Communications Clinic, with a far more sympathetic statement, which said that the nuns were:

> shocked and deeply saddened by recent reports about St Mary's Mother and Baby Home, which operated in Tuam, County Galway from 1925 to 1961.
>
> The Bon Secours Sisters say they are committed to engaging with Catherine Corless, the children's home graveyard committee and the local residents as constructively as they can on the graves initiative connected with the site. They donated €2,000 to the committee. The Sisters welcome the recent Government announcement to initiate an investigation, in an effort to establish the full truth of what happened.

The treatment of the remains of the Bon Secour nuns based in Tuam was vastly different from that of the remains of the 796 forgotten children. When the nuns left Tuam in 2001, they exhumed twelve members of their order and reburied them in Knock, County Mayo. The nuns had been interred in a small, 20 square-foot plot at the back of the Grove Hospital in Tuam, less than a mile from the septic tank site. For the exhumations to take place, the order had to seek the approval of Galway County Council by obtaining a court order. Subsequently, the mass exhumation took place over two days in the summer of 2001. The remains of the nuns were transferred to the cemetery in Knock, County Mayo, where they were buried with a blessing from a local parish priest. The names of the nuns who were reburied in Knock were engraved on the base of a memorial cross that had been at the Grove site. The whole matter was dealt with sensitively and respectfully, which cannot be said of how the children's bodies were handled.

As time went on, one by one, statements began to issue from various groups. The Archbishop of Tuam, Michael Neary, said there was 'a clear moral imperative on the Bon Secours Sisters in this case to act upon their responsibilities in the interest of the common good'. He said in a statement: 'I was made aware of the extent of the situation by media reporting and historical research. I am horrified and saddened to hear of the large number of deceased children involved.'

President of Ireland Michael D. Higgins said:

My first reaction was one of enormous sadness. These are children who, while they were alive, had rights, the rights to protection, and who, if dead, had the right to be looked after with dignity.

Time doesn't remove any of those rights, but I think now what is important is that all of the questions that are provoked by this are answered and that they are answered adequately with the assistance of science and forensics.

I think too there is a reminder in it of history and our past and there is so much to be revealed and there is so much to be learned from these really terrible reports that are appearing.

Fergus Finlay, the head of Barnardos Children's Charity in Ireland, later said:

I find it all so shocking ... it's the thoughts of children being buried in a septic tank in an unmarked grave, we can't seem to live with that, we can't accept that.

Children were abused, children were neglected and children were buried in unmarked graves. We can't live with that.

Some priest at some point had to have come in to the homes and said, 'These children are not going into consecrated ground'. The Tuam Graveyard is across the road from the Home. I find that appalling.

In 2014 there was concern about a plaque; in 2017 there was global revulsion at the disrespectful manner of the burial of these little angels. Yet, all Anna Corrigan wanted was for someone to ring and say, 'It's me,

William, your brother' or 'I know your brother William'. The reality, however, was that even if William had been adopted and brought to the USA, as her late mother had told a family member, he was likely unaware he had been born in Tuam or to know anything about his past life.

Amidst all the talk and speculation, there were allegations floating around that death certs had been falsified, and the nuns' documents were certainly pointing in that direction, too. For Anna, this gave fresh hope. Could William be living somewhere under a different name, with no clue as to who he really was? Could John, too, be alive?

They had come so far, but maybe the truth, when it was finally revealed in its entirety, would be better than they had feared?

# 1

# The Path to Home

On the day Anna Corrigan's mother, Bridget Dolan, was born, on 5 September 1918, the German army was in full retreat after suffering a devastating defeat to the Allied Forces on the Western Front. The First World War had effectively been won, and would be over within weeks. For the majority of Europe, there would never be a return to the old world order. Along with the millions of deaths, the Great War transformed technology, the class system and economic structures. It changed the world completely, and it would never change back.

But in the small corner of rural Ireland where Bridget Dolan took her first breath, the industrial revolution had yet to arrive. Her parents were living without electricity or running water, eking out an existence as subsistence farmers on a tiny parcel of land with their large family. They were living a life largely unchanged from the lives lived by their grandparents.

When the First World War came to an end on 11 November 1918, Bridget was two months old. Ireland had avoided the massive destruction most of mainland Europe had experienced during wartime, but great change was coming to Ireland – and this change would be felt even in the most isolated and rural parts of the country.

The war had transformed Ireland politically. The Easter Rising in 1916 had sparked a drive for full independence from Britain. As a result of the British government's failure to deliver Ireland Home Rule, Sinn Féin won a landslide victory in the Irish general election in December 1918. When Bridget was four months old, on 21 January 1919, Sinn Féin formed a

EIRE      IRELAND    Uimhir Number L 222

Uimh. No.   22

## DEIMHNIÚ BREITHE
## BIRTH CERTIFICATE

Na hAchtanna um Chlárú Breitheanna agus Bása 1863 go 1952
BIRTHS AND DEATHS REGISTRATION ACTS 1863 to 1952

Ainm agus Sloinneadh
Name and Surname *Bridget Dolan*

Gnéas
Sex *Female*

Dáta Breithe
Date of Birth

Lá
Day *Fifth*

Mí
Month *September*

Bliain
Year *1918*

Míle      gCéad
One Thousand *nine* Hundred and *eighteen*

Ceantar Cláraitheachta
District of Registration *Laurencetown*

i gContae      Éire
in the County of *Galway*    Ireland

Uimhir an Taifid
Number of Entry *199*

Is fíor cóip í seo de thaifid atá i gClár Leabhair na mBreith in Oifig an Ard-Chláraitheora i mBaile Átha Cliath, 1.
Certified to be a true copy taken from the Certified Copies of Entries of Births in Oifig an Ard-Chláraitheora, Dublin, 1.

TUGTHA faoi Shéala Oifig an Ard-Chláraitheora,
GIVEN under the Seal of Oifig an Cnláraitheora,
Baile Átha Cliath, an      lá seo de
Dublin, this *twentyeight* day of
*May*, 19*72*
Scrúdaithe
Examined

Is cion trom é an doiciméad seo a athrú nó é a chur chun feidhme taréis a athraithe
**TO ALTER THIS DOCUMENT OR TO UTTER IT SO ALTERED IS A SERIOUS OFFENCE**

breakaway government and declared independence from Britain. This sparked the War of Independence, which ultimately led to the Anglo-Irish Treaty in December 1921. The Treaty would ultimately spark a bitter civil war in Ireland over the terms of the deal, which saw six counties in Ulster remaining part of the UK, with former comrades in the War of Independence dividing into pro- and anti-Treaty forces. The Civil War was won by the Free State forces.

Bridget, her parents, and brothers and sisters lived in the small village of Clonfert in County Galway at around the time of the creation of the Irish Free State. Back then, Clonfert had a population scattered across a number of townlands in east County Galway, which is halfway between Ballinasloe and Portumna. This small village is famous for its cathedral, which was part of the mid-sixth-century monastery founded by St Brendan. It is estimated that at one time there were 3,000 monks based in Clonfert, until they were raided by Vikings who burned the monastery to the ground in 1016, 1164 and 1179. All that's left of the monastery now is the cathedral, which has been transferred into the hands of the Church of Ireland, although local Catholics still get buried in the graveyard.

The Dolans' pretty, single-storey, whitewashed house in Clonfert was situated on the corner of what was known as the 'Three Roads'. The house had one wooden gate into the farm and one gate into the front garden. It housed Bridget's parents, Thomas and Katie Dolan, and her eight siblings, Molly, Kit, John, Michael, Nancy, Maggie, Julia and Attracta. Their small farm gave them a meagre living. The family had to walk one mile to the nearest well in order to bring water home every day. It would be years before one of Bridget's brothers erected a pump in the front garden and made the long walk no longer necessary. The house had tiny windows dotted all around it. The surrounding scenery was not important to families back then; the only thing that mattered was taking shelter from the high winds.

Unlike her parents, Bridget would grow up in a country where the Catholic Church attempted to become inseparable from the Irish state. Her parents had been born at a time when the Church of Ireland was the state religion, with the British monarch at its head, and the majority adherents of the Catholic Church were outsiders who just over a hundred years earlier would have been subjected to severe restrictions.

As Bridget grew into her teenage years, the Irish state continued the system inherited from the British in which religious bodies controlled health and education services. As the largest religious grouping, the Catholic Church administered the majority of important institutions with little or no oversight from the government.

After 1922, the Irish government gave responsibility for education, health and social welfare policy to the Church in order to project the image of Ireland as a 'Catholic and morally pure society'. Children born out of wedlock, in particular, were treated as a moral problem that could only be solved by the Church. James Smith, Associate Professor at Boston College and author of *Ireland's Magdalene Laundries and the Nation's Architecture of Containment* (2007) described it as a time when 'They contained and confined and rendered invisible what Irish society didn't want to be confronted with. They allowed most people to buy into the fiction of a holy, Catholic Ireland.'

In 1940, when Bridget was twenty-two, the family pulled together and built a second storey onto their home. In years to come Bridget would tell her daughter, Anna, how she had to carry blocks to her father and brother as they laboured. She would wear her long overcoat and lift the blocks one by one to whoever was laying them, right up until every piece of brick was laid.

The finished building had what was known as half-doors. The door was split across the middle, with the open top half allowing air into the house during the day, while the bottom half stayed closed to keep out the chickens. If the bottom half of the door was opened, the chickens would quickly make their way into the house and walk around the large flagstones on the floor until someone chased them out again. At night, both halves of the door would be closed to keep in the heat, but the door was never locked. The latch could be lifted at any time, letting in a friend who was out 'rambling' and came for a chat, to share a favourite pastime.

In the living room there was a huge open fire, which was always on the go, and there was a constant smell of the fresh turf throughout the house. The fire was both heater and oven. Michael and John Dolan's job was to keep the fire in the house going at all times. The pair would take turns bringing in the sticks for the fire, while the girls cleaned and helped their mother with the cooking. Over the fire hung a large cast-iron crane from which the pots were suspended, hanging on big hooks. There were two small hobs on either side of the fire where you could sit on a cold winter's evening and listen to the crickets. Mrs Dolan baked bread every day in a griddle pan on the fire. Tilley lamps, which ran off kerosene, were used to light the house and to help heat the rooms in the autumn and winter. They used lime to sterilise the walls because paint was too expensive. Thomas Dolan, Bridget's father, was a quiet and gentle man whom she adored. He was self-sufficient and made all his own furniture for his new home – whatever was needed. He was quiet, hard-working and could turn his hand to anything. As an adult, she would remember the happy and easy conversations she had with her father as she was by his side when he was working. She told her daughter, Anna, that she loved her father so much, her hair went grey overnight after he died.

In later years, Thomas Dolan got a transistor radio which he loved to listen to and which provided a form of escape in the evenings when all the work was done. He had a love of music, which meant the house was often filled with it. When Bridget and her siblings were put to bed on the nights of gatherings, they would listen and stare through a spy-hole that looked into the living room. There were so many people coming to and going from the house for the renowned sing-songs, it provided the children with much entertainment at night. Bridget and her sisters, Nancy, Kit, Molly, Maggie, Julia and Attracta, would watch as the neighbours came in for a rambling in the house and spent the night singing.

Bridget had many happy childhood memories, but as an adult she would also vividly recall the grinding and relentless poverty the family endured. She described how her family went barefoot in the summer and made their clothes out of flour sacks. The children had to bring sods of turf to the local school in winter so they could have some heat. Without that they were sure to 'freeze to death' in the cold school.

In the 1920s Ireland was in a ruinous state. The *Freeman's Journal* of 22 July 1924 reported that Connemara, in County Galway, was one of the worst hit regions in terms of poverty: '75% of the people had now no potatoes, their chief diet for the last 2 months, and the harvest prospects were never worse in living memory. There is no employment.' As early as 20 August 1924 *The Meath Chronicle* reported 'a famine condition is imminent as bad as 1843'. Through the early autumn, local newspapers were littered with similar predictions of mass starvation. In September 1924, *The Anglo-Celt* predicted a famine and the local branch of Cumann na nGaedheal said 'the shadow of famine is overspreading the outlook of the poor peasantry'. The people of Ireland, particularly the rural people, were ground down by cold and hunger and uncertainty.

Bridget Dolan was a quiet child who did whatever her parents asked of her. Like many girls back then, she lived with her parents for most of her young adult life. She was happy to stay at home to help run the house. Her family were known as 'decent and hard-working' people in Clonfert, something they instilled in all of their children. But employment was hard to come by, especially in the West of Ireland, and Bridget's brothers, John and Michael, eventually moved to England in search of work.

The Dolan children went to the local school, where Bridget excelled at Irish. It was here she first encountered the rigid mindset of the Church. She was left-handed, and her teacher would pin her left hand to her back and beat her to write with her right hand. Back then, any *citóg* (left-handed person) was known as the 'Devil's child'.

Bridget went to primary school, but as she grew into her teens she, like all but the richest young women, had to leave school to work and contribute to the running of the family home. As a young woman she was tall and good-looking, with fine bone structure and high cheekbones. She had drooping eyelids, which she believed were the result of exposure at birth. Her eyes would flicker upwards so it would appear that she was looking up. Her good looks had not helped her meet a husband just yet, as she was so busy with her family.

The Catholic Church was an inescapable part of life in rural Ireland. A priest would have had more power and influence in Clonfert than a politician, police officer or teacher. The Dolans, like most of the people they knew, were observant and faithful Catholics who tried not to deviate from the Church's teachings. On Sundays, the family would attend Mass, where women who fell pregnant outside marriage were named and shamed by the priest on the altar during his sermon. It was a horrifying experience for any woman who was in this situation. The Church was happy to remind its parishioners that there was no place to hide if you were an unmarried woman with child. The whole community was going to know about it, and never let you forget about it either.

It may seem hard to believe, but Bridget was devoted to her faith and remained a devout and observant Catholic for the rest of her life, embracing the teachings of the Church. In her later years she would often tell anyone in difficulty to try and 'put their faith in God and he would resolve their issues'.

Bridget (known as Biddy to her closest friends and family) was a likeable woman, who wanted others to like her in return. She never judged anyone and tried to get along with everyone. She was no wild-living rebel. So how she ended up pregnant at the age of 26 is a mystery. Did she fall head over heels in love with some local man and throw a lifetime of caution to the wind? Did she know enough about the mechanics of sex to know the risk she was taking? Or was she the victim of rape, like many of the women who ended up in the Mother and Baby Homes?

We will never know. Bridget went to her grave without ever telling her daughter, Anna, that she had been pregnant before Anna was born. All that is known is that Bridget was neither married nor courting anyone when she missed her period in early 1946. Terrified and alone, she kept the pregnancy under wraps for as long as she could, all the time knowing that the life she had always known was about to come to an end.

The moment when she had to tell her family must have been horrific. The disappointed faces on her siblings would have hit her like a hammer blow. We do know some family members just walked away and never mentioned it again. The fear of what the neighbours would say, as well as the priest naming her publicly on the altar, would have caused her a sickening dread.

Once she had uttered her confession, her secret would have been shared with the people who mattered. When the local priest and the doctor arrived at the Dolan house, Bridget's future was completely taken out of her hands. There was only one place for someone like her: she would be sent away until her child was born and she would not bring her child back to Clonfert when it was all over. To save her family from the shame of her sins, it was decided she would be sent to the Tuam Mother and Baby Home.

Moving to Tuam for a year was not something Bridget believed would happen to her. Anna's cousin would later speak on her behalf to one of her aunts about her mother's experience, but was curtly told that 'if her mother wanted her to know, she would have told her. Let that be an end to it.' Another relation when asked replied, 'Some things are best left in the past.' Walls of silence surrounded that part of Bridget's life, erected by all her family and her neighbours. Anna describes it as 'mass amnesia'. But there were real and terrible effects of this refusal to talk. As Anna said sadly, 'People don't realise how hard it is to try and understand what your own mother went through. I can only imagine because she never, ever told me about what happened to her.'

Perhaps those words were beyond Bridget because to speak them would have been to drag up the most painful scenes of her life. She obediently accepted her fate, as she had always accepted her parents' wishes, and she prepared to leave for Tuam. When she came to say goodbye to her family, her father turned his back on her and stared out the kitchen window. Her mother, in her apron, continued to cook bread at the fire. Fighting back tears, her mother simply said that this was for the best.

Having disgraced her family and been publicly named on the altar by the local priest, Bridget was driven away from her home for the first time in all her 26 years. She was taken to a place she didn't know that was a massive 74km away from the only place she'd ever known. There, she was left outside the Tuam Mother and Baby Home, shivering in the bitter January wind. She was eight months' pregnant, alone, abandoned, with no money, no support and no partner. She had no choice.

Drawing in a deep breath, she knocked on the front door.

# 2

# The Place of Shame

From the time it was first built, in 1841, the grey, blocky building on the outskirts of the town of Tuam was always a place that housed people who had been robbed of all other options. The people who resided within its walls were like a shameful secret that had to be locked away from the view of moral, upstanding people. They were the ones the authorities deemed to be unfit for normal society, and that was exactly how they were treated.

Originally it was used as a workhouse for the poor, whose numbers multiplied hugely in the wake of the Great Famine. After that it was used to house the homeless, 'idiots' and even IRA prisoners during the civil war (1922–1923).

However, from 1925 until 1961 it housed hundreds of women who had fallen off the edge of Irish society and were unlikely to haul themselves back up anytime soon. It became an institution for women who had got themselves 'in trouble', an Irish euphemism for getting pregnant outside of marriage. These women, who were usually very young, were cast as sinful, shameful and deserving of punishment. They were sent there to be delivered of their babies and repent for what they had done. Once inside the cold walls of the institution, the women were effectively prisoners for one year after they gave birth, at which point they were thrown out into society again, or back to the Magdalene home where they came from while their 'bastard' children were kept. The young mothers could not take their babies with them when they were forced to leave. It seems ironic that the locals called it 'the Home' – it was very, very far from homely. It was also known as the Children's Home, the Mother and Baby Home or St Mary's Home.

Only half-noticed by the locals most of the time, the institution played a central role in the economy of Tuam, providing customers for local farmers and shops. But the women who lived in the Home were never part of the town's normal social life. They were isolated and locked away because they had had sex outside of marriage.

Mother and Baby Homes and county homes run by religious orders and overseen by local councils were dotted all over Ireland. Typical residents were unmarried mothers, their children and also other orphaned or destitute children. The Tuam Mother and Baby Home was owned by Galway County Council, which paid the Bon Secours Sisters for overseeing the running of the institution. The nuns were mostly fully trained nurses and midwives, and some were also trained children's nurses.

At first, three sisters were in charge, but this was increased to four a short time later. There were also three lay women working there, who had either stayed on in the Home or were born there. Between 1925 and 1943, the average number of women and children residing in the Home was 200. In 1944, the total population suggested as desirable by an Inspector Humphreys was 243. However, when the Home was inspected in 1947, there were 271 children and 61 women resident, making a total of 333. It is clear that conditions became more and more overcrowded as time went on.

There could be up to 150 infants in the Home at any one time, and these babies, who were supposed to be cared for by the state and religious orders, died at a rate of five times that of babies living in the community. This is not surprising given that the Home was a breeding ground for infectious diseases. There were only a half-dozen toilets and they were often blocked, so some children urinated and defecated in the corners. If any child wet their bed, the nuns would make them sleep in their own urine for up to four days before changing the bedding – if they ever changed it. The children were hungry and cold all the time, which meant they were very skinny and therefore vulnerable to any illnesses going around. Some children were adopted out of the home, but no one ever wanted to adopt a sick child, so the most vulnerable were left behind and often died.

Once inside the doors, all normal liberties and rights were suspended, and the women were forced to endure rampant disease, sub-standard meals and harsh working conditions and hours. The Tuam Mother and Baby Home was not exceptional in this. The sad fact is that it was normal for the time, for these 'fallen women'.

Since the truth about these homes was uncovered, people have asked again and again: how could this have happened? There can be no doubt that both the political class and the Church set out to isolate 'fallen women' from normal society. A conscious effort was made to treat pregnancy outside wedlock as a social ill. The close relationship between the Church, the media and the political class allowed this view to be reinforced constantly. Bishops took an active role in enforcing these views and the Church sought to be intimately involved in every single bit of Irish life.

While the bishops took an interest in many political projects, it could be said that the war against sexual 'immorality' was viewed as their greatest battle. This attitude remained up to the 1990s, although there was a steady waning of their influence from the 1960s onwards. The Church's influence, along with the conservative elements in the media and politics, lead a largely successful resistance to social reforms, such as contraception, divorce and abortion, which were introduced in many other European countries. Unmarried mothers were regarded as a threat to public morality, and this was reinforced by the Church's teachings. A woman who got pregnant outside of wedlock was the 'greatest scandal', according to Associate Professor James Smith, who has written about the Magdalene laundries: 'It threatened the respectability of the family. It impacted opportunities for siblings.'

Another academic, Paul Garrett at NUI Galway, has also studied this era: 'If an unmarried mother found herself in a Mother and Baby Home in Ireland, the minimum amount of time that she'd have to spend in such a home was two years. That's a considerable chunk of someone's life. If they got a ferry over to England, after staying in a Mother and Baby Home [there], they could go after three months.'

The Irish government outsourced its responsibilities towards single mothers to the Church, which made examples of these women and their children. While the women in the homes were badly mistreated, beaten, abused and often forced to give up their children, the Church had the full backing of the government. This is how it had happened. The women were abandoned by their families, their communities and their government. They were left with nowhere else to go.

The Church and state worked together to control women's bodies in order to enforce 'correct' sexual values throughout the country. The Church also knew that public shaming was one of the greatest weapons in its arsenal. All over Ireland, women were terrified of becoming pregnant. Since the dawn of time, if a woman fell pregnant out of wedlock, the responsibility and shame tended to be hers and hers alone. The men, the fathers, did not have to carry the can for their child or for the mother of their child. The fathers of these babies were, in fact, obliged by law to pay for the maintenance of their children, but that law was not enforced and the women were sentenced to hard labour as a result. The 'sin' the fathers had committed didn't affect their lives at all.

For the women who were sent to the Mother and Baby Homes, however, it was a life-long sentence. First there was the time spent living in the home, but getting out didn't mean breaking free. The young women were often haunted by the fate of their child, left wondering what had happened to their son or daughter. They weren't allowed to remove their child to be with them, so were faced with the gut-wrenching prospect of walking away and leaving their vulnerable, powerless child in the home. The stories of these women, and their children, are truly heartbreaking. Any sort of committal at the home, long or short, meant a lifetime of sorrow and guilt – there was no escaping that.

Daily life in the Tuam Mother and Baby Home followed the same routine as many of the homes around the country. The last woman to leave Tuam when it closed in 1961, having spent most of her life there, was Julia Devaney (*née* Carter), although she didn't leave as such, merely moved to the Grove Hospital less than 1km away. The Grove was owned by the Bon Secours Sisters and some of the mothers went to work there after their incarceration. Julia stayed with the nuns and worked in the gardens of the Grove because she was institutionalised and didn't know what else to do with her life.

Years later she did manage to get away from the nuns when she married and settled with her husband, Tom Devaney, in Tuam. She met Tom at the Grove Hospital. In the 1980s she gave an insightful interview to a local woman about her time in the Home, and that interview was uncovered by local historian Catherine Corless in 2015. It gives a very clear picture of what it was like to live inside the Home and to be seen as an object of shame. She described it as a 'house of tears, a house of sorrows'. From her lifetime of unofficial servitude, she had vivid memories of the nuns and how they had treated the women:

> Mother Hortense … she was a big hefty woman, a slave driver with a heart of gold. She was friendly, but still she put those poor girls into Ballinasloe and the Magdalene laundry!
>
> Sister Priscilla was childlike … a lovely old nun … and I would canonise her, she hadn't much to do with the children, she was old, but worked with the chapel and the convent side of it. But she was the essence of kindness to everybody.
>
> Sister Anthony would say to the women, 'Don't be crying, wouldn't it be worse if it was a bad marriage?' Sister Gabriel, in charge of the babies, was always praying. Sister Patrick was a lovely nun, she was elderly, she would walk down the garden to me as she said she hated being above in 'that place', and she would always be telling me her

love stories. She was natural … the only nun who ever spoke to me about life as an equal.

There was a beautiful nun, Sister John Baptist, she was magnificent, and they sent her up to the children's home to try her vocation, and by God she left it. She left the convent!

Sister Celestine was a bit peculiar, whatever thing she had about clean clothes, she used to change her clothes on a Saturday night, and take all she took off her and burned them in the furnace. She was daft. She started the 1p dinners in Dublin. A little red-faced woman. Sister Celestine was red-faced from washing herself.

One nun in the home, Mother Ann, was the most beautiful person – she wouldn't see a hole in a ladder. She ruled by gentleness, she'd do with love what Martha did with an iron rod. She was the nun that closed the door in the Home in 1961. The bad Mother Martha … she ruled us with an iron hand. She'd keep you down. On a wet day when I couldn't go out on the land, I might go inside and maybe do a bit of crochet, and my heart would be in my mouth for fear Martha would walk in. Martha … life wasn't worth living with her … You couldn't argue with her, she would give you a thump to put you into the middle of next week!

The mothers-to-be were generally sent into the Home either by their doctor or parish priest or their family, normally arriving at the forbidding front door around a month before they gave birth. When their time came, they were offered no pain relief during labour, another facet of their punishment. The attending nun would remind them that this pain was a result of their own sinful behaviour – a small taste of divine justice. Women often gave birth to breach babies in agonising pain. It didn't matter how hard a woman screamed on the birthing table, no medication was given to help her in any way.

The women then remained in the Home for twelve months, to mind their child and do all the jobs required to keep the place running. It was backbreaking work, unrelenting, day in, day out. Once a woman left the home, she was expected to send money to the nuns for the upkeep of her child until the child left the Home or died.

Although they are often lumped together, the Mother and Baby Homes were not the same as the Magdalene Laundries, also known as Magdalene Asylums, which were founded in the eighteenth century. The first Magdalene Laundry was a Church of Ireland institution founded by Lady Isabella Denny. It was renamed Denny House in the late 1950s. During the nineteenth century, as penal restrictions were relaxed, Roman Catholic versions emerged often in reaction to proselytising in Protestant institutions. Homes were run by a number of different religious orders and received a payment per child from the local council. The purpose of the homes was to ensure the mothers were completely isolated from society. The Magdalene Laundries were institutions set up across Ireland by the Church to house women for all sorts of reasons, including having good looks, being cheeky and having sex outside marriage. There are no official numbers, but it's accepted that around 30,000 women were confined in these institutions.

Julia Devaney described the women's daily routines in the Tuam Mother and Baby Home:

The women had to have an admission ticket from the doctor to get in. There was no such thing as being signed in, but once they were there they would have to wait a year to look after their baby. One girl escaped, went out, but she was brought back again that night by An Garda Síochána.

Breakfast consisted of porridge, milk, tea and bread – trays of bread. Then down to feed the babies.

Children went to mass, too. The children got porridge, milk, bread and tea before school.

Mothers then fed their babies, they were barged into breastfeeding. If the babies weren't breastfed, bottles would have to be made up and sterilised. She'd [Reverend Mother] nearly starve the infant to make the mother breastfeed. The doctor had to certify that the mother could not breastfeed before bottles were given.

The mothers used to belt the hell out of the little children and they could be heard screaming by passers-by on the Athenry Road. Probably mothers frustrated and taking it out on the other children.

None of the women ever attempted suicide. They had a very hard life, there was no consolation, no advice, and no love there for them. They just got through, counting the days and weeks until they were free to go. The parents would come back to the Home to bring the woman out after her term of a year was up, whether it was to put them on the train or what, and the nuns would get a job for anyone else who had no one to meet them.

Sometimes people from Tuam would come up looking for a servant girl. The mothers would never tell me anything. They were afraid of the nuns and they were suspicious of us, even though I would be nice to them. They were always talking among themselves. The garden wasn't hard for me for I loved it, but the girls were unhappy at it. It was an unhappy ould place, that's what it was now. The girls found no interest there, they were just putting in the day.

The children of these women fared no better. Their lives were marked from the start. One survivor spent the first five-and-a-half years of his life in the Tuam Mother and Baby Home. He gave a chilling account of his early years to *The Journal.ie* in March 2017:

You were just a bastard in their eyes. People would just make little of you and look down on you. They wouldn't even talk to you. They knew that I was out of wedlock and it is the Church that is to blame for that, because that is the way they were raised to think. We were nothing but a kind of scum, you weren't normal because you didn't belong to a wedded family. It is totally crazy.

It was this 'crazy' that Bridget Dolan was about to step into. A girl from a small farm, who had never been apart from her family, who had no experience beyond her own village, would now have to learn to fend for herself in a place she couldn't even have imagined.

# 3

# Life and Death

On 26 January 1946, Bridget Dolan walked up the path to the front door of the Tuam Mother and Baby Home. Standing on the steps, alone with her suitcase, she was following in the sorrowful footsteps of more than a century's worth of lost souls. Her family had sent her to Tuam to have her baby and then come home when that shame had been lifted off her. Like many people, they would likely tell the neighbours she was in England, or helping a family member in another part of Ireland, some lie to try to cover over the fact that their young daughter was pregnant – if she hadn't already been named from the church pulpit. The truth was impossible and could never be acknowledged.

Although the young women no doubt held on to the promise of eventually returning to their homes and families, the reality was that women in Bridget's situation rarely came home. The shame for their families was permanent and could not be erased by the passage of time. Even though Bridget had been a dutiful daughter who had spent her life working hard for her parents, she, like many others, could not be forgiven because her great sin could not be forgotten.

As she stood on the steps of the Home on that cold January day, in her hand Bridget held a tiny piece of white paper, a handwritten note:

Children's Home Tuam, Please Admit Bridget Dolan, 26 years of Clonfert.
She expects to be confined at end of present month.

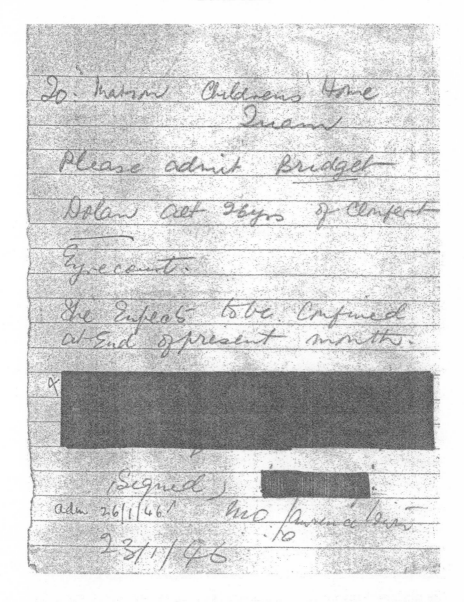

Those two simple sentences, which could be written by either a doctor or a priest, were all that was needed to confine an unmarried mother-to-be like Bridget Dolan into an institution that had more in common with a prison than a charitable hospital. In Bridget's case, her local doctor had signed off on her admission, and his word alone was enough to deprive her of her liberty – and her baby.

However she had ended up there, when she knocked on that imposing door and it was pulled open by a nun, her fate was sealed. Dressed in a long brown overcoat to hide her bump, Bridget was admitted into the Tuam Mother and Baby Home that day, just weeks before her baby was due. The nun led her through the Home and to her sleeping quarters, where she opened out her small brown suitcase on the old iron bed with its thin, narrow mattress. Twelve beds were lined against the walls of the room. As Bridget stood in that room, she must have been shocked at the reality that this was where she would rest her head for the next year, in a room full of strangers who were all pregnant and outcast like her.

The windows in the room were only tiny wooden frames, but Bridget would still have felt the January wind pushing easily through them. It was freezing in the winters and the building was as cold as ice. There was no large turf fire lighting in the corner like there was at home. No, this horrible old stone building, with its three-metre thick walls, was freezing, devoid of warmth, with the sadness and tears of many a woman who had cried herself to sleep at night seeping from the walls. Bridget was no fool: she knew bad things happened in a place like this. Her life as she had known it was over, and she was about to be faced with a place and a routine that were totally unlike anything she had experienced in her own home. No doubt she was pining for her own bed and her own family, wishing desperately that things were different.

She was surrounded by girls and women in the same situation, but that was cold comfort. Just like all who had gone before her, she had to quickly figure out the ways of the Home and how to get through each day. There was no great sense of camaraderie – each woman was fragile and damaged and unable to offer a huge amount of support to others. It was just a matter of grim survival. Like everyone else, Bridget was there to give birth, mind her child after it was born and help with all the other babies who lived in the Home, condemned by society. These were the babies and children who had been left there by their mothers, women who had no choice but to leave them behind, and who were waiting for a foster home or an adoptive parent to come and take them away.

All of this must have seemed so alien to Bridget on that first day, but like many of the women she would live with over the next year, 'the Home' would become Bridget's life. In time, Bridget would struggle to leave the institution and rejoin the real world. She would become used to all the ways of the place, to being totally under the control of the nuns, their hard labour, strict rules and tough regime.

In the early years of the Home, when a woman's time came to give birth, she was sent to a maternity unit in a hospital outside the Home. This practice disgusted many councillors and committee members, who believed that the hospital's maternity ward was tainted because it was being used by unmarried mothers. As a result, several discussions took place with regard to building a separate maternity ward for unmarried mothers, and the Bon Secours Sisters advocated for such a unit to be built in the Home. An inspection took place at the Tuam institution and it was agreed that the nuns could build a maternity ward for the unmarried women, so they could stay out of the local hospitals. The maternity unit in the Home was completed in 1929.

The daily routine began at 6.00 a.m., when the night shift woke the mothers. They had to take care of their own baby's needs first, then attend to the toddlers, dressing and feeding them – although if their babies were small, mothers would be up to do the night-time feeds as well and would have got precious little sleep. That didn't matter – the day began at 6.00 a.m. for everyone, no excuses.

Mass was at 8.30 a.m. Then the work of the day began, with a heavy schedule of cleaning, laundry and cooking. The feeding times were very regimented and strictly adhered to. The nuns ensured that every moment of the women's day was accounted for, with no down time whatsoever. Mothers were never allowed any kind of recreation and there was a strict no talking rule during meal times and when nursing babies. Bedtime was at 7.30 p.m., by which time the women were so tired, they fell into their beds with exhaustion. There was no special treatment for pregnant women either – they worked right up until they gave birth.

This was the case for Bridget, who worked hard for the first month of her stay at the Home. When she went into labour, she was helped to the Home's maternity ward by another inmate. She was told to lie down on the table and there she laboured, while the nuns watched. There were no sterile utensils used during delivery and Bridget, like all the labouring mothers, was not allowed to make any noise as she gave birth to her baby.

Bridget's son, John Desmond Dolan, was born on 22 February 1946, just four weeks after his heartbroken mother was admitted into the Home. His birth was recorded as 'normal' and he weighed a healthy 8lb 9oz, and he had a beautiful mop of black hair – a loving detail mentioned to Bridget's grand-daughter decades later, which she told Anna after Bridget died.

Bridget cradled her beautiful little baby boy in her arms, and even though she must have felt that rush of love all new mothers feel, her heart would have ached knowing that there was no way she could keep him. Little John was born in the wrong place at the wrong time, through no fault of his own. Unknown to this innocent little bundle, he was viewed as proof of a mortal sin rather than as a miracle of life. Given Bridget's socio-economic and religious background, the path she was forced to take was inevitable from the second she told her family she was expecting. And now that heavy inevitability would fall on John's head, too. There was no hope of her keeping her child unless the baby's father agreed to marry her. But there was no sign of him.

John was baptised on the day he was born by the Rev. M. Loftus from the Cathedral of the Assumption on the Dublin Road, Tuam, County Galway. His baptismal certificate describes Bridget Dolan as his mother, while a woman called Winnie Casey was his sponsor. There are no details given of John's father on his birth certificate.

Bridget spent ten days on the maternity ward before she was ushered back out to work her long days again – this time with a tiny baby to

| | | |
|---|---|---|
| **Deimhniú Breithe** | | **Birth Certificate** |
| Arna eisiúint de bhun an Achta um Chlárú Sibhialta 2004 | | Issued in pursuance of the Civil Registration Act 2004 |
| | **Éire** | **Ireland** |

| | | |
|---|---|---|
| Ainm/Name | **John Desmond** | |
| Sloinne/Surname | | |
| Dáta Breithe/Date of Birth | **Friday, 22 February 1946** | |
| Gnéas/Sex | **Male** | |
| Ionad Breithe/Place of Birth | **Childrens Home Tuam** | |

| | **Máthair / Mother** | **Athair / Father** |
|---|---|---|
| Ainm/Name | **Bridget** | |
| Sloinne/Surname | **Dolan** | |
| Sloinne Breithe/Birth Surname | **Dolan** | |
| Sloinnte Roimhe Seo/ Former Surnames | | |
| Sloinne Breithe Mháthair Tuismitheora / Parents' Mother's Birth Surname | | Sonraí Neamh-chláraithe / Details Not Registered |
| Slí Bheatha/Occupation | **Farmers daughter** | |
| Seoladh/Address | **Clonfert Eyrecourt** | |

| | **Faisnéiseoir A/Informant A** | **Faisnéiseoir B/Informant B** |
|---|---|---|
| Ainm/Name | **Bina** | |
| Sloinne/Surname | **Rabbitte** | |
| Cáilíocht/Qualification | **Present at Birth** | |
| Seoladh/Address | **Childrens Home Tuam** | Sonraí Neamh-chláraithe / Details Not Registered |

| | |
|---|---|
| Bina Rabbitte | |
| Sínithe ag/Signed by | Sínithe ag/Signed by |

| | |
|---|---|
| Cláraitheoir/Registrar | **Bridie Corcoran Asst.** |
| Cláraíodh i gCeantar an Chláraitheora / Registered in the Registrar's District | **Tuam No. 1** |
| Limistéar an Phríomh-Chláraitheora / Superintendent Registrar's District | **Tuam** |
| Contae/County | **Co. Galway** |
| Dáta an Chláraithe nó Athchláraithe (más maidir) / Date of Registration or Re-registration (if applicable) | **1 May 1946** |
| Cláruimhir/Registration Number | **5891374** |

Deimhnítear gue taomariodh an sorrai seo á cláraichar coimithe faoi alt 13 den Acht um Chlárú Sibhialta 2004/Certified to be compiled from a register maintained under section 13 of the Civil Registration Act 2004

Eisithe ag/Issued by **Michelle Connelly**, General Register Office    Dáta /Date **27 February 2013**

Is cion troimchúiseach é an deimhniú seo a athrú nó é a úsáid agus é athraithe / To alter this certificate or to use it as altered is a serious offence

mind as well. There was no fear of seeing women like Bridget pushing a pram up and down the town centre of Tuam. The birth and baptism took place within the walls of the Home, and there the women stayed, never appearing in public. That was the extent of the help they received – the

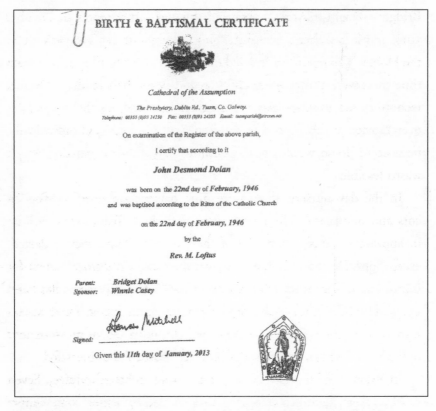

**BIRTH & BAPTISMAL CERTIFICATE**

*Cathedral of the Assumption*

The Presbytery, Dublin Rd., Tuam, Co. Galway.
Telephone: 00353 (0)93 24250  Fax: 00353 (0)93 24355  Email: tuamparish@eircom.net

On examination of the Register of the above parish,

I certify that according to it

**John Desmond Dolan**

was born on the *22nd* day of *February, 1946*

and was baptised according to the Rites of the Catholic Church

on the *22nd* day of *February, 1946*

by the

*Rev. M. Loftus*

Parent:    **Bridget Dolan**
Sponsor:  **Winnie Casey**

Signed: _____

Given this *11th* day of *January, 2013*

cold, disapproving nuns witnessing their silent labours, and then the cold disapproval of the priest who came to baptise their child. There was no other medical help of any kind. The only other interaction would have been a visit by a health inspector.

Records from the Home show that a health inspection was carried out just over a year after John's birth, in April 1947, by an Inspection Board official (name illegible on form). Despite being born a healthy baby, in this report John is described as a 'miserable emaciated child with a voracious appetite and no control over his bodily functions'. The document referred to John as 'probably mental defective'. At this stage, Bridget was no longer in the Home, having been forced to leave after twelve months, as was normal for all mothers. Her baby, little John, had no one to fend for him now – he was alone and deeply vulnerable.

Bridget's daughter, Anna, uncovered this inspection report in October 2013, and it gave her a very disturbing insight into her brother's life at the Home. The report was carried out on 16 and 17 April 1947, at which time there were a total of 271 children and 61 mothers resident. Normal recommended capacity was 243 residents in total, so the Home was overcrowded at this time. The children were not inspected individually, because to do so would mean examining 135 children per day, which wasn't feasible.

In the day nursery, there were nine babies 'contained in wooden cots and one pram'. The report states that these 'Babies were healthy in appearance, except two'. All of the children's names were redacted, except John Desmond Dolan, who was the subject of Anna's request for information. The report noted that one baby had a 'misshapen head and wisened limbs', while another child was a premature infant. There was no inspection of the children's hearing, eyesight, heart rate or measurement of limbs. It does not state if the babies were bottle fed or breastfed.

In Room 2 of the day nursery there were eighteen toddlers. Seven children were identified as having various medical issues, some simply detailed as 'mental defective', another described as having a physical disability and that arrangements were being made for 'admission to Orthopaedic Hospital'. A ten-month-old baby was described as a 'child of itinerant, delicate'.

In Room 3 of the day nursery, the sun room and balcony had 31 infants. Twelve of these were identified as having health issues, mostly 'emaciated', 'delicate' or 'wasted'. Ten children were 'wholly breastfed', with the remaining either being 'bottle fed or partially breastfed'. It also records that there had been an outbreak of measles in the Home earlier that year, which John Desmond Dolan had contracted.

Unloved and uncared for, John never had much of a chance.

Bridget was discharged from the Home on 28 February 1947. Her baby, John Dolan, died on 11 June 1947. Bridget's daughter, Anna, also got hold of John's death certificate. It shows that a Ms Rabbitte was present at the time of his death, the same woman who was also present at his birth. Ms Rabbitte was a long-term 'inmate' in the home and had no medical experience. John's cause of death was recorded as 'measles', but he was also described as 'congenital idiot'. He had been born healthy, but died less than two years later.

Bridget was not given the chance to be with her child when he died, or afterwards. In this she was not alone, just one of thousands of unmarried mothers who did not get to say goodbye to their children, give them a funeral or even pay their respects.

For Anna, finding the records describing John's life and death was incredibly important, but they still leave her with more questions than answers. Did he die alone, only for someone to discover him dead in his cot? Was he sick for long, and did he receive any medical treatment? Or did he die of neglect and malnutrition? Was anyone with John Desmond, holding him lovingly as he slipped away? Was his mother informed? Again, Anna has hit a brick wall in her efforts to uncover the truth about her brother. There is no medical file available for such a sick baby nor is there any medical certification of death for him, as required by law.

Eye-witnesses claim the children who died in the Home were wrapped in shrouds when they died – was John one of these children? Is he one of the bundles that was placed among other little baby bundles in a septic tank? This little baby boy is included in the list of 796 children who are registered as having died in the Home over a forty-year period. It seems likely that his fate was to end up in that unmarked grave (and Sr Marie Ryan of the Bon Secours order has told Anna he is more than likely in the children's grave at the back of the home). When the story of the mass grave in Tuam emerged in 2014, even the survivors of the Home were dumbfounded. One of them, John Pascal (JP) Rodgers, later said: 'I didn't want to believe Catherine Corless, but it is all true and I could have been one of those babies and am blessed to have survived.' John Desmond wasn't so lucky.

John Desmond Dolan's story was at the heart of media explosion

surrounding the Tuam Mother and Baby Home, a little boy left behind
by his mother because he had reached the tender age of twelve months
and it was time for her to go. A little boy left without his mother to die
in the hands of the Bon Secours nuns, who were paid by the state to care
for him. From paperwork Anna has received, it appears that Bridget also
sent back five shillings per month for John's upkeep. There was no further
information available to her on this matter.

The baptism certs kept by Tuam Cathedral have been a key source of
information in uncovering the truth about the burial of the children who
lived in the Home. John Desmond Dolan's baptism cert was among them
(see p. 42), and Anna was able to gain access to it in recent years. It is now
widely accepted that most, if not all, of the 796 children who died at the
Home had been baptised. This contradicts claims made that the children
may have been buried in an unmarked grave because they had not been
baptised – and therefore would not have been eligible for burial in a
Catholic graveyard. There were also suggestions that the Tuam Babies
were buried in what was known as a *cillín*, meaning 'little churchyard'
or 'little burial ground', an unconsecrated burial place for children who
were unbaptised at the time of death. Anna argues that those theories

have now been disproven:

> A lot of people seem to think that these children were unbaptised so that makes it OK for them to be in an unmarked grave, but they were baptised, and I've no doubt all of them were. Even one baby buried in an unmarked grave like this is too much and even worse when that final resting place is a disused septic tank. You have to consider things like rats and vermin crawling through the sewers at that time. No one has told me that didn't happen and after all this was a cesspit, so what rodents were in there?
>
> These were Catholic nuns, who were trained in nursing, and it would have been a natural thing for them to do by having them baptised. I don't think the nuns would have just baptised one baby. I've no doubt they all were christened.

The Registration of Maternity Homes Act 1934 states that 'whenever on or after the appointed day of death occurs in a maternity home in respect of which a person is registered in the register kept by a local authority such person shall give in writing to the chief executive officer of such a local authority notice of such death and the cause thereof by delivering by registered post within twelve hours after such death'. The Act also states that 'if any person fails or neglects to comply with the provisions of this section such person shall be guilty of an offence'.

Despite requesting evidence that her brother's death was notified to the county council, Anna has not received any paperwork to show that the 1934 Act was adhered to in relation to John's death.

After her baby died, Bridget's ties to Tuam were completely dissolved. She had survived the horrors of the Home, but her son had not. She was now a free woman, with a job and a new life. What she could never have foreseen then was that she would become a resident of the Home once more, and would have to endure the terror, pain and heartbreak all over again.

# 4

# The Stories behind the Headlines

The tragedy of the Mother and Baby Homes story is that it affected so many lives. Through Bridget Dolan's story we can appreciate the reality of life in the Home and the isolation it forced on these women and their children, but Bridget was far from alone in this. The homes afflicted so many lives, and those repercussions are still being strongly felt to this day.

In his book *The Lost Child of Philomena Lee* (2009), Martin Sixsmith writes about how the women in the homes were encouraged to feel shame even when among others who had suffered the same fate as them: 'The girls were forbidden to talk among themselves and told not to reveal their real identities or even where they came from. Their lives here were cloaked in secrecy, loneliness and shame. They had, as everyone said, been "put away" to spare their families and society. Few if any received visits from relatives; the fathers of their babies never came.'

The experiences of brave Philomena Lee, who is now an elderly woman, led to her touring the world and encouraging women who had given birth in secret, like Bridget, to come forward and share their experiences. She lovingly told them there was no need to be afraid or to feel shame anymore. As she told the *Irish Daily Mail*:

We were so browbeaten never to tell the story and to keep [it] secret. Too frightened we were in those days because we were classed as immoral. You believed everything the nuns taught you. I think I've reopened the floodgates. I just want the women in my age group to come out and talk too, and don't be afraid. Once I told my daughter, I felt relief.

In later years, other women did find their voices and added them to that of Philomena Lee. They didn't always give their names, but they lent their voices to the movement to destroy shame, which was a brave and honourable thing to do.

One such woman gave a detailed account of her own experience in Tuam in the years after Bridget had moved on. Her memories of the Home are documented in *The Unmarried Mothers: 1920s to 1960s, Irish Culture of Confinement, Institutionalisation and Denial of Family Life, The Tuam Mother and Baby Home* by Kay Geoghegan-Kelly. The woman – who uses the name 'Mary' – was sent to the Home in April 1955, nine years after Bridget was admitted. She describes it as a 'big gloomy building surrounded by big iron gates'.

Mary recalled being brought into the office, where the Reverend Mother asked for her personal details, including the name of the baby's father. She was shown to the maternity ward, where she was placed in bed. It was 3.00 p.m., but she was told the doctor would be with her in the morning. She had to wait two days before the doctor appeared: '[he] examined me and told me when the baby would be due ... I never saw the doctor again in the whole 12 months I was in the Home.' That was Mary's admission procedure – details taken, quick examination and a date given for birth.

Once Mary had been checked by the doctor she was taken to St Patrick's ward, a room in the Home, where there were around twenty children, aged between two and two-and-a-half years old. There was a long table in the room, 'where the children sat to eat their meals'. She described the scene as she saw it:

48

There were no toys in the room, in fact the children never had any toys to play with. The children who could walk trotted around and those that couldn't or were handicapped just sat and rocked back and forth, there was nothing to stimulate them with. There was a bucket in the corner with some kind of disinfectant to mop up the accidents the children continuously had.

They were always soiling themselves, even though there was a potty in the room which they were put on every half an hour. They couldn't help it, their diet consisted of porridge for breakfast, mashed potato for lunch and bread and milk mashed together for dinner, they never had any solid food. I was working in St. Patrick's and was known as a waiting girl. My duties included cleaning up after the children, feeding them and covering the other girl I worked with … At feeding time we would go round with a big pot of porridge and mashed potato and spoon-feed the children, they never had their own plate, cup or cutlery. Some girls worked as waiting girls while others worked in the launderette, sewing room or kitchen.

Mary says the women used to talk among themselves about how the nuns were eating much better than them:

One girl helped the nuns' cook, she would tell us about all the lovely food they would get to eat while we were fed slops. We had a tin mug of porridge for breakfast, lunch was like a water stew, and dinner was bread and butter served on a big plate that was put in to the middle of the table. You had to be quick or you wouldn't get any. We also had a mug of tea. Once a week, our cook would make a fruit cake. This was done without the nuns' knowledge. How she did it I will never know, but we looked forward to it all week.

You didn't have a wash, only once a week were you allowed to the washroom. We were all covered in a huge itchy rash, including the children. We were given a lotion to put on it once a week after your bath, but there was a bottle of the stuff in the nursery that you could put on the babies every day, this was only allowed so that they wouldn't be crying from the itch and disturbing the nuns.

Mary remembered that, when it was her time to give birth, the inmate who helped out in the maternity ward came in with 'filthy' hands – she had been called in from planting potatoes. She tried to get Mary's child to breastfeed, but the child was sleepy, so the inmate slapped the baby very hard across the face to wake her up. Like all the new mothers, Mary spent ten days on the maternity ward and thereafter was expected to resume normal chores, working a long, hard day. Mary remembers only too well the gruelling work schedule the young mothers had:

We were treated so badly. We were never allowed any kind of recreation; no talking was allowed during meal times or when you were in the nursery attending your baby. We were allowed to write one letter a month, which was censored, as was the one coming in. This was done by the nuns' secretary, who had remained on in the Home. She never attended to any of the children nor did she attend any births, she only stood for the children when they were baptised. You were allowed visitors but they seldom came, no one wanted to know you while you were in there. I had none. Christmas was no different to any other day. We never had a Christmas dinner or a tree nor were any decorations put up. The children were never given any presents. They may have had presents sent in by their mothers, but they certainly never received them.

Some mothers sent parcels in after they had left the Home, they would have new clothes and some toys in them, but the children never got them.

A few of the children stick in my mind, there was one child that was a result of a sister/brother relationship and she was so pale, like a porcelain doll. They said she probably wouldn't live past five [years].

Another child had a terrible condition where every time she went to the toilet her bowel would protrude through her bottom. She was never seen by a doctor, they would just push her bowels back inside her. The children were never seen by a doctor or had any kind of medical checks. It was very hard knowing you would have to leave your child behind in that place.

Mary said there was a huge hall in the Home, which served as a communal area for about one hundred children, who were all 'running around … dirty and freezing cold'. There was a complete lack of basic care or compassion, and the facilities were unsuitable for sheltering vulnerable young children:

> There were only four nuns minding the children [in the hall]. The building itself was very old and freezing, especially at night because of the large stone walls. It felt like an ice block when you put your hand on the wall. We were allowed outside on extremely rare occasions. Everyone ate in the big long hall and each person had a bowl for their soup, which was dished up from a big pot which was made earlier. It tasted disgusting, but when you are starving, you would eat just about anything.

Despite the limited care the children received, the nuns were always careful to ensure the children were brought into the faith. The babies in the Home were baptised and the older children made their Holy Communion and Confirmation, if they were unfortunate enough to remain in the Home that long.

The children who survived babyhood and stayed on in the Home were sent to the local primary school in Tuam from around the age of four. When the children walked in together it sounded like a march, according to a retired school principal and long-time resident of Tuam, Mr O'Dwyer. The marching sound came from their hobnail shoes, and the Home children also stood out because their hair was cut short. Mr O'Dwyer told *The Irish Times*: 'We'd hear the boots on the road in the morning, they were always kept back so they wouldn't arrive at school the same time as the rest of us. That also meant they got a slap for being late – every single day.'

Mary describes how the nuns would only clean and dress the children properly if there were visitors coming.

> Some visitors would come to the Home and when that happened the nuns would demand that all the children were scrubbed down, the halls and floors were shining. A big effort was made to clean up the Home, but typically the children were rarely washed and wore the same clothes for weeks. Everyone apart from the nuns were filthy dirty. The young children often soiled themselves and wet the bed. I saw the nuns duck one young child into a big cold bath because she had dirtied herself.
>
> No one was segregated. Boys and girls were all in the same room and younger children were in different rooms. The babies were in wall-to-wall big wooden cots.

One of those babies in the wooden cots was John Rodgers, who was born in the Home on 5 May 1947, just one month before John Desmond Dolan died on 11 June. JP Rodgers would likely have been in the same nursery as John Desmond Dolan. JP's mother probably would have been in the Home at the same time as Bridget, so the two women might have known each other. Bridget Dolan had to leave the Home in February 1947, but JP's mother, Bridie, was in the Home for around six months before her baby was born, so they were bound to have been there at the same time.

JP went on to write the story of his mother's life in his book, *For the Love of My Mother* (2007). Unlike in Anna Corrigan's case, JP's mother told him about her time in Tuam. JP stayed in the Home until he was six years old. When he finally learned of his mother's story, he promised not to write about it until she had passed away.

His mother, Bridie, who was born in Dublin, was found begging in Smithfield when she was two-and-a-half years old and was sentenced by Justice Cussens in the Metropolitan Courthouse on Chancery Street to be detained in St Joseph's Industrial School, Galway, until she reached the age of sixteen. A year after she got out of St Joseph's, Bridie went to work as a domestic for a family in Galway, where she fell pregnant to a local man who worked for the same family. It wasn't until JP was in his thirties that he began building a relationship with his mother:

I believe my mother Bridie was in the Tuam Home for around six months before I was born.

I was very fortunate to have learned her story and to be able to write about it. My mother refused to sign adoption papers for me so I was fostered and she followed me to the ends of the earth until I met her and got to know her.

We had ten wonderful years together after that. She had a friend who used to visit her every month and I would be there. The story of Tuam always came up and I would listen and retain everything. I was always listening. The story was engrained in my memory and anything I was unsure about I tentatively asked the questions. I even had photos.

In his book, JP recreates his birth using his mother's testimony, which he recorded before she died.

Bridie was on her feet, a tortured expression on her face as she bent over holding her tummy.

Oh! The pain! Hold me hand, Quick. Quick. Oh God …

Twelve hours later the nurse delivered a seven-pound baby boy to Bridie, who cried out in agony, and then with joy at being handed the tiny infant.

'Thank you, Sister. I never thought I'd be a mammy. Isn't he lovely?' she whispered, as tears of happiness filled her eyes at the thought that she had produced such a beautiful child after all the distress.

'What are you going to call him?' asked the sister, showing her how to put the child to her breast. 'I think I'll call him Patrick or John. I can't make up my mind yet.'

'Why not call him John Paschal, after the feast of the Passover? Besides, the name Paschal is French and as the Bon Secours Sisters originated in France, it would be a nice name.'

Bridie took her advice and two weeks later, when the baby was christened, he was named John Paschal. Mother and baby stayed together for 13 months in the nursery, where Bridie helped with the feeding and bathing of all the other children.

When JP's mother was due to leave the Home, she told him that she was summoned to the office of Sr Hortense, the head nun in the Home. Sister Hortense had been there since the beginning. Her name can be found on a plaque in the graveyard that she had erected for the IRA men who were imprisoned in the Home in its earlier incarnation. She oversaw the separation of mother and child.

In his book, JP records how Sr Hortense said to Bridie: 'I think it's about time we discussed your baby's future, and of course your own. What are you going to do with the child?' Bridie replied that she wanted to keep her son. It was made very clear that this could not happen. Eventually, Bridie was told that a good job had been secured for her, as a domestic in Galway. She was told: 'You have no means of support, you have no home and you're destroying any chance of future happiness you might have of being free to find a husband and get married.'

In the end, Bridie had no option but to agree. The 'good job' turned out to be a transfer to the Magdalene Laundry in Galway, leaving behind her 13-month-old baby. By the time she reached 34 years of age, Bridie Rodgers had spent nearly 30 years of her life in institutions – just over 13 in St Joseph's, around 18 months in the Tuam Mother and Baby Home and 14 years in the Magdalene Laundry in Galway. In 1962 she finally escaped by climbing over the wall of the Laundry with two of her friends, and they fled to England.

Another former resident of the Home is Pat Duffy from Maghermore, County Galway. Born on 6 April 1952, Pat Duffy's mother, Teresa, who was married to his father Edward, died of a brain haemorrhage during his birth at their family home. The youngest of five, Pat never got to know his mother and almost died at birth himself. He was told he had to be rushed to be baptised because he was in such a 'delicate' state.

Pat's aunt and uncle, Thomas and Mary Kate Duffy, took him for three months because his father could not cope alone with five children following the tragic death of his wife. Three of Pat's sisters were sent with him. But their aunt and uncle, who had ten children of their own, couldn't manage such a large family, so the girls were placed in a convent. Pat told the *Irish Daily Mail*:

My father got vexed because my aunt and uncle put my sisters in the convent so in pure rage he took me away from them and put me into Tuam. I was doing fine until then, they loved me and were broken-hearted over what my father did. I was in Tuam from three months old to seven years. I remember two years very clearly. I was naked a lot of the time in the Home, I don't know why, it was freezing and my nose was dripping all the time, my ears had stuff coming out of them. When you got your dinner, it wasn't much, you would still be hungry and if food fell on the floor, the nuns would make you take it off the floor. All I remember is porridge and it was horrible, but you would eat anything because of the hunger. I was always sick and hungry.

You got no nourishment, you just ate whatever you were given because you were starving. You would be going around the place in that dark and cold building and you would be locked up most of the day, they let you out into the garden the odd time and you would be running around the place.

There were no birthdays, no Christmas, I didn't know what Christmas was until I came home. I had absolutely no life experience whatsoever. I had no idea about life. Even as a child you just didn't get that motherly love, you had no boundaries. I didn't care about anything, I didn't even know what caring was.

There were no cuddles or hugs. The building is as clear as anything in my mind, it was like a concentration camp. The nuns pulled me down by my ears, my ears were sore all the time. When I got out of Tuam, my ears were out of place and sticking out. I went to the GP and he wasn't happy, he said there were numerous infections in my ears. The pain was terrible, they were really badly infected and so painful. To this day I still have a thing about my ears. I couldn't let anyone touch them.

Pat's story is different from the majority of others born in the Home because he was resident there for so long. He wasn't born within its walls, but he remained within them from three months old until the age of seven years. It seems almost miraculous that he survived, given how sickly he was and how little care he was given.

When Pat was seven years old he was due to be sent to Letterfrack Industrial School, a place that is now infamous for its mistreatment of its young inmates. However, his step-sister, from his father's first marriage, insisted he wasn't going there because he would never survive. Quite possibly, Pat owes her his life. St Joseph's Industrial School for Young Boys in Letterfrack, County Galway, was one of the most notorious homes for children. It opened its doors in 1887 and was run by the Congregation of Christian Brothers. Dozens of men came forward years after it closed to reveal they had suffered sexual abuse and extreme physical punishments at the hands of the Brothers. The final, correct figure might never be known, but around 147 boys died from abuse and neglect in the school, which finally closed its doors in 1974. Pat knows how lucky he was not to end up in Letterfrack:

> Somehow my father just relented when my sister put her foot down and I was allowed to come home from the Tuam Home. I just remember all my aunts and uncles crying when I got home, they changed me and cleaned me.
>
> I didn't have a clue what was going on. They were all there looking at me and crying. Everyone was crying and hugging me. I was wild, they had no idea how to manage me. I didn't know anything. My father gave me two packets of biscuits and I ate every one of them and then got sick everywhere. I never had a biscuit in my life and all that sugar, sure I would never have had sweets or treats. I just got sick everywhere.
>
> I went outside, there was animals all around me, I didn't know what they were. I didn't know anything. My father was there. I seen all those wild animals [and I] caught them, broke their necks and killed them all. They were turkeys, no one said anything. My father said, 'Oh my God, he was up to no good.' I didn't know right and wrong. My aunt said he is only a child, he doesn't know what was going on. She was always very good to me, she was my mother figure. When she died I broke down, it was devastating, I felt very broken. I was out of place and something was gone and it took a long time to get myself back.
>
> I love children, I feel hurt, I can't bear anyone touching kids or animals, I cry when animals are sick to this day.
>
> I had no idea about life or the difference between right from wrong and had no empathy. I didn't understand how to show care. Now I am so different, I can't cope with any sort of hurt, like that I love animals and children.
>
> I had a lot of damage done to me in Tuam. I never was able to ask a girl out when I got older. I was just too shy, I could not ask anyone out. I didn't know what to say or how to go about it. So I ended up on my own. I liked the women but could never have the courage to

ask one out and so I never got married and I have no children. I regret that very much.

I have been on the Disability Allowance for 40 years, it is a sad life on your own. I did nothing wrong, this was done to me.

The truth has to come out now. My childhood was robbed from me and it had a life-long effect, it followed me all my life.

I want to be something, I want to be more than I am. I wanted to be strong and famous, but I wasn't. I thought people didn't care about me because I was only a number. I am disgusted with how we were all treated.

Like Pat, the Tuam home played a huge role in Annette McKay's life. Her mother, Maggie O'Connor, gave birth to a little girl in the Home on 7 December 1942. The child, who was named Mary Margaret, sadly died of whooping cough and heart failure six months later, on 6 June 1943. Maggie, who 'probably spoke out of turn' to the nuns, had been sent to Loughrea Industrial School as a punishment; she didn't know for sure, so assumed it was a punishment for cheekiness. One day she was told bluntly by the nuns in Loughrea that her daughter, whom she'd had to leave behind in Tuam, was dead. Maggie's daughter Annette said:

My mam never saw her baby again and was thrown out of the Home straightaway. The nuns just told her, 'The child of your sin is dead.'

That was it, she was kicked out and was not allowed to ask any questions. When she finally did tell us she had a baby that died, she remembered how the baby was heavy on her hip and she said she was a bonny baby.

The nuns had five babies who died in a six-week period of whooping cough and my sister was one of them. The research we have shows 11 babies died in that year. My sister was six months old. Where would you have 11 babies die and no one batted an eyelid? The Health Board didn't.

They didn't even tell my mother if she was sick or unwell. No one cared for Mum's feelings. My mother was haunted by the memories of that home and when she did get dementia in her later life, before she passed away in 2016, I believe it was probably the only time in her life that she had peace and stopped suffering with trauma.

The many, many stories that can now be told about Ireland's hidden children, hidden away in homes and institutions around the country, describe what happened, but they don't explain why. That's a bigger picture, and it has to take in the social mores of the time. It is very difficult for the modern generation to understand how this could have happened, and for so long, but if no one in a position of power is willing to speak out, such travesties of justice can occur.

At the centre of the misery that was the Mother and Baby Homes was the view of the Catholic Church that sex before marriage was a mortal sin, and that an illegitimate child was all the proof needed to reveal that sin. The idea that an unmarried mother would keep her child and raise him/her on her own was not considered. It simply did not happen. (The rare exceptions might be a wealthy woman who could afford to stand separate from society, or a brave woman who was prepared to ignore the teachings of the Church, but those were rare indeed.)

The real source of the Church's power, however, and of its ability to enforce this view on vulnerable young women, was the fact that the state also actively conspired to penalise pregnancy outside marriage. Any moves by progressive politicians to improve the welfare of single mothers were met with attacks from both the political and clerical world. It was an extremely powerful alliance.

This alliance between the Church and the political class was exposed in one of the most notorious political scandals in the history of the Irish state, when Minister for Health Noël Browne tried to introduce socialised healthcare in Ireland.

In 1950, Noël Browne of the Clann na Poblachta party became Minister for Health in John A. Costello's inter-party government. Browne introduced his proposals for mother and child healthcare services, which included free state-funded healthcare to be provided for all mothers and for children aged 16 years and under. Known as the Mother and Child Scheme, this had the potential to radically transform the ability of single mothers to support their children. Through Free State services, bypassing the Church, the proposals were also opposed by family doctors, Catholic and Protestant, who saw the thin edge of the wedge of a Welfare State and a National Health Service, like Britain's. They clearly left the Church to defend religiously run private enterprise medicine.

The Bill sparked a fightback from the Church. The government backed down under pressure from the bishops. In the wake of this scandal, Browne was forced to resign. He revealed confidential Church–state correspondence, giving rise to an impression that the Church dictated government policy.

In *The Lost Child of Philomena Lee*, Martin Sixsmith described how the powerful Archbishop John Charles McQuaid, Archbishop of Dublin from 1940 to 1972, attempted to exercise a veto over any legislation he did not like:

> Archbishop McQuaid railed against it, stating it would encourage single mothers and illegitimate births, allow state interference in moral issues (the preserve of the Church) and usher socialism into Ireland by the back door.
>
> McQuaid had denounced Browne's proposal as 'Totalitarianism' and had written to the Vatican that it was 'an attack on the Church under the guise of social reform'. Browne was summoned before an inquisitional court of bishops which read him a formal statement saying his scheme was contrary to Catholic social teaching. He had been forced to resign and the collapse of his scheme had brought down the government two months later.

It can be argued that Sixsmith overstates McQuaid's influence as he did not achieve his ambitions. He was outmanoeuvred on the 1937 Constitution and was forced to resign from an inquiry into youth employment. However, there can be no doubt that the Church had a direct line to Irish politicians when it came to issues of public morality.

When Bridget Dolan agreed to be signed into the Tuam Mother and Baby Home, it is likely she didn't see any other option. While some women who found themselves pregnant in wealthier families were sent abroad to have the child, before returning home as if nothing had happened, this would not have been a feasible solution for a woman in Bridget's position. She was separated from her family because her pregnancy out of wedlock would have been viewed as damaging to them, as well as to herself.

Bridget, like the other women she shared the Home with, would have had no idea what her future would hold. Their lives were 'ruined' and there was no going back to the way things were before. This resulted in many women leaving Ireland for good after giving birth, to try and salvage some sort of new beginning elsewhere, where their 'shame' could not follow them.

The Irish government, with the help of the Catholic Church, attempted to prevent illegitimate pregnancies by introducing various laws that actively discriminated against unmarried mothers. Their lives were made hard by design, not by accident.

To this day, Anna Corrigan is still trying to piece together her mother's experiences during this bleak part of her early life. The power of the shame she was seen to have brought on her family means there is not a single living person who can tell Anna what her mother had suffered at that time.

This is why hearing about the experiences of other women in the Home is so important to her. The women and their surviving children have stories to tell, and it is crucial that we listen to them and hear them. This is the only way that cloak of silence can be shredded forever.

# 5

# Haunted by What Was Left Behind

I t must have been a bittersweet moment for Bridget as she picked up her suitcase and walked out the front door of the Tuam Mother and Baby Home – free at last, but without the child she had given life to twelve months earlier.

The mother-of-one was formally discharged by the Bon Secours Sisters on 28 February 1947, after securing a position in Loughrea, County Galway, as a domestic – the common term for a housekeeper. She had impressed the nuns so much by staying out of trouble and working hard that they had arranged a job for her on the outside. This is how Bridget was offered a position working for the mother of Sister M. Gertrude Kelly of the Presentation Order, who held the offices of Mother Superior and Mistress of Novices in that order.

Mrs Sabina Kelly lived in Grange Park in Loughrea and was in her eighties and struggling to manage her home. For some women, leaving a Mother and Baby Home for a new job in a new town would have been seen as a chance to start again and close the door on the past. In Ireland at the time, a positive reference from the nuns, whose word was deemed to be God-approved, would go very far for an unmarried mother like Bridget. Without this backing from the nuns and the networks they had influence over, a woman leaving a Home would have had limited employment prospects. Her past would have dictated her present and her future.

'Fallen' women would not have been deemed respectable enough to work with families or with the public. For many, after they left the Home their only option was emigration. The Church's control over the fate of the women in their care was absolute and unquestioned by any section of civil society. It was inescapable. And that iron grip strangled Irish society and Irish women for decades.

In 1973, three decades after Bridget Dolan's experiences of the Home, 18-year-old Terri Harrison was put on a plane for the first time in her life and flown back to Dublin from London when her family learned she was pregnant. She was taken to Bessborough Mother and Baby Home in County Cork, where she stayed for five weeks before running away. She describes how it felt to be cast as the sinful, shameful woman:

The big door closed behind me and I was absolutely frightened. I never saw a place like it in my life. I was only there for five weeks. I flew back to Ireland – it was my first time flying on a plane which they ensured I was on and I had no idea where it was going to land, my mother and her sister were the only family members that knew. The fear I was feeling, the same fear had wrapped itself around this country, it wasn't just in the institutions, where it was a more intense fear. People felt it in national schools, hospitals, everywhere. It was a deep-rooted fear of the clergy that people today can't really fathom.

They had a superior hold and control over you. If a priest walked past you, you bowed your head. In the institutions you were locked behind the doors and gates and they had free rein over you.

You lived in fear that if you stepped out of line, you would be put in a strait-jacket and locked up in a psychiatric unit where no one would ever come near you again.

You were put in those homes because no one cared about you, no one missed you, so you quickly had to try and play ball. You were desperately afraid because they had this divine right over you and they were nearer to God than you would ever hope to be.

You're a criminal without a jury, like a prisoner of war. Those nuns took their badness out on you. No one understands unless they were in there.

Bridget was extremely lucky, then, that she had impressed the nuns enough to secure their patronage.

On the day appointed for her to leave, Bridget said goodbye to the friends she had made in the Home before holding her little boy, John Desmond, for the last time. It must have been a terrifying, exciting and devastating moment all at once – as freedom beckoned, but at a terrible cost. For the nuns, Bridget's deeply conflicted emotions would have been commonplace. They had seen thousands of mothers pass through these institutions, suffering the same hurricane of emotions.

This forced separation of mother and child was a shameful, indefensible feature of a system that sought to punish unmarried mothers. Terri is a case in point. She was eventually caught after running away and brought to St Patrick's Mother and Baby Home in Dublin, where she delivered a baby boy. Like all the other women, she was forced to leave him behind. This separation has affected her whole life. She is riddled with guilt for 'not fighting back to keep her son':

I gave birth to Niall John Kiernan on 15 October 1973.

A Nun and Priest drove from Bessborough in Cork and took him away for adoption. I never signed a document, he was taken from me.

Part of me dies every birthday and I still wait for someone to come to my door and say, 'This has been a terrible mistake, here is your son.'

Like Bridget, Terri was told that this was 'for the best'. The mothers were all told that their child would have a 'better life' if fostered or adopted. There was no choice – as Terri said, the babies were taken. The bond between child and mother, built up during their time in the Home, was regarded as disposable and incidental. Tragically, this logic would cause irreparable damage to thousands of adoptees and their birth mothers, who suffered wounds that would never heal.

The babies and children who were left behind faced a precarious future. The strong survived; the weak did not. Those who did manage to survive the depredations of the Home were often advertised in the local newspapers, looking for foster parents for 'boarded out' children. An article in the *Connacht Tribune*, published on 14 November 1953, appealed for families to come forward to foster children:

Application on Form A to be obtained from the undersigned are invited from female persons for boarding out boys up to 4¾ years: and girls up to 7½ years of age. Maintenance Allowance: 1. Children boarded out under five years of age: £2 per month, until they reach the age of 9 years, and £1-5-0 per month thereafter. 2. Children boarded out over five years of age: £1-5-0 per month. Clothing Allowance: From 6–12 years: £7-10-0 per year. From 12–16 years: £9 per year.

A similar classified advert in the *Tuam Herald*, on 26 April 1958, was headlined 'Boarded out Children' and read: 'Suitable home required for a little girl, 10 years of age, who is at present in Tuam children's home.'

Such adverts were common all over the country. Artist Kevin Sharkey, who was born in St Patrick's Mother and Baby Home in 1961, was one of those children who was fostered out after appearing in an advert. Kevin was told his mother was 15-and-a-half when she gave birth to him in secret. The young teen concealed her pregnancy after she had a relationship with a Nigerian man who was training to be a doctor in the Royal College of Surgeons in Dublin. Having spent four months in the Home after his birth, Kevin and another boy were advertised in a newspaper for adoption:

Adoption, Catholic Registered Adoption Society seeks good adopting parents for two fine healthy coloured baby boys,

Nicholas aged two and Kevin four months old. Apply Box 3962 – A.

Comparing his advertisement in a national newspaper as a child who could be adopted to being like an item for sale, he said: 'It is like Done Deal.ie ... it's so dreadful and the ones that weren't adopted, where are they? You don't see the sick babies.'

He is right. The truth is that for the children who stayed behind in the homes and fell ill, their chances of survival were very limited. After she left the Home and her 12-month-old baby, Bridget Dolan never saw him again. She was not allowed to come back and see him. And that too was 'for the best'.

Bridget kept many letters, memorial cards and photos throughout her life, but there was nothing to say she gave birth in a Mother and Baby Home in any of her belongings when she died on 19 May 2001. In all of the boxes of memorabilia she brought from place to place with her throughout her 82 years, there wasn't a single shred of evidence that she gave birth before her daughter, Anna.

Bridget's son, John, wasn't one of the strong ones. He passed away four months after his mother was discharged from Tuam. Little John's harsh and brief life was doomed from the start. He was denied his most basic needs – a proper diet, a mother's love, a safe environment to grow and learn and decent medical care. John wouldn't live long enough to become an advert in the newspaper. He couldn't survive alone in the Home.

For those who did survive, it was no easy matter to get over the trauma of their early lives. The experience of being so cruelly and suddenly separated from their mothers had a deep and lasting impact on the children who made it out of the Home. In *Understanding the Pain of Abandonment*, Claudia Black writes:

Children are totally dependent on caretakers to provide safety in their environment. When they do not, they grow up believing that the world is an unsafe place, that people are not to be trusted, and that they do not deserve positive attention and adequate care.

These feelings would blight the lives of survivors of the homes.

For the babies and children left behind, the chances of survival were quite bleak. The health inspection report carried out on 16 and 17 April 1947 by a visiting committee, and provided by the Department of Health to Anna, examined the high mortality rate in the Tuam Mother and Baby Home, which far exceeded the national average at the time. In an article on that report, published on 4 March 2017, thejournal.ie noted that:

> The infant mortality rate at the Home (Tuam) was double that of even other Mother and Baby Homes around the country at the time.
>
> Young children in the Tuam Home succumbed to deaths from afflictions as heartbreakingly familiar as the flu and, although only in a small number of cases, ear infections.
>
> The most common causes of death were 'debility from birth' (25%), 15% from 'respiratory diseases', 10% each from influenza and the measles, 8% born too premature to survive, 6% from whooping cough and in small numbers of epilepsy/convulsions, gastroenteritis, meningitis, congenital heart disease and congenital syphilis, skin diseases, chicken pox and one per cent – 10 children – of malnutrition.

Statistics from that 1947 report show that over a 12-month period that ended on 31 March 1943, the number of births and admissions was 159 while the number of deaths was 54, or about 34%. In the figures for the same period up to 31 March 1944, the number of births plus admissions was 169 while the number of deaths was 42, or 25%.

In the year up to 31 March 1945, the number of births plus admissions was 153 and the number of deaths was 36, or 23%. For the next year up to 31 March 1946, the number of births plus admissions was 143 while the number of deaths was 39, or 27%.

A note at the end of the report stated:

The death rate had appeared to be on the decrease but has now begun
to rise again. During the ½ year ended 30.09.46 the number of births
and admissions was 66, the number of deaths 21 or about 32%.
Appended is a list of causes of death of each of the infants who died
in the year ended 31.03.46.

It is time to enquire into the possible cause before the death rate
becomes higher. First there is the constant risk of infection brought in
from outside by admission of whole families of itinerants, destitute,
evicted persons, etc. Dr Dillon drew attention to the following on
inspection in July 1945 – there is no isolation unit and the children
mingle with the others in the home.

Despite the damning evidence of sick and dying children, the report
concluded that the 'care given to infants in the Home is good, the sisters
are careful and attentive, diets are excellent. It is not here that we must
look for the cause of the death.' The Home itself was described as filthy
and rife with infection, even as the report described the care as 'good'. It
was inevitable that vulnerable youngsters would suffer serious illness and
death in such a place.

The indignity the children suffered did not come to an end with death.
When it was discovered that 796 babies and children had died at the
Home in Tuam, the obvious question was: where are they buried? It was
this question that led to the subsequent scandal. When local graveyards
had been searched and discounted, another possibility came to light: that
the nuns were getting rid of the ever-increasing number of children's dead
bodies by dumping them in an abandoned cesspit underneath the Home.

Following the first wave of the Tuam scandal, long-forgotten
architectural plans of the old workhouse on the site of the Tuam
Mother and Baby Home were uncovered, in June 2014, by blogger Izzy
Kamikaze – a campaigner for LGBT rights who was born Ruth O'Rourke

but has since changed her name. The plans show at least nine previously unknown cesspools, or large boxes, underground on the site.

A cesspit, or cesspool, is a pit or covered cistern that can be used to dispose of all sewage and refuse generally. The drawings of what lies beneath the Home offered a fresh perspective on the mystery of the location of the bodies of the 796 children whose deaths were recorded at the Home, but for whom no burial records have been found.

The plans of the workhouse, which date to 1840, show that the original sewerage system seems to have been updated in 1918. This means the system marked on these plans may have been decommissioned at that time rather than later, as previously thought. The plans lay untouched for years until they were discovered by Izzy Kamikaze at the Irish Architectural Archives. At the time, Izzy told the *Irish Daily Mail*: 'The plans show the construction design of several vaults and cesspools as well as the plans for the infirmary building.' As the system was upgraded, a map from 1892 shows that there was a 'sewage tank', which is clearly marked in the southwest corner of the site. If you overlay the map of present-day Tuam, it is clear there was a septic tank at that location. The 'sewage tank' is actually a septic tank – in other words, a water-based system – and is not part of the original workhouse.

It has been one of the most deeply shocking findings of the history of the Home, that the bodies of these babies and children were treated with such disrespect, such casual neglect. One survivor of the Tuam Home, who was born there in 1951 and remained as a resident for five-and-a-half years before he was 'boarded out', noted that rats must have been rife underground in these cesspits. 'It only makes sense that rats were down there, we are speaking about a sewage area after all.' It is a chilling thought.

For the families of those buried there and the survivors, it is an incredibly distressing scenario to accept. Bridget's daughter, Anna Corrigan, is both shocked and angry that the children's bodies were treated in this manner. In life they were labelled as the products of sin, as mental defectives and congenital idiots, and when they died, those labels meant they could be disposed of without any care or decency whatsoever. As Anna put it:

If these children who were sick were given these awful titles, like congenital idiot, then it's easy to think no one cared enough to give them any sort of loving bedside manner. And how many of these 'congenital idiots' were in the Home with my brother? Were they all left there to die? There is no medical file for John, how can that be? He was a very ill child according to the nuns and they were a nursing order and there was a resident doctor.

I can't get my head around it, I am fully convinced my brother died from neglect and malnutrition. But even then, with everything that has emerged about Tuam and other homes, such as Bessborough, where the *Irish Examiner* newspaper stated that following research they claim that death certificates were falsified to broker clandestine adoptions, I have to ask: is John even dead?

The distressing thing about the harsh lives and deaths of these innocent babies and children is that they were so unnecessary. These poor little ones had families – mothers, grandparents, uncles and aunts – who could have taken care of them. It was the social stigma attached to their birth that made that choice impossible. Instead, they were abandoned, totally and utterly. The families of the girls who ended up in the various institutions around the country were incapable of going against the received wisdom of the Church. It was a failure not just by the Church but by the government and by all Irish people. The blame cannot attach to one single place – the sad truth is that everyone colluded in damning these pregnant young women and their babies. It brings to mind that famous quote: The only thing necessary for the triumph of evil is for good men to do nothing.

The unmarried mothers living in the Tuam Mother and Baby Home were permitted visitors, but it was rare for anyone to show up at the door.

For Bridget, the distance would have been too far to travel for the Dolan family, and there is no evidence that any of Bridget's family visited her while she was in Tuam. She told a family member in later years: 'My family completely and utterly abandoned me and I owe a lot to the nuns for taking care of me.' When she recently learned this information, Anna said she felt 'totally helpless for my mother's pain'.

It would be at least ten years before Bridget reconciled with her family after arriving in Tuam, which one can only assume left her completely devastated. None of Bridget's family attended the births of her children and no family relatives stood for them when they were baptised, according to their documents.

Expectant mothers like Bridget 'disappeared' to another town or county during their 'shameful' pregnancies, and they were never spoken of back home. For example, Sheila O'Byrne gave birth to her only child, a boy, in St Patrick's Mother and Baby Home on the Navan Road, in Dublin, in 1976. He was taken from her and she never saw him again. She said: 'I loved my family, but they never, ever asked me about my son. They just carried on as if it didn't happen. I disgraced them in their eyes. It was wrong. And I was worked like a slave in the home, from morning to night, hard, tough labour, and no one gave a damn about us, we were sinners and slaves, when the reality is, we were neither and there wasn't a thing we could say or do about it.' This deep and wide silence was observed by everyone, and that's why these practices could take place right under people's noses.

There is no evidence that Bridget was told about her son's death, but like any mother who was separated from her child in such a cruel way, it is likely she made discreet enquiries of her own. Whatever she heard, Bridget went on about her chores in her new post in Loughrea and tried to put the past behind her. It is unclear if she visited her family when she was discharged from Tuam, but they probably learned of her release. In a letter written to Bridget at Christmas 1947, six months after John's death, Sr Gertrude thanked her for looking after her mother, Sabina:

My dear Bridget,

This is a line to thank you very sincerely for your goodness in minding mother R.I.P so well in her last illness and all along.

I got a great account of you and all you did for mother R.I.P. May God Bless you for it and I'm sure she will not forget you in Heaven. You were wonderful to be able to carry her up and down stairs every time she wished, and all the other work you did besides.

May the good God leave you your health and strength always. It is a great charity to be kind to the old and weak and God will bless you for your charity.

You have a very good kind mistress now, it would be hard for you to get the like of her, so mind her well.

Again, thanking you Brigid and wishing you a very happy Christmas. I remain yours sincerely in J&C

Sr M Gertrude.

When Anna first came across this letter in her mother's belongings after she passed away, it didn't mean much to her at first. But later, after she had learned of her mother's secret life, the first thing that struck her was that the nun had not mentioned Bridget's child, who had died in June that same year. There is also no reference to Bridget's gruelling year in the Home and the devastation of having to part company with her own flesh and blood forever.

Bridget also kept a memorial card for Sabina Kelly, Sr Gertrude's mother, whom she had evidently cared for so well. According to the card, Mrs Kelly died on 17 December 1947, aged 84 years. Also among Bridget's belongings is a death notice for Sr M. Gertrude Kelly from the Presentation Convent in Galway – but there is no date for when she died.

Bridget was not typical in finding work outside the Home. Not every mother who entered the Home in Tuam was permitted to get a job on the outside; some mothers were sent on, or back, to the Magdalene laundries. The Bon Secours Sisters were paid by the local county council for their work running the Home, but the nuns supplemented this by charging the women as well. Brigid, for example, sent back five shillings (around €10) every month for John.

Whatever happened to them afterwards, it is true to say that many women who left the homes or the Magdalene institutions suffered psychological trauma as a result of their experiences. Annette McKay, who is a qualified counsellor, said her mother, Maggie, endured countless dark periods in her life after spending most of it in institutions run by nuns. For Annette, it was heartbreaking to witness her mother's torment.

Maggie O'Connor was born in County Galway on 25 February 1924, but spent most of her life believing she was born on 24 February, until the Residential Institutions Redress Board confirmed her actual date of birth. She was one of eight children, who were all abandoned by their father after their mother, Annie, died. Annie and her unborn baby had died after she contracted sepsis during her ninth pregnancy. Maggie's grandmother lived a few doors away from the family, and she wanted to help them, but her other daughter, Annette's auntie, wouldn't hear of it and barred Annette and her siblings from their grandmother's house. After losing their mother the children were starving, with no one to take care of them. Annette said:

One day they were all marched to Court and sentenced to Lenaboy Industrial School on Taylor's Hill in Galway and the boys went to the Christian Brothers. No one wanted to take care of them and my mother ended up in one of these nasty religious-run homes. It didn't stop there for my mother. She went on to the Tuam Home after she was raped in the Home [at Lenaboy]. My mother suffered so badly, people have no idea, it was endless trauma and it was all because of those evil nuns.

Lenaboy Castle, also known as St Anne's, was an orphanage and industrial school on Taylor's Hill, in Galway, run by the Sisters of Mercy and catering for both boys and girls. There, Maggie worked 'like a slave' in the kitchens, but received no payment for her work. Her father, Paddy O'Connor, would come and visit the children in the Home sometimes and Maggie told her daughter that the nuns would stand behind her father holding a stick – a warning that she wasn't to speak a word of truth about her situation. Annette said:

> My grandfather would say, 'Are you OK, Maggie? You have bags under your eyes, you look nervous.' But she would tell him she was fine, so he wouldn't have known how bad it was for them or what was happening to them.
>
> The trauma they must have went through, having been taken from your home and put in a dormitory with kids crying and wetting their beds.
>
> Nora and Bridgey [Maggie's younger sisters] would wet the bed and wake Mum and she would be so terrified. If they were caught, they would be made stand in the corner of the room with the wet sheet over their heads. The nuns would come and put her in the bed, or put her in the cold bath and shave her head in punishment.

Maggie left when she reached the age of 16, as she was legally entitled to do, but she came back to care for her sisters, Nora and Bridgey. Following her return she was raped by a male worker at the Home, which resulted in her becoming pregnant at 17 years of age. Maggie was immediately sent to the Tuam Mother and Baby Home, where she gave birth to her 'bonny' baby, Margaret Mary. Annette said: 'Mam didn't stand a chance, she would have given them [the Bon Secours nuns] some cheek and that is why she was moved to Loughrea Industrial School with the Mercy nuns. She was never clear how long she got to spend with the baby, but she kept it from us until she was 70.'

Baby Mary Margaret died the following year and is one of the 796 children named in the list of those who died in the Home at Tuam.

Annette is plagued by some of the same awful doubts and questions as Anna Corrigan. She says that Maggie was never shown any human decency: 'After she was put out of Loughrea by the nuns, she was not permitted to visit her baby's grave or to ever know any details about the baby she had so tragically lost. Is my little sister even dead?'

Maggie O'Connor fled to the UK as soon as she was told those awful words: 'the child of your sin is dead'.

Years later, Annette uncovered her mother's early papers, dating to the time shortly after she moved to the UK, and she discovered that Maggie had made a very serious attempt to take her own life and was committed to a psychiatric home as a result.

She really suffered, it was life-long. Even when she lived in normal life, she would see a convent or nuns and would freak out.

After she came out of the [psychiatric] unit she came straight to pick her children up [Annette and her siblings], which says a lot about her character. She just kept going.

But she was always talking and talking about her own life, she would run off sometimes and the neighbours would have to put us to bed. She was a wreck, she suffered so badly.

A lot of the women who came out of those homes were on Valium, I know my mother was. The neighbours used to say, 'Give your mum her tablets.'

I think when she got dementia in the end, in a way it was a blessing, right up to her eighties there was memories that were traumatising for her, so she had peace.

You would go to the house and say, 'Mum, why are you crying?'"and she would say, 'It's the nuns, it never goes away'. I just can't forgive the nuns for what they did on my mother. To think of the damage they caused my mother, who was one of the most beautiful women you could ever meet. Everyone knew her and the way she dressed, she was so stylish, she was just a beautiful woman.

It wasn't until Maggie's first great-grandchild, Josh, was born – Annette's grandchild – that she broke down sobbing and revealed the secret she had kept all those long years.

> Imagine not being able to tell anyone what she had been through, and that she had lost her little daughter. It was so awful, she told us she had a child who had died. It just never occurred to us that she was going through this pain of losing a child for all those years. What can you do with that sort of information?
>
> My poor mother thought, somewhere there is a little grave with a headstone. When we learned that wasn't the case and there were hundreds of babies in a septic tank, my God, it just makes me so angry.

Maggie suffered with dementia for the last number of years of her life and sadly passed away on 8 April 2016 in a hospital in Manchester. Annette said:

> Mum must have been insanely stressed and traumatised, there was nothing humane about the treatment of these women at all. Whenever you read about it, it's so similar to the behaviours of the Nazi camps.
>
> My mum was lost over here [in the UK] as an Irish woman and the Irish government has a responsibility to those people.

That call for the Irish government to take responsibility for its role in the treatment of unmarried mothers is echoed by Anna Corrigan. She believes both the nuns and the state let her mother down and also believes, in hindsight, that her mother suffered something akin to Stockholm syndrome when it came to the nuns. Stockholm syndrome can occur in people subjected to a hostage or kidnap situation, whereby they feel a positive bond with their captor. Psychologists see it as a survival strategy at a time of distress and crisis. Anna recognised this in her mother's thinking:

My mother still spoke highly of the nuns as the years went on, probably for survival because the reality of thinking of all the horrible things that happened to her could have been far worse. And all she could do now was to thank the nuns because she was obviously alone. That's not OK. Sometimes it's easier to believe someone is a good person rather than accept they did wrong because what would happen to them then? It's easier to pretend bad things didn't happen.

Bridget was a survivor, that's for sure. She was a strong woman who moved on after her experience in the Home and carved out a new life for herself. Anna does not know for sure where her mother went after she left the service of Sister Gertrude's mother, but it is certain that Bridget never went back to ask after John Desmond. She wouldn't have dared. She would no doubt have known that any desperate woman turning up at the door of the Home begging for information, or sight of her child, had the door shut firmly in her face. There was only one way for Bridget, and that was forwards and onwards, trying to build a new life as best she could.

But life wasn't to turn out as Bridget hoped. The new life she was building in Loughrea, away from the trauma and misery of Home, was not to last. In a stroke of huge misfortune, in 1949 Bridget found herself pregnant again. She was living in Main Street, Loughrea, at the time, but other than that nothing is known of the circumstances of her pregnancy.

What is known is that, once it became obvious that she was pregnant, she faced the same sentence: to be sent to the Tuam Mother and Baby Home, a place she hoped to have left behind for good two years previously. This time, she knew all that awaited her, and walking up to that door and knocking to be let in must have broken her heart all over again.

# 6

# The Mystery of Tuam's Lost Babies

The system of separating and isolating unmarried mothers was supposed to promote 'moral behaviour' in society, but it never seemed to achieve that goal. Young women who had been sent to an institution because of pregnancy were damaged by the experience, which made them vulnerable. When they were turfed out of the institution after twelve months, they were more vulnerable than ever. It isn't surprising that many found themselves pregnant again, just like Bridget, and back under the 'care' of the nuns.

On 27 March 1950, Bridget, who was by then seven months' pregnant, once again dragged her suitcase up the path to the Tuam Mother and Baby Home. She was admitted back into the Home and the same old damp building full of bad memories, terrified mothers and neglected children.

Years later, her daughter Anna uncovered her readmission form with the help of Barnardos, which secured the information from the HSE office of Clann Western Adoption Committee (now Tusla – the Child and Family Agency), in Merlin Park, Galway. The form read:

Form 3 – Order for Admission to an Institution other than a Hospital.
Galway County
To the Matron or other Officer in charge of the Children's Home, Tuam.

I hereby certify that to the best of my belief, Brigid Dolan, Main Street, Loughrea, aged 28 years is a person in the County eligible for Relief who is an expectant mother and cannot be effectively received at less cost to the rates otherwise than in the above-mention Institution and I hereby require you to admit the said person to the said Institution.

FORM 8.—Order for Admission to an Institution other than a Hospital.
GALWAY COUNTY.
To the Matron or other Officer in charge of the Children's Home, Tuam.
*I hereby certify that to the best of my belief* Brigid Dolan Main St, Loughrea, *aged* 28 *yrs.,*
*is a person in the County eligible for Relief who is* an expectant unmarried mother *and cannot be effectively relieved at less cost to the rates otherwise than in the above-mentioned Institution and I hereby require you to admit the said person to the said Institution.*

Member of Public Assistance Authority
or other authorised person.
Date 26th March 1950.
*State here the qualification for admission to the Childrens' Home, i.e., whether a married or unmarried mother, or (if a child) whether legitimate or illegitimate or an orphan, or a deserted child*

On the form, which was released to Anna in 2014, the signature was redacted, but an explanation was provided by describing the person who had signed it as a 'member of Public Assistance Authority or other authorised person'.

How would the nuns have reacted to Bridget falling pregnant a second time? In her book *Mother and Child: Maternity and Child Welfare in Dublin 1922–60*, author Lindsey Earner-Byrne quoted a 1943 report by the Joint Committee of Women's Societies and Social Workers, which referred to 'repeat offenders' like Bridget Dolan:

When referring to the institutional care of unmarried mothers, the report stressed that the detention of mothers for a period of one year was in no sense 'penal'. However, the validity of this argument was somewhat vitiated by a subsequent recommendation the 'repeat offenders' be detained for two years.

The report explained that 'the object of our recommendations is to regulate control according to individual requirements, or in the more degraded cases, to segregate those who have become sources of evil, danger and expense to the community'.

The expense could of course be interpreted as a moral or financial one, but the emphasis was on the latter.

The commission urged that no woman should be discharged until she had given a guarantee that she could provide for her child 'either by paying wholly or partially for maintenance in the Home or boarding it out with respectable people approved by the Board of Health'.

These recommendations were predicated on the assumption that legal powers would be introduced, to allow for the detention for at least one year of unmarried mothers who sought assistance. No such legal powers were ever introduced.

Christine Hennessey, a counsellor with the Post-Adoption Unit in Barnados, feels that everything was stacked against these women breaking away from the experience of being ostracised, deprived of their babies and made to feel like outsiders who deserved nothing at all from their communities:

Many women had hopes the father of their baby would marry them, but it just never happened. Some women tragically were raped. It was a terrible time and I see first-hand the damage done to these women and children.

I have a major issue in particular with what happened in the Industrial schools especially as these children had no life skills and many girls were pregnant as soon as they left. They had no idea about life. Other women went on to have two children and three children out of wedlock. There was a lot of suffering and still is. I am working in this area 30 years and I see all the mothers coming back and the survivors using our tracing service and our workshops. Tuam lifted the lid on what was going on, but we have not even scratched the surface of any of the bigger homes, like St Patrick's on the Navan Road, North Dublin.

While the exact circumstances of how Bridget fell pregnant for a second time are a mystery, we do know that Bridget was not in a relationship. She had no one to support or shelter her.

Once back inside the Home, Bridget was signed in and shown to the maternity ward, where she was placed in a bed. A doctor would have examined her, to ascertain her likely due date. Then the drudgery of life in the Home would have begun again – the hard labour, the enforced silence, the unrelenting work to care for so many distressed and ill children.

Less than a month later, Bridget was admitted to Central Hospital, Galway, on 12 April 1950.

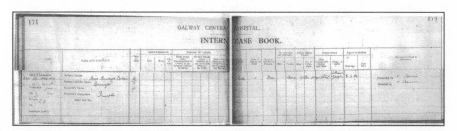

In the nuns' ledgers it says: 'mother discharged to Galway Hospital'. It was rare that a woman from the Home went to the Central Hospital, now known as Galway University Hospital, to give birth, so the indication is that something must have been wrong. Bridget would have only been brought to the hospital if there was a medical emergency that posed a risk to either the mother or the baby.

**Deimhniú Breithe** — **Birth Certificate**

Arna eisiúint de bhun an Achta um Chlárú Sibhialta 2004 — Issued in pursuance of the Civil Registration Act 2004

Éire — Ireland

| Clárúmhar Registration Number | 5970905 | Breith a Chláraíodh i gCeantar Birth Registered in the district of | Galway No. 2 |
| i Réimhéar an Phríomh-Chláraitheora in the Superintendent Registrar's District of | Galway | i gContae in the County of | Co. Galway |

| Uimh. No. | Dáta Breithe Date of Birth / Ionad Breithe Place of Birth | Ainm Name | Gnéas Sex | Ainm, Sloinne agus Ionad Chónaithe an Athar Name and Surname and Dwelling-Place of Father | Ainm agus Sloinne na Máthar agus a sloinne roimh phósadh di Name and Surname and Maiden name of Mother | Céim nó Gairm Bheatha an Athar Rank or Profession of Father | Síniú, Cáilíocht agus Ionad Chónaithe an Fhaisnéiscora Signature, Qualification and Residence of Informant | An Dáta a Chláraíodh When Registered | Síniú an Chláraitheora Signature of Registrar | Ainm Baiste má agadh é tar éis chlárú na Breithe agus an Dáta Baptismal Name if added after Registration of Birth and Date |
|---|---|---|---|---|---|---|---|---|---|---|
| 245 | 1950 (*torty*) Twenty first May Central Maternity Hospital Galway | William Joseph | M | — | Bridget Dolan Clonfert Eyrecourt — Farmers daughter | — | As to Physical occupier Central Hospital Galway | Twenty sixth may 1950 | H' Hurley Clárutheóir (Registrar) | |

Deimhnítear gur thúrslíodh na sonraí seo ó chlárleabhar coimithe faoi alt 13 den Acht um Chlárú Sibhialta 2004/Certified to be compiled from a register maintained under section 13 of the Civil Registration Act 2004 Eisithe ag / Issued by **Michelle Connelly, GRO** Dáta / Date Of Issue **27 February 2013**

Is cion tromchúiseach é an deimhniú seo a athrú nó é a úsáid agus é athraithe / To alter this certificate or to use it as altered is a serious offence

---

UNIVERSITY COLLEGE HOSPITAL, GALWAY

## Certificate of Baptism

WILLIAM JOSEPH DOLAN

son / daughter of BRIDGET DOLAN

and

was born on the 21 day of MAY 20 1950

and was baptised according to the rite of the Catholic Church on the

25 day of MAY 20 1950

by the Rev. M. C. CONNOR

the Sponsors being THOMAS BARRETT
BRIDGET RUANE

Record of Confirmation

Record of Marriage

Given this 14 day of JANUARY 2013

Signed Rev. Fr. Peter Tyler
CHAPLAIN
UNIVERSITY COLLEGE HOSPITAL
GALWAY

At the hospital she gave birth to her second son, William Joseph Dolan. His birth certificate shows he was born on 21 May 1950. The little boy was baptised four days later, on 25 May 1950, by the Rev. M. O'Connor and his sponsors were Thomas Barrett and Bridget Ruane.

Medical documents secured by Anna under the Freedom of Information Act show that Bridget stayed in the hospital until 5 June 1950, a period of two weeks after giving birth, and was then readmitted to the Home in Tuam. Again, there is only a one-page medical record to go with Bridget's medical file in Galway University Hospital. It is one of the only pieces of documentation to survive from William's brief life.

The Home's records show that William was resident there for a number of months after being discharged from the hospital. However, the nuns' ledgers subsequently include a brief, limited note, merely saying he 'died' on 3 February 1951. Crucially, however, there is no death certificate for William. Anna has checked and double-checked, but her brother William is not registered in the General Registry of Births and Deaths.

These checks were also subsequently carried out by Barnardos and by An Garda Síochána, who failed to uncover any documents to prove conclusively that William is either alive or dead. He is not on the list of the 796 children who died in the Home.

The only record of William's death is in the nuns' ledgers, where he is referred to as 'illegitimate' and simply that he 'died'. No medical explanation is given. And to confuse matters further, there is a second date of birth – 20 April 1950 – recorded for William in the nuns' documents.

When Bridget was readmitted to the Home from the hospital on 5 June, her age was recorded as 29 years and her date of birth was recorded as 23 August 1921, instead of 5 September 1918. Anna has secured this information from the Department of Health and from Tusla – Child and Family Agency. Exactly 13 days after William's supposed death, Bridget was discharged from the Home again. This meant she would have been there when her son was meant to have passed away – unlike John, who died four months after she was discharged.

The nuns' ledger states: '226 Dolan Bridget, 29 years of age, date of admission, 5th June 1950, her date of discharge 16th February 1951, Clonfert, name and address of nearest relative, No of children, 1, William Joseph Dolan, 9 months.'

Anna remains unsure about what happened to her brothers, given the confusion around the records that she has unearthed. Poorly kept or inaccurate records in Catholic institutions are often an indication that illegal adoptions may have occurred, and there can be no doubt that the practice was widespread across Ireland at the time.

While unregistered adoptions were illegal in Ireland after the 1952 Adoption Act, the law was often ignored by nuns – as well as by some doctors – who knew that they were very unlikely to face prosecution if caught. The practice was an open secret in Ireland at the time, despite being nominally a criminal offence. Consultant Archaeologist and Anthropologist Toni Maguire is a leading expert in marginalised infant and adult grave sites in Ireland and has recorded 97 *cillíní* grave sites for County Antrim alone, involving new information for *cillín* burials at established historic sites and a number of previously unknown and unrecognised locations.

In Toni's expert opinion, she believes that death certificates of children who died in the Home may have been falsified and that it's quite possible Anna's brother, William, was trafficked to the States under the smokescreen of an infant death:

There is a real concern here. Where you have a Mother and Baby Home scenario, the baby is the commodity, he or she is a saleable item, they had value, and without objective scrutiny to monitor the various aspects of management within these institutions, systems such as these are open to misuse.

If the baby was healthy and there was a demand for that child and that child added value to the Church or order involved, you must remember the priest and nuns are human, they are not going to miss an opportunity to make money. I've no doubt babies were trafficked like this. You move babies around enough, perhaps to a hospital or to another home, and then paperwork goes missing and suddenly the child is missing. It would have been all too easy to do.

On foot of advice from experts such as Toni, and having reflected deeply on William's situation throughout the process of this book, in January 2018 Anna began writing to orphanages across Dublin in case her brother was transferred to a Dublin orphanage from Tuam and then on to the USA. She is awaiting replies from the various institutions, but has not given up hope.

It is a fact that the babies and children who survived in the Home were offered for fostering, or 'boarding out', as we know, and it seems likely that full and permanent adoption was also offered. There is much evidence to support this disturbing trend.

On 8 October 1951, *The Irish Times* reported that in the previous year 'almost 500 babies were flown from Shannon [airport] for adoption', a number that the paper said 'is believed to have been exceeded' during the first nine months of 1951. In the first week of October alone, it reported 18 'parties' of children had departed from the airport. These figures far exceed the number of official 'adoption passports' issued by the government to let adoptive parents take children out of Ireland. In the whole of 1951, only 122 such passports were issued, a fraction of the number of children actually taken from the state.

In 1952 a headline in the German newspaper *8 Uhr-Blatt* read: '1000 children disappear from Ireland'. And in 1955 the *New Haven Register* wrote how '50 American couples buy Irish babies through international adoption ring'.

An indepth study by Mike Milotte, published in his book *Banished Babies: The Secret History of Ireland's Baby Export Business* (1997), described how in the 1950s, 1960s and 1970s thousands of 'illegitimate' children were illegally trafficked to the USA. Wealthy American families travelled to Ireland in their droves to adopt, legally or illegally, babies born in the

Mother and Baby Homes or in private nursing homes, and they were permitted to take these children away with little or no paperwork.

Information held by the National Archives shows that during the 1950s up to 15 per cent of illegitimate children were taken to the USA with the blessing of the Irish government. It's estimated that at least 2,000 children were adopted to America, but these are only the children we know about. There are still children unaccounted for. Eyewitnesses claim hundreds of babies were taken through Shannon Airport and into the North of Ireland and adopted to America with no official records. Who they are and if they even know they are adopted remains a mystery to this day. There are also eyewitness reports that children were brought by car over the border into Northern Ireland and flown abroad from there to their adoptive families.

These illegal adoptions effectively erased the history of the illegitimate child, which was seen as preferable by some adopting parents. However, as some of these children, who were told they were adopted despite their falsified records, grew to be adults and began to enquire about their biological parents, the failure of the state and the religious orders to regulate adoptions in the 1950s and 1960s, and the impact of this on the now-adult adoptees, became heartbreakingly apparent.

Even to this day, there are thousands of files relating to around 48,000 adoptions in Ireland (which came into operation on 1 January 1953, following the implementation of the Adoption Act, to the present day) that are still unaccounted for, while an unknown number of files are lying in warehouses still waiting to be processed after some of the religious orders who were running these orphanages and homes finally handed them over to the state. Many of the adults affected were left bereft by their inability to discover anything about their origins. The law in Ireland favours the privacy of the birth mother, which means an adopted person is not automatically entitled to their birth details. In the 1980s and 1990s the adoptees began to organise support groups, speak to the media and apply pressure on the government to try to resolve this issue.

THE MYSTERY OF TUAM'S LOST BABIES

In an article in *The Irish Times* on 6 March 1996, headlined 'Adoption Board Confirms false names were given', the state publicly admitted, for the first time, that false documents had been issued during adoptions:

> Claims that religious and other institutions illegally provided false names for the birth certificates of so-called illegitimate children were supported last night by the Adoption Board (now known as the Adoption Authority of Ireland).
>
> The board has called for birth records and counselling to be offered to adopted people and birth parents who cannot contact each other because of the practice.
>
> The practice came to light when Ms Norah Gibbons of Barnardos said attempts to establish the origins of children sent to the United States in the 1950s and 1960s were hampered in some cases because their birth certificates carried false names.
>
> Ms Gibbons said … that the practice also affected many adopted people in Ireland.

Illegal adoptions or false registrations happen when an adopted child is illegally registered as the birth child of their adoptive family. It is unknown how many people in Ireland were illegally adopted, but the effects have been devastating to many who have made the discovery later in life – while others are perhaps unaware that this happened to them. A birth certificate is a legally binding document: it means that your adoptive family is now legally your birth family, thereby erasing your true biological history. It is a deception that can never be undone, can never be amended unless someone comes forward with the truth. Even then, the General Register Office (GRO) would require DNA proof and legal interventions to restore the natural identity of someone in this situation. The process is so onerous and time-consuming, it would be an impossibly huge burden for the majority of people. In reality, then, once that information is lost, obscured, hidden, it is very rarely ever recovered.

In recent years a number of cases relating to illegal adoptions have come before the Irish courts. On 6 May 2016 *The Irish Times* reported on one such case in the High Court under the headline: 'Adopted boy passed off as couple's "natural child", mother says':

> A woman has claimed her new born son was passed off as the natural child of a couple after she believed he was sent for adoption 54 years ago.
>
> The mother and son, who were reunited in recent years, are suing a private adoption organisation over what they allege were fraudulent documents stating the baby was the natural child of the couple who brought up the boy.
>
> Eanna Mulloy SC, for the mother and son, said the woman, when aged 21 in 1961, gave birth to the child in Dublin by arrangement, having travelled from England. She later spent years trying to find out who had adopted him, counsel said.
>
> Asked by Justice Gilligan was it the case the natural mother never consented to adoption, counsel said she did consent but it was not done in accordance with law.
>
> Documentation relating to the baby was fraudulent in that he was 'passed off as the true natural first child' of the couple from the country town, counsel said. It was only in 2006 the birth mother 'got wind from a nun in the adoption society of what actually happened'.

Meanwhile, Sister Gabriel of St Patrick's Guild Adoption Society, which registered adoptions for a number of Mother and Baby Homes in Dublin, told *The Irish Times* in 1996 that she had 'come across false names on birth certificates on occasions'. The article said: 'She assumed the false information had been given by the mothers. "We would never have had experience in registering births," she said. "The false names sometimes made it impossible to trace the birth mothers."'

Tragically, Ireland was not alone in this practice. In fact, claims have been made all over the world that death certificates for children were falsified in order to accommodate illegal adoptions. In 2011, the BBC exposed a 50-year-old scandal in Spain, revealing how 300,000 babies were stolen from their parents and trafficked by the Catholic Church. The trafficking was enabled by a whole network of doctors, nurses, priests and nuns during General Franco's dictatorship (1939–1975). It was not only the babies of single mothers who were taken in this way, but also babies of people considered 'undesirable' parents. The programme told how mothers were informed their baby had died and then shown the corpse of a dead baby in a freezer. The BBC programme-makers showed photographs of the dead baby. The scandal was exposed when two men, Antonio Barroso and Juan Luis Moreno, learned they were stolen as babies and illegally adopted. DNA tests confirmed their claims.

Another widely reported incident sent shockwaves through many in the Tuam Babies Family Group. In September 2017, Lydia Reid was granted a court order to exhume the body of her son, Gary, who died aged seven days old in Edinburgh's Hospital for Sick Children in July 1975. The grave was opened, but no human remains were found. Instead, a hat, shawl, crucifix and name tag were discovered, with baby Gary's name misspelled on the tag.

Lydia, now 68, said she had asked to see her son when he 'died' and had always believed she was shown a child that was not hers. But when she objected, she was told that she was suffering from post-natal depression. She told BBC Scotland: 'This baby was blonde and big, my baby was tiny and dark-haired. This was not my son.'

The exhumation was conducted by respected forensic anthropologist Prof. Dame Sue Black. Her report concluded that the coffin had been buried without human remains. Professor Black said: 'I have not had this experience before and I fully understand the fear that this might generate in others. Our intention had been to take a sample of bone for DNA to establish once and for all whether it was Lydia's baby. We had not considered what we found as an option. There will now be an investigation by the police and, at present, our job is done, except to assist with inquiries in any way that we can. My heart goes out to Lydia, who was looking for answers but instead just found more questions.'

While illegal adoptions have happened all over the world and have been carried out by many different organisations, the involvement of Catholic institutions in such adoptions has occurred in Canada, Scotland, Spain, America, Ireland, north and south, and in the UK. The moral values associated with the Irish Catholic hierarchy seem to have played a key role in illegal adoptions becoming so prominent in Ireland in the 1950s and 1960s. From the birth of the Irish state in 1922, the government had viewed illegitimacy as a 'problem' and believed it had to take an active role in deterring unmarried women from getting pregnant. Both the Church and the state believed they had to act in unison to ensure single women faced penalties for falling pregnant as otherwise others, surely, would follow their lead.

Within the framework of this sort of thinking, adoption could act as a safety valve for dealing with unwanted children. However, the Catholic Church had a tight grip on every area of social policy in Ireland, and its desire to protect the 'religious rights' of Irish children slowed down a number of official moves to modernise adoption policy. Basically, the Church wanted guarantees that any adopted children abroad or within the country would be raised as Catholic. This policy, along with the fact that there continued to be a demand for Irish children in the USA, led religious bodies to take matters into their own hands. The fact that the religious orders operated across both countries allowed them to use their contacts to arrange hundreds of illegal adoptions to 'suitable' families. In this case, suitable meant observant Catholics.

But it was not just the fact that these networks existed that drove the policy of illegal adoptions. The moral and religious view of 'fallen' women meant that the nuns and bishops saw separating an illegitimate child from a sinful mother was 'for the best' – a term repeated to literally tens of thousands of heartbroken mothers during those decades. For the religious orders involved, the sending of children to the UK or America was a sensible solution to the problem of 'unwanted' children, getting them out of the homes and into God-fearing families. They saw it as a win-win situation.

Sadly, time has shown that these enforced separations of mother and child were absolutely not 'for the best'. Testimony from women and their children over the last few decades reveals that this policy had a traumatic and life-long impact on many – though clearly not all – of the survivors. The sense of loss and alienation it created has haunted many survivors, feelings also reported in other countries where these policies were allowed to flourish without restraint.

In 2013, one mum-of-two went public to appeal for information about her biological mother after discovering she was illegally adopted. Her case shows the deep sense of loss that can result when adopted children are denied the option of tracing their origins.

Margaret Norton, from County Longford, began trying to trace her birth mother following the death of her adoptive parents. Margaret had discovered that, as a baby, she had been handed to her adoptive mother and father in a hotel car park in Dundalk and registered as their biological child. She was reared in Dublin by her adoptive family. Margaret is a straight talker, who refuses to feel like a victim. 'You have to laugh sometimes about it, even though it is absolutely awful,' she says. 'I mean, I have lost out on my identity. I don't have a clue who I am.'

Margaret, or Maggie as she's known to her friends, is a textbook mother. She cooks, bakes, drives her children to all their activities, looks after her husband, runs her beautiful home with energy and efficiency. She is highly intelligent, organised, thrifty. But when she speaks about the loss of her past life, the life that was robbed from her when she was signed away on a birth certificate, the hurt she feels is very evident. Maggie wears her heart on her sleeve:

The moment that changed my life was the time that I realised I was illegally adopted, my birth cert was illegally registered and I began to realise that searching for my birth parents wasn't going to be as easy as I thought it was.

People take for granted that they know who they are, they know who they look like, they know people's characteristics. But in my case, I don't have that luxury. I don't know who I am, where I came from or who I look like. I don't know any ordinary stuff. It is a massive game changer in anybody's life.

How do I feel? I feel lonely, I feel lost. I wonder where I am going to turn next. I am searching for my birth parents and it is not an easy task. How does it affect me emotionally? Only every day, it affects every aspect of my life. I try sometimes to look on the brighter side, that I have had a very privileged life and I have wanted for nothing. But then on the other side, it's that small little bit which turns into a massive bit. I just want to know where I came from.

Margaret can't say for sure that she was never a resident of a Mother and Baby Home, but she knows she was illegally adopted by a local doctor – a fact the doctor's family has confirmed. The doctor involved in her case was Irene Creedon, who turned out to be involved in quite a number of such arrangements.

Dr Irene Creedon, a well-known family GP from Carrickmacross, County Monaghan, was involved in at least 19 illegal adoptions in Ireland. Dr Creedon lived in a large home in County Louth with her two children, a boy and a girl, and her husband. Given her position as local GP, she was familiar with most families in her hometown and was considered a 'formidable woman'. As one local noted: 'You would see her out and about mixing with the gardaí and solicitors. What she said, went. She walked with a straight back and you would see her coming, everyone knew her. She was always well dressed in nice skirts, jackets and blouses, but you didn't cross her.'

Dr Creedon took in a string of babies from vulnerable mothers, sometimes gave their place of birth as her surgery, and then allowed adoptive parents to register the babies as their own biological children. By going outside state services and allowing couples to falsely register babies, Dr Creedon was knowingly breaking the law. She herself died more than ten years ago and no records appear to be available that would allow the children she arranged adoptions for to trace their true biological parents.

And Margaret Norton has looked everywhere. She spoke to the local priest, she has written to people who may have information, she has contacted Dr Creedon's family, but she has come up with nothing. It is exceptionally frustrating and heartbreaking for her. The results of these illegal registrations were catastrophic for the children at the heart of the scandal. The only clue Margaret can work on is her place of birth, which is registered as 31 O'Neill Street, Carrickmacross, County Monaghan – Dr Creedon's surgery.

The late GP's actions were confirmed by her own daughter, Marie McDermott, in 2013. Ms McDermott said she was not certain how many adoptions her mother had organised, but she praised her mother's efforts to simultaneously help childless families and single mothers in distress. In an interview with the *Irish Mail on Sunday* in 2013, Dr Creedon's daughter said:

She helped a lot of people. They were different times and a different era. People came to her when they needed help, whether it was to give up a child or to adopt a child. My mother was a wonderful person, a heroine, she was an extraordinary woman.

Asked about the fact that the births were registered illegally, Ms McDermott said:

Paperwork wasn't something they were strict about back then; that's changed for the better. Some people don't want to be found, but I do understand that people have a right to know who they are. Lots of girls had babies who were hidden or given away back then. It was very sad and people were ashamed. Mammy helped a lot of those people.

She rejected suggestions that her mother received money for arranging the adoptions, saying:

The things she did to help people was unreal: she helped people who were elderly and hungry as well as people who could not have children and were not allowed to have children. She did not ask for money; it was not about money, she had her own. Sometimes she came home with a bag of potatoes or turnips as a gift.

That is one view of Dr Creedon, but Margaret Norton has a totally different perspective on Dr Creedon's actions:

I'm angry that this went on when it shouldn't have. It was completely wrong. This is baby trafficking and no excuses can be made for not allowing someone to know who they are. I have absolutely no idea who my birth parents are and there is no way of me finding out without them coming forward or passing me some information.

Following a high-profile public appeal for help in the newspapers, on radio and TV, Margaret received two letters from a woman claiming to be her mother, which helped fill in some gaps about her past life. She learned from this woman that she gave birth to Margaret in Dr Creedon's surgery and afterwards was put up in a local hotel for the night and given £20. Sadly, however, and much to Margaret's regret, she received no more information from this woman and is still unsure if she was her biological mother, or a woman who had gone through a similar experience.

As a result of Margaret speaking out about Dr Creedon and her adoption, at least 19 people came forward to confirm that they too had been illegally put up for adoption by the doctor. Margaret was shocked by the extent of it:

> Why would it matter, some people might say, you've had a nice life, you've had a privileged life, you have a nice family now, a good husband, two beautiful kids, but it is a big thing when you don't know your own roots. You try and make sense of it all in your own head. Why people wouldn't leave the door open for you to search, what about the people on the other side, your birth mother, your birth father, what about them? What are they thinking? Are they still alive? What can I do next, where do I turn? How will it change the rest of my life, will I ever know the answers? Emotionally, I need to know, I need to sort it out. It does affect me every day and will continue, I'm sure, to affect me every day. Can anyone help me? I am not sure. What do I do next, where do I turn next? Why didn't they leave the door open for me to check? Someday I might have all the answers.
>
> I just need someone to come forward. I just want to know who I am.

Another high-profile professional who was involved in illegal adoptions was Professor Eamon de Valera Jr, who was a consultant gynaecologist at the National Maternity Hospital (Holles Street), Dublin. He bypassed the courts in order to arrange for the children of unmarried mothers to be adopted by wealthy families.

Professor de Valera Jr was the son of the former Taoiseach and President Eamon de Valera. A document revealed by the *Irish Mail on Sunday* showed how the high-ranking doctor arranged for a baby boy to be illegally adopted in the 1960s by facilitating his adoptive parents to sign his birth certificate. In the letter, dated 17 July 1982, the late professor, responding to a query by the adoptive family of the child about his medical history, said:

I am aware of the boy you have noted in your letter. I can confirm no adoption certificate was necessary at the time because there was to be no further communication between the boy and his biological mother.

An arrangement was made for a birth certificate in the late 1960s for his new family. Given his illegitimate background we felt it best the child was placed with a good family as a matter of urgency.

The letter, signed by de Valera, was sent to the family doctor of the adopted boy.

In a statement, the GRO said: 'There has never been an investigation of illegal adoptions by the GRO. The GRO is only aware of two such cases, one of which took place before the Adoption Act 1952 came into effect.'

A publication by the Royal Irish Academy, *Documents on Irish Foreign Policy Volume 10*, which covers the years 1951 to 1957, shows that forced adoptions happened all over Ireland during the period of the Mother and Baby Homes. The documents reveal that as many as ten Irish children a month, most born to unmarried mothers at the Catholic institutions, were being adopted by Americans and removed to the USA. Some 330 such children left these shores between 1950 and 1952, with these records only being kept safe from the former date.

At the time, the then Department of External Affairs (now Foreign Affairs) saw its role as an administrative one and supplied each child with a passport. In March 2016 the CEO of Barnados, Fergus Finlay, claimed that the nuns in several homes had faked death certificates for scores of children so they could be adopted to the USA. Mr Finlay also believes there could be hundreds of people in the UK and USA who have no idea they are living under false identities after being illegally adopted from Ireland. Speaking to the *Irish Daily Mail*, Mr Finlay said:

Barnados has been working with mothers and families from Mother and Baby Homes for 30 years.

I feel it's important to say I have no doubt at all that a large amount of children's death certs were falsified by the nuns and there's a whole community in the UK and US that don't know they were ever adopted.

There are people who don't know they were adopted, and those people had a life in a Mother and Baby Home here at some point.

As far as the Irish state is concerned, they died as children in the homes and that's where their lives ended – when in reality they were taken away under a new name and living under a new identity in another country. I've no doubts about that.

These baby passports were issued to all children who were adopted to the USA. The paperwork completed and kept by the nuns may have been in order, but it does not mean the details on these passports were accurate.

Michael Byrne was born James Patrick Owens on 22 July 1957, and his birth certificate says his mother's name was Annie Owens. There are no other details, no home address or age for his birth mother and no father's details. He was adopted to Boston in 1961, but only discovered in November 2017 that he had been born in the Mother and Baby Home in Tuam.

Ironically, as part of his job as a travel agent, Michael has been carrying out tours all across Ireland for the past 40 years. Due to his interest in Ireland, he had read about Tuam, but had no idea he was born there. The soft-spoken American said he does not feel like a victim because of his adoption, that he had a good life and was not treated unfairly. He has his adoption papers and baby passport because his adoptive parents kept them for him. The passport reads:

Certificate of Blessing of an Adopted Child
Church of St. Jeremiah,
That Michael James Byrne (name changed on adoption) and his parents were Raymond and Marilyn Byrne from Boston. Born Galway, Ireland, 22nd July 1957.

The certificate of blessing was signed on 14 October 1962.

Michael knew that he was born in Galway, but was unsure where. At just a week old he was very ill with severe physical problems, so the Bon Secours nuns sent him to Temple Hill Orphanage in south Dublin, where he would be closer to a hospital for treatment. Michael says he feels a sense of empathy for his birth mother and is keen to search for any other information that may have been held in the orphanage, where he was resident for four years.

During an exclusive interview with this author in O'Callaghan's Hotel on St Stephen's Green, Dublin, on 4 November 2017, Michael stared down at his stamped baby passport and its details of where and when he left Ireland. It was stamped on 23 August 1961, upon his arrival at Boston Logan International Airport; the same year the Home in Tuam closed down. He was shocked to discover that it formed part of his own life story:

> I was trying to figure out the odds of me being in that home. In the Mailonline article about the mass grave in Tuam, I wondered if I was a part of that. That was a massive deal in the States when it came out. It was all over the news. I starting thinking about it all then properly. Was I born out of wedlock? Most likely. I wasn't born in a hospital; most hospitals were run by the Catholic Church.
>
> I have a picture of me as a baby. This was taken when I was moved to Dublin. I was born on 22 July 1957 and I was told by my adoptive parents in Boston that at seven days old I was sent to Dublin. I spent four-and-a-half years in a Temple Hill Orphanage in Dublin. I was adopted through St Patrick's Guild Society.
>
> I was out in Bray, in south Dublin. We went back and visited the place when I was 12 or 13 years old. My mother was a travel agent, so we had the opportunity to travel a lot. …
>
> But the bottom line is, I was handicapped when I was born. I had a deformed right foot. This foot is size seven, my other foot is size ten.

I have had seven operations, on my legs, down through the years. I had several operations in Boston when I was taken there.

I think this fact meant I wasn't picked to be adopted, that's why it took so long. But my parents had arranged for an adoption through Catholic Charitable Bureau, now Catholic Charities, in the Archdiocese of Boston for my adopted brother. He was born in County Meath. He was adopted by my parents at six months old.

I knew all my life I was adopted. My brother is two years younger than me, he has tried to reach his birth mom a few times, but didn't have any luck.

Michael said he has some memories of being a resident in the orphanage in Dublin before he was moved to the USA:

I only have [mental] images of how the building was laid out. I remember where we used to sleep and that there were rows of cribs. I went back at 12 or 13 years old and went back to meet one of the nuns.

Unlike a lot of the people who seem to be traumatised, I have no negative memories at all. To me the nuns were loving and took care of me, whether that was because I was sick, I don't know.

When I read the story about the Tuam Babies, I couldn't help thinking, I need to find out more. I began to push myself and look.

His adoptive parents always told him he was adopted, but they never gave him – or possibly never had – details of his origins.

It wasn't a secret, everyone knew. My dad Raymond was Irish, his family were Irish. They never told me why they chose to go to Ireland to adopt, it could have been word-of-mouth. I am grateful that I ended up where I am. I am not in that grave. I am not ungrateful for being adopted, I don't feel I was sent away, I don't feel banished.

I have thought about my birth mother. How did she get into the situation she did? God forbid was it a rape or was it young love? It's always been the wonder. She could still be alive. I would like to find her.

Anna Corrigan knows exactly how this feels – the desire to know for sure. She still searches for definite information on Bridget's two sons, John and William. After Bridget died, Anna discovered that in her later years her mother had confided in a relative that she believed William had been adopted to the USA. Anna's own research into William's life has turned up only confusion and conflicting information, which means she has to continue her quest to find her missing brothers:

If John is in that mass grave in Tuam, I want him reinterred with our mother in our family plot in Glasnevin in Dublin, and if William was adopted, I want him found. Either way, I want both of them found.

My mother stayed in her tenement flat all her life and would not move into a newer home perhaps because she believed her son would one day come back for her and this was the only address he would be able to find. So, she didn't go. I never knew any of this, but it really is gut-wrenching to think how my mother would have kept him in her heart all her life and couldn't bring herself to tell me. I could have helped her find him, I could have done something.

Anna wrote to the Department of Foreign Affairs in November 2013, requesting any documentation that might show a passport was made for her brother, William. The reply she received was that there were no records for William Dolan there. On 22 March 2017 she wrote to the Adoption Authority of Ireland, asking if any court order had been made for her brother's adoption. As William was born before the Adoption Act 1952, there are no court records to say he was adopted. The little boy, it seems, has vanished into thin air. There is no proof that Anna's brother was adopted and her investigations to find him, including providing DNA samples to a number of genealogy services, have amounted to nothing:

> I reported the matter to An Garda Síochána in September 2013. William is now being treated as a missing person and John's death is being treated by the gardaí as a criminal matter since June 2014. I believe he died from neglect and malnutrition.
>
> I have said this over and over again, and despite my story stacking up and international stories to back up similar cases of dead babies showing up alive in another country, I have still been met with some very shocking denials.

Anna learned that a well-known Catholic orphanage in New York, the Angel Guardian Home, was also involved in adoptions from Ireland and she decided to write to them about William. Sr Margaret Dempsey wrote back to her on 18 December 2015: 'After a lengthy search of our records I believe it is correct to say that your brothers John Desmond Dolan and William Joseph Dolan were not adopted through Angel Guardian. I found no mention of their names in our documents. I am enclosing a copy of the International Adoption Registry Folder which may be a help to you in finding them. I am sorry that I cannot be of more help to you. May the hope of Christmas fill you with peace.'

The Irish authorities can no longer claim ignorance of the illegal adoptions that took so many Irish children out of this country, sending them into homes and families that hadn't been in any way vetted or checked in advance. Some of those adoptees are thankful that it turned out this way for them, because the alternative seems very grim. And it is possible that those children benefitted from being adopted, as Michael feels he did. But it remains the case that those children, those Irish citizens, had rights, and those rights were steamrolled in favour of solving the 'problem' of illegitimacy. You can't give an illegally adopted child their identity back, you can't show them the way to their birth mother, and that is a tragic situation that is still causing huge grief and heartache for so many people to this day.

# 7

# Forwards, but Never Forgetting

Whether she knew it at the time or not, when Bridget walked out of the Home in Tuam on 16 February 1951, after giving birth to William, it would be for the last time. After giving birth twice and having both sons deemed 'dead' while in the care of the nuns, Bridget finally broke free of the institution that had dominated her life as a mother and tentatively joined the world again.

For Bridget, like the majority of women in her situation, her old life was simply not available to her anymore. There was no going back to Clonfert and her family. Her shame was absolute and permanent – the passage of time would not erase it. She had to start from scratch: there was no other choice.

As she left Tuam for the last time, Bridget walked in the footsteps of all the bereft women who had to leave their babies behind and rebuild their broken lives from nothing. They went into the homes with tiny suitcases and the clothes on their backs, but they carried heavy burdens out of the homes with them – the loss of a child, the shame of their families and the abandonment of the communities where they were born and raised. It's understandable, then, that for many of the survivors, the institutions – despite their obvious horrors and deprivations – often seemed less scary and threatening than the outside world. Many of the women were so damaged and institutionalised that they refused to leave. As a result, some would spend the rest of their lives in the places that had broken their spirits, finding in those cold walls their only home in life.

Bridget Dolan would never return to live with her family in Clonfert, and she would never again see the sons she gave birth to. She was told both her sons had died, but she would never know, for sure, if they were alive or dead. She would also have to bear the impact of these losses alone. There was no one there for her. She didn't know it as she walked out of the Home, but it would be at least six years before she was reunited with her family. (Anna uncovered a letter from her father to her mother while she and her mother were on holidays in Clonfert in 1957, which suggests there was a reconciliation at that time.) Bridget went from being a loving and loyal daughter to being an untouchable outcast. There are no records of any family members reaching out to Bridget, no letters among her possessions. They cut her off completely, as if she'd never existed in the first place. At the age of 32 she was forced to live with the deep wound of losing two children, her home, her family and her self-respect.

However, while Bridget had no doubt witnessed the casual cruelties of the Mother and Baby Homes, they would also help provide her with a bridge to normal living. As she left this second time, she was once again offered a job by the nuns. This time she would get a chance to go to Dublin, where her past would not be known to anyone. She would get a fresh start, although, in return, she would have to leave behind everything she had ever known. At that time and for a woman her age, Dublin should have brought some sense of excitement, but for Bridget life was about raw survival, not adventure.

So it was that in 1951 Bridget began working in a newly opened hospital in Glasnevin, in North Dublin. This was the Bon Secours Private Hospital, run by the Bon Secours Sisters, the same religious order that ran the Mother and Baby Home and the Grove Hospital in Tuam. The sisters had given Bridget a job in their laundry, where she would sweat and toil for the next four-and-a-half-years. The hospital would also be Bridget's home because she would live in the staff accommodation as well as working there.

'It is for the best' she would have been told yet again – after all, who would want someone with a chequered past like Bridget's? The question as to whether Bridget was paid or just lived a life of servitude was queried by Anna in 2013, when she contacted the Bon Secours order and asked if her mother was an official employee, who paid her taxes to the government, or if she was an indentured servant, like the girls in the Magdalene Laundry. The nuns have never provided Anna with any of the information she requested, claiming they do not have any records.

It is estimated that around 30,000 women were confined to the Magdalene Laundries in the 19th and 20th centuries. These 'fallen' women were given a place to live and basic meals, but in exchange had to work hard from morning to night, washing clothes. The women never received any money for the endless hours they slaved in the laundries. It was effectively a form of indentured servitude, and these laundries remained in operation until 1996. Of course, Bridget was working in a privately run laundry, not a state laundry, so the set-up may have been different there.

Bridget settled into her new job and learned to live, yet again, under the rule of the nuns. By now she had learned to adapt to their strict regime and this helped her to settle in easily. Bridget made friends with the other women who worked there and became particularly friendly with a girl from County Offaly who worked as a domestic in the Bon Secours hospital.

This girl had a history similar to Bridget's. She had left Bessborough Mother and Baby Home in County Cork after her baby was taken away for adoption. It must have been a great comfort to both women to find a sympathetic ally in their new job; one could mind the other. The daily grind at the hospital, while gruelling and relentless, must have also provided a stark contrast to the sorrow and deprivation that existed in the Tuam Home. The desperation that was palatable in Tuam was not present in the hospital. Instead, private patients were taken care of with the gentle, loving care that money has always been able to buy. Here,

Bridget was permitted to take some time off work, a huge change from the constant incarceration at Tuam. She began to go on sightseeing trips around Dublin, to see what the big city had to offer a country girl like her. It must have been exhilarating to be able to breathe in fresh air as a free woman, to watch cars driving on the roads, people busily getting to their places of work, glamorous clothes in shop windows and people not knowing who she was or where she came from. By this time Bridget was 33 years old and she wanted exactly the same as any young woman – to be loved and cared for and have somebody to call her own.

As time went by, a little more freedom was given to the girls and they were allowed to go into Dublin city centre for evenings out, although they had to be home on the last bus at around 11.00 p.m. Bridget and her friends went to the AOH (Ancient Order of Hibernians) Dance Hall and to the Galway Arms in Parnell Square and slowly eased themselves back into normality. The AOH had a whole mix of music that tried to cater for everyone's tastes. By the 1960s, when the showband era was in full swing, the club hosted the Blarney Club, which specialised in *céilí* bands.

Dublin was a whole new world. She would later tell her family how she was filled with amazement by all that she saw, especially when Christmas came. The lights and music around the city centre struck her as being like something from a Hollywood film. There was never any Christmas in the Home in Tuam, and even in her homeplace in Clonfert the holiday would have been a muted and modest affair. But in Dublin, Christmas was a spectacle, and Bridget couldn't drink it all in fast enough.

It was at the AOH Dance Hall where Bridget Dolan first met William Corrigan, known to his friends as Bill. She was 34 and he was 49 years old.

Bill first laid eyes on Bridget as she sat talking with her friend, before he plucked up the courage to ask her up to dance. She immediately agreed. To Bridget, the older man seemed confident and comfortable in his own skin. He was a great dancer, and Bridget would later tell their daughter, Anna, that he moved her around the floor with ease. She would remember feeling free as she danced in a room full of people where you could let your hair down and forget your troubles. The dance halls were a huge release, and gave her a sense of being part of a bright life that contrasted starkly with the harsh and oppressive routine of the Home. It was the rhythm of a life that was new, and that Bridget had probably never even known existed.

Although she was enjoying the dancing immensely, Bridget and her friend had to leave the dance hall early to get back to the hospital before lights out. She said goodbye to Bill and his friend and reluctantly left to catch the bus. The following morning would be an early start, back to the chores and the routine after her wonderful few hours of escape.

A few Sundays later, the girls had some time off and went back into town. There was an afternoon dance in the AOH and they decided to go. Once inside, Bridget spotted Bill and smiled to recall the dance they had shared a few weeks before. He came over and spoke to her, and Bridget was delighted that he remembered her. Over the last couple of years, she had begun to believe she was invisible, her confidence having suffered a number of severe knocks. Bridget hoped Bill would ask her for another dance, and when he did, she was thrilled. Bill was well turned out and wore a dapper suit and a nice shirt and tie. He was carefully groomed and she remembered him as having 'a pleasant way' about him. He was a kind man, and that was something Bridget had not experienced for a long time. For a woman like Bridget, who had been abandoned by her parents, her siblings and the men she had loved, Bill's kind and soft nature held a massive appeal.

That afternoon at the AOH passed quickly and soon it was time to go. Bill didn't ask too many questions, for which Bridget was thankful. She carried a heavy secret and lived in fear of anybody ever finding it out. After all, she was a fallen woman who had given birth to not one but two children and lived in mortal sin. To her surprise, Bill asked if he could see her again. On the walk home to Glasnevin, she began to feel something of a little spark of life rising in her and suddenly she thought that, perhaps, just maybe, there might be a light at the end of the tunnel.

Work in the hospital was gruelling, as there was a constant round of washing and ironing, along with any other jobs they were told to do. These were the days before modern conveniences, so the work was, for the most part, hard manual labour. But for Bridget, anything was better than being confined in Tuam. Sometimes toilets had to be cleaned, and that often included wiping up vomit. One time when Bridget was cleaning the toilets she accidentally hit her wrist off something and heard a crack. She realised she had cut her wrist right through to her artery. She was rushed to an examining room and had to undergo major surgery. For a change, it was now the nuns' turn to care of Bridget. But soon enough, she was rolled back out to the hospital floor to continue her hard work.

As Dublin edged further into the 1950s, the city was starting to change as parts of the economy began to recover from 'the Emergency'. Cars and department stores were becoming the order of the day in the city centre. For Bridget and others like her, the great pastime of the day was 'window shopping', which meant looking at things in shop windows you couldn't afford but could dream freely about owning someday. For Bridget, life was exciting and she began to feel that the darkest of her days might be behind her. During those dreamy days strolling around O'Connell Street, looking at beautiful but unaffordable gowns in the windows of Clerys, Bridget thought a lot about Bill, who was also quite taken with her. He liked her soft West of Ireland accent and gentle manner. She had an air of mystery about her because she didn't speak a lot about herself. Bill was a quiet man, happy in his own company. He also said very little about his past and would later admit that he mistook Bridget's quietness for shyness.

Bill lived alone. He had a small room in a tenement in 32 North Great Charles Street, in Dublin's north inner city. Unknown to Bridget, Bill had suffered huge losses in his own life that must also have left deep emotional scars. In an effort to get on with his life, he chose to fill it with work, friends, fun and travel. He took regular trips to the countryside and a yearly trip to Guernsey. Bill had got a passport with the intention of going to Switzerland with his friend, but this plan fell through. He had not yet met anyone he wished to spend his life with, and he was comfortable with that.

Bill was born on 10 February 1904 in Dominick Street, in Dublin's north inner city, to Annie and John Corrigan. He had two siblings: Mary, known as Mollie, who was born on 4 June 1905 at the Rotunda Hospital in Dublin, and his brother John, who was born 19 September 1906. They were a happy family until tragedy struck and their mother, Annie, contracted tuberculosis. She died on 11 February 1911.

Without Annie, the Corrigans' world quickly came crashing down. Annie's mother, Elizabeth Healy, died one month after her daughter and by the following October the children, Bill, aged 7, Mary, aged 6, and John, aged 5, were taken from their father and sentenced, through Dublin District Court, to ten years' incarceration in industrial schools. Bill and John were sent to St Patrick's Industrial School in County Kilkenny, and when they reached the age of ten they would be sent on to Glin Industrial School in Limerick. Little Mary was sent to St Brigid's Industrial School in Loughrea, County Galway, run by the Sisters of Mercy.

Even in a country with such a tragic past as Ireland, the history of the industrial schools is one of the darkest chapters. The schools were established under the Industrial Schools Act 1868 to care for 'neglected, orphaned and abandoned children'. They were, in the vast majority of cases, run by the Catholic Church, which used its healthy cash reserves to buy a number of country estates that had been put up for sale in the decades after the Famine. The institutions were paid a fee by the state for every child they 'cared for', giving the Church a regular income and allowing the state to outsource the care of children to others.

For the most part, children were sent to the schools by the courts – often for the most minor of infractions of the law. Even petty crimes could see a young child taken off their parents and sentenced to years in an institution. It is estimated that thousands were sent away simply because they were not attending school. Needless to say, these sentences were only given to impoverished children, not to the children of the middle and upper classes. Families were brutally ripped apart and the damage caused has affected several generations down through the years.

Over time the industrial schools became extremely profitable businesses for the religious orders. This meant they required a steady supply of children, serving significant sentences, to keep them economically successful. The profits could then be funnelled back into the different congregations, to fund their different projects and to maintain the clerics attached to the orders. In a report drawn up by the Commission on Child Abuse in 2005, a government-funded investigation into abuse in the schools, it concluded that the Church put pressure on the courts to impose long sentences. For children who were found guilty of not attending school, for example, the average sentence was 4.2 years.

The noble aims originally stated in the Industrial Schools Act were rarely, if ever, realised and the institutions became notorious for their harsh treatment of vulnerable children. Devoid of meaningful oversight, they served as a dumping ground for impoverished children who had fallen off the edge of society. By 1884, there were 5,049 children in industrial schools throughout the country. This figure would wax and wane throughout the twentieth century, but it is estimated that between 1936 and 1970, some 170,000 children were detained in these schools.

Following a series of child sex abuse court cases and exposés by RTÉ in the late 1990s, in 2000 the Irish government established the Commission to Inquire into Child Abuse, in order to explore the issue of historical abuse in Irish institutions. While the Commission looked into institutions run by a number of different organisations, inevitably the majority were run by the Catholic Church and overseen by the state. The Commission was originally headed up by Ms Justice Mary Laffoy, but she resigned in 2003, claiming she was not being given access to vital documents by the government. Mr Justice Seán Ryan was subsequently placed in charge, and in 2009 a report was issued which found that there was endemic rape and abuse of children in these institutions. The

Ryan Report laid out, in painstaking detail, how thousands of children were systemically tortured and abused by clergy while the state ignored repeated warnings and failed to take any action. The 2,600-page report drew on the experiences of thousands of children in 250 Church-run institutions across the country. Although much of the abuse had been made public over the preceding decade, Mr Justice Ryan's harrowing report still proved to be a watershed moment for the Catholic Church in Ireland as it laid out in stark and grim detail the undeniable horrors that occurred daily, particularly in the industrial schools. St Patrick's Industrial School – where Bill and John were sent as children – was opened in 1879 and closed in 1966. It was situated on an 80-acre farm about a mile outside the city of Kilkenny. The school housed up to 200 boys up to the age of 10. In the period 1933–1966, there was usually one nun and one staff member to every 30 or so children. It was one of two schools in Kilkenny highlighted in the Commission's report, where it stated that 'sexual abuse of and violence against children was rife'. According to the Ryan Report, the Sisters of Charity, who ran the school, said they looked after the boys 'to the best of their ability'. However, the Commission outlined how failures by the order, by the Department of Education and by An Garda Síochána allowed abusers in the school to continue their cruel practices:

> Despite the introduction of innovative childcare training and guidance guidelines by the Sisters of Mercy in Kilkenny there were still serious instances of sexual abuse.
>
> A significant feature of this school was the very young ages of the children and the large group of them all being cared for by a small number of nuns. Due to them being so young when they were there, witnesses tended to remember specific episodes rather than have overall memories of St. Patrick's. Some of these incidents pointed to a regime that was harsh and unpredictable, with corporal punishment the usual response to misbehaviour.

Three male complainants described incidents of sexual abuse and the significant factor in each account was the child's inability to confide in the Sister who was caring for him. Men who were employed in the school appeared to have ready access to these small boys and there was no awareness of the risks posed by this.

Like many young children who were shamefully incarcerated in Ireland's appalling industrial schools, at the age of ten Bill was moved to another home, St Joseph's School in Glin, County Limerick. St Joseph's was founded in 1872 in Sexton Street, Limerick, then moved to Glin in 1928 and operated until 1966, and was described by the Commission as having a 'severe, systemic regime of corporal punishment'. There was very little attention given to the welfare of the children. Two Christian Brothers were transferred to Glin having been investigated for accusations of sexual abuse in other industrial schools at earlier dates. In *The Boy from Glin Industrial School* (2013), survivor Tom Wall describes how he and others were beaten, abused, raped and denied food, proper clothing, care and education during his years at St Joseph's. Bill was sent to Glin in 1914, followed later by John, who arrived in 1917.

Alone and missing her brothers, six-year-old Mary, who was charged by the courts (along with her brothers) with 'want of proper guardianship' and sentenced to ten years, was shipped off to the other side of the country. On 14 October 1911 (all three siblings were sentenced on that date), Mary was enrolled in St Brigid's Industrial School for Girls in Loughrea, County Galway, which was run by the Sisters of Mercy.

Independent Dublin City councillor, author and playwright Mannix Flynn, who was a resident in several industrial schools across the country, including Letterfrack and Artane, summed up the experiences of the industrial schools as a 'horrendous grim presence that was always present whether it was day and night ... Life in the Industrial Schools and these homes run by the nuns and priests was made extremely uncomfortable and miserable.' Mannix Flynn has devoted his life to highlighting the injustices inflicted on those who were locked up in these institutions and the damage it has caused down through the generations in the aftermath:

> For a person taken from their family it was extremely difficult. The ones who had no visitors were particularly isolated and abused and got the worst time. You were stigmatised twice as much if you were an orphan, you were seen as a bastard with no family.
>
> The idea of thinking you could let out how bad you were feeling was out of the question. You could never afford to let it out, it would completely overwhelm you. The closest description of this is the Holocaust and the burning of the bodies. That is how I would compare it.
>
> The workhouses were full of misery, then you had the Church shame on top of that, followed by society shame, as well as all kinds of abuse, physical, emotional and sexual.
>
> You are really talking years and years of absolute horror. That was a situation everyone contained and controlled. It was an emotionally deep and profound depressing sadness that was carried through the generations. You carried something you couldn't speak about, these places were in isolation, with no oversight, and they were controlled by the Church.
>
> You were ghosted and sent away to die. Some people ended up taking their own lives or drinking themselves to death because of it.

Little Bill, John and Mary were separated from their father for good and the three siblings were separated and spread out across the country. The knowledge of what they suffered and what they were forced to endure is lost at this stage, but there can be no doubt that any safety, security or love they had ever known was taken from them at an age when nobody has the resources to cope with such losses.

St Brigid's Industrial School in Loughrea was managed by the Sisters of Mercy. It operated in 1869 and closed in 1967, and was originally certified to accommodate 150 girls. There is an extremely limited number of records of Mary's stay in the Industrial school. In a school report provided by the Mercy nuns and dated 12 October 1915, little Mary was described as 'a good child, very satisfactory and a little bit giddy'.

During 1916, a record exists of a visit by a doctor to Mary – who was also known as Mollie – who reported: 'found her with a high temperature which I find to continue up to the 8th Inst. and I can find no definitive disease to account for it' (5 July 1916).

On 8 July the doctor reported: 'Again visited Mollie Corrigan, she has a coated tongue with a temperature 101.6.'

And on 13 July 1916 the doctor reported: 'Children healthy except Mollie Corrigan who has a temperature and should be sent to Hospital.'

Mary was just 13 years old when she died from influenza, most likely Spanish flu, on 1 November 1918, without ever seeing her family again. William and John could never pay their respects at her grave because the child's place of burial has never been identified. They probably never wrote to each other and would have spent years apart not knowing if their sister was alive or dead.

Mary's death certificate confirms her place of death as the 'Industrial School Loughrea'. There are no other burial records for the child in the county. Locals in Loughrea claim that there is a site on the grounds of the Sisters of Mercy convent that was used to bury the children who died in St Brigid's Industrial School. However, no burial records for children at the school could be located by Galway County Council. When questioned by the *Irish Mail on Sunday* in 2014, the nuns refused to respond to detailed questions on the issue. One local source said:

> The school ran for 100 years, yet there's only a grave for six children in a cemetery that opened in the 1950s. Where are all the other children? There are six cemeteries in Loughrea. None of them date back to 1869, the oldest is from the 1950s, so it is not possible they are there. Half the kids in there would have had every disease going

and the mortality rate would have been high, too.

In a letter to Anna Corrigan on 21 January 2013, from the Mercy Congregation Archives, the order confirmed that Mary 'Mollie' Corrigan did attend the school, but said: 'We do not have information to show where Mary Corrigan was buried.' A second, follow-up letter from the nuns, dated 11 February 2013, reads:

You may wish to know the outcome of the search for information about graves in Loughrea, made by our Galway office.

We have been informed that there are two cemeteries in Loughrea. Mount Pleasant is the one currently in use and an older cemetery called Garrybreeda.

Our Galway office made contact with the county council and were informed by the caretaker of the graveyards [James Regan] that there is no record of burials dating back to 1918.

He checked the headstones of the graves in Garrybreeda and unfortunately found nothing to indicate that Mary is buried there.

There is a children's plot in Mount Pleasant and we have been informed that the information on the headstone dates only from 1952.

I am very sorry Ms Corrigan that we cannot be of more help to you with your enquiry.

Anna later contacted many organisations in an effort to trace Mary's place of burial, but just like the story of her brothers, the Mercy nuns were unable or unwilling to provide her with information. Anna is now dealing with three missing relatives – her two brothers and her aunt – and no one can tell her for sure where they are.

Bill left Glin on 9 February 1920, at the age of 16, and went back to live with his father, a tailor, in 2 Ardilaun Terrace in North Circular Road. He became a pawnbroker's assistant in Buckingham Street, where he worked until he joined the newly formed National Irish Army on

17 August 1922, serving for 18 months. He was honourably discharged and went back again to live with his father, at his father's latest rental property in 583 North Circular Road. Bill served in the Medical Corps of the National Army and was stationed in Templemore, County Tipperary. His physical development was 'fair', given his tough life in the industrial schools. His brother John did not leave Glin until 18 September 1922.

Bill had a very curious mind and a great interest in all things mechanical, but his particular passion was radios. He was one of the first people in Dublin to have a crystal radio set. He later learned how to drive and spent the rest of his life driving trucks. His father died on 29 August 1943 of coronary thrombosis, and Bill spared no expense for his funeral. There was a hearse and two horses, which cost £18.10.0 (around €900 in today's money). It is unknown if Bill and his father ever discussed life in the industrial schools or the death of little Mary. Perhaps it was too difficult to ever mention these things again.

Bill and John shared a love of gadgets and mechanics. After his release from Glin, John went on to become a film operator and spent his whole life regaling people with the fantastical escape that was the cinema. Anna believes this escape gave him some peace from his traumatic childhood. He married Nancy Darmody on 14 November 1934 and went on to have a family, who grew up loved and well cared for.

John idolised his wife and children and Bill was a regular visitor to their house. The brothers spoke often of their sister and a picture of their mother held a special place in each of their homes. There was no photograph of their father – perhaps they blamed him for what had happened to them, but it is difficult to know, given how much effort Bill put into preparing their father's funeral. Although that, too, may have been a therapeutic way for Bill to deal with his pain.

Bridget carried on working at the Bon Secours hospital in Glasnevin, and the daily grind seemed a little easier now that she had Bill in her life. Having spent nearly fifty years as a bachelor, Bill had fallen for Bridget and wanted to spend the rest of his life with her. When he finally plucked up the courage to propose, Bridget said yes. The happy couple went to McDowell's 'The Happy Ring House' on O'Connell Street to buy the wedding ring. (They never bought an engagement ring, but Bill presented her with a gold Claddagh ring later on in their married life.)

As their wedding date drew near, Bridget feared having to tell the nuns that she was getting married. She had heard that another girl had told the nuns that she was getting married and they had quickly reminded her of her past and the baby she gave up. But the nuns had a soft spot for Bridget, and they accepted her decision and her plans for a new life.

Anna will always wonder if her mother shared her secrets with her father. With the love and friendship they shared, Anna believes her mother confided in her father because of his caring nature. She said: 'My father was such a lovely person, he was a lot older and had gone through some painful times in his own life. I think they were meant to meet and I believe he shared my mother's burdens because he loved her and me so much. I like to think they both found peace and strength in each other.'

Bridget and Bill were married on 7 September 1955 in the Church of Our Lady of Dolours, known as The Wooden Church, in Glasnevin. Bill's friend Eamon McElory was best man and Laura Corrigan, John's daughter, was bridesmaid. They had their reception at a friend's house in Spring Garden Street, Ballybough, in Dublin's north inner city. Looking through their wedding photos in late 2017, Anna realised that there was not a single member of her mother's family at the wedding. Despite all Bridget had been through, her family were not willing to be by her side on what should have been the happiest day of her life.

# 8

# Dirty Old Town

D ublin's north inner city was a far cry from rural Clonfert. It was nothing like the life Bridget had once known, but it meant a fresh start for her after her two tragic losses and all the years of heartache.

The newlyweds settled into married life in a tenement in North Great Charles Street, which lies between North Circular Road and Mountjoy Square, near to Summerhill. The nearest hospital was the Rotunda on Parnell Square, which was where Bridget went to give birth to her third child. Anna Corrigan was born on 1 September 1956, and she arrived at the right time and place. This time, no one but Bridget and Bill would have a say in her future.

The tenements in Dublin's north inner city were one of the poorest and most overcrowded dwelling places in Western Europe. Unlike Bridget's family cottage in Clonfert, the tall, narrow buildings were packed to capacity with families living on top of each other. Conditions were so bad, it was a breeding ground for disease, particularly tuberculosis (TB), which had taken hold in the country. Every year thousands across Ireland died of TB and related illnesses alone; the majority of the victims were children.

Tuberculosis was known as 'the Consumption' because the victims were consumed by weight loss and breathlessness. It was a dangerous, contagious illness that spread fear and dread, especially among the working classes. Inevitably, it spread throughout the tenements like wildfire. On 24 August 2010, in an article entitled, 'The silent terror that consumed so many', *The Irish Examiner* described how:

The highly infectious tuberculous bacillus thrived in the crowded tenements of inner city Dublin and in the poorly ventilated, thatched cottages in the country. Its effect was all-embracing, even among those who were healthy. A coveted job in the civil service or a bank was not yours until a chest X-ray film was reported as normal. In the 1950s, a work colleague might disappear for some months of sick leave. After treatment, most victims returned to the workplace, their gaunt features and weight loss confirming the unspoken diagnosis.

Despite years of tireless efforts by Noël Browne and his army of medical carers to beat the scourge, it was not until the 1950s that TB started to decline. By the 1970s, it had all but vanished from our shores.

Anna's granny and Bill's mother, Annie Corrigan, had died from TB while living in the tenements, and this was the reason her father and his siblings had ended up in industrial schools. 'Thankfully, we never were affected by it at all,' said Anna. 'Most of the people in the tenements had big families, and we weren't, so that was a blessing that there was only three of us in the room. It was what it was.'

The Corrigans lived on the fourth floor in one room, sharing a toilet and stone sink with cold running water on the next floor down. They had no hot water, no fridge, washing machine or shower, but their tiny home had a large fire, which had the added advantage of being warm all day given that it was on the top floor. When Anna was born in 1956, the new Republic of Ireland had come a long way, but the tenements were still one of the most dangerous places to live because of extremely poor health and safety standards. Anna recalled:

I stayed in the tenement until I was 23. I remember we had a big old Belfast sink to wash in downstairs, but no hot water. I remember when I got older, I would be washing my jeans in the sink and my hands would go blue from the cold. There was no way of washing, no showers and we used a basin. You would start washing at the top and work your way down. But you didn't know any different.

Most people had tin baths for the weekly bath time and you would put them out in front of the fire. We had to hand-wash the clothes too.

There was an open fire in the house and there were open fires in all of the rooms, so the place was warm. We had a double bed which was up in one corner and my cot was up against the wall near the fireplace. There were no lights on the stairs and eventually the Corporation told the landlord he had to install them.

As I got older I slept in a single bed which was pushed against the end of the double bed. There was a small bit of room to open the door of the wardrobe and barely enough room for the door to open.

We could see Croke Park from our room in the tenements. There was an amber street light which shone directly into the room and it would light up the street outside which gave you a cold survey on the street.

That light is still there to this day. I often drive my bike up around there and have a look around and take it all in.

If you were looking for a job, you couldn't give out your address in the tenements because no one would give you a job. We were lucky on the other hand, no one seemed to know North Great Charles Street, no one had a clue it was a tenement.

Our house was privately owned. In the end our landlord got electricity on the stairs and landings. Then my mother's bills started coming in and her bill was huge. When my uncle John investigated it, he discovered the landlord had connected all those lights to my mother's bill.

Anna said her mother was 'spotless clean' and took the responsibility of washing the stairs in the tenements. 'There were bed bugs and they lived in the old skirting boards, my mother would put DDT on the beds, she was always at it. Then she would go out and wash the four flights of stairs in the building. She was very clean and house proud, she couldn't stand the dirt.'

At their peak, prior to the First World War, around 20,000 families were living in single tenement rooms all over Dublin. The tenements contained some of the worst urban poverty to be found in Western Europe, but thousands of people came out of these homes and made a better life for themselves. An article in the *Irish Independent* in November 2013 described the tenements:

> The houses were graded in the census of the time from 'first-class' to 'fourth-class' according to their size and the materials used in their construction.
>
> Official figures show 22,701 people lived in 'third-class' houses, which were termed as unfit for human habitation.
>
> One inspector described a first-class tenement house at 41 Camden Street Lower occupied by five families, consisting of 20 persons, as follows: 'It has one water closet, is in good repair and I regard this as a first-class tenement.'
>
> The fact that one water closet (or toilet) for 20 persons was deemed to be 'first-class' is indicative of the scale of squalor in which thousands of Dubliners lived.

Irish Republican and socialist leader James Connolly said the living conditions in the Dublin tenements captured the contradictions he saw in Irish society as a whole:

> Ireland is a country of wonderful charity and singularly little justice. And Dublin, being an epitome of Ireland, is it not strange to find that Dublin, a city famous for its charitable institutions and its charitable citizens, should also be infamous for the perfectly hellish conditions

under which its people are housed, and under which its men, women and children labour for a living?

Connolly, who was Commander of the Dublin Brigade in the GPO during the Easter Rising of 1916, was badly injured before the evacuation to Moore Street. He was executed by firing squad in Kilmainham jail, while strapped to a chair, on 12 May 1916 for his role in the Rising. In *James Connolly, A Full Life* (2005), Donal Nevin notes that 'A circular issued by the British army recruiting authorities quoted a speaker at a recruiting meeting in Dublin as declaring that the Dublin slums were more unhealthy than the trenches in Flanders.'

This might have been the grim reality of the tenements, but for Bridget and Bill it was the start of their new life together, and it burned brightly with the promise of a better future than the difficult pasts they had both endured. Bridget was a stay-at-home mother while Bill went to work as a truck driver for Water Bros. Tea and Wine Merchants, O'Connell Street, Dublin 1. He left for work at 7.00 a.m. every day. He lit the paraffin heater and made tea and toast for his wife and daughter, which he served to them in bed before leaving. Bridget would spend the day caring for Anna and their home.

Bridget was always neatly turned out. As a young woman her hair was permed, but later in life she had it cut short and left it straight. She still loved her fashion and dressed mostly in skirts and blouses and pretty floral dresses with a cardigan. She cleaned and cooked all day while Bill was out. Bridget loved a cup of tea and the kettle was always on the go. She didn't have many friends, but the ones she had were close to her. To her friends, she was 'Biddy', a warm and welcoming woman who loved to chat and laugh.

Mrs Kellett, who was married to Sgt Kellett, lived on the nearby North Circular Road and the women popped in and out of each other's homes regularly. Mrs Gallagher, who also lived on North Great Charles Street, was from Mayo and became a good friend. She would call in to the Corrigans' place regularly. Although Bridget's own family weren't in her life, she was close to Bill's sister-in-law, Nancy. Bridget loved her cigarettes and smoked up to twenty Golden Flake a day. She would sit back and have tea with her friends while they caught up on the latest news. The women always loved cake with their tea and there was always a bit of lemon sponge in the cupboard.

When Anna was sleeping, Bridget would get the dinner on for Bill. She was a very good cook, preparing simple, plain, nutritious food of the meat, potato and two veg kind. Bridget loved making stews and was well-known for her apple tarts. She had a sweet tooth and relished Iced Caramels, Liquorice Allsorts and Fry's Chocolate Cream bars.

During the day, Bridget would go to Coxes, the local shop across the road, where the family ran a tab that Bill paid up every Friday. As the years went on Bridget would venture out to a supermarket in Henry Street, where she collected Green Shield stamps in a book that could be traded for gifts from a catalogue at a later stage. Afterwards, if she had any spare time, she would knit and sew while listening to the radio. She was never bored and made clothes for all her nieces and nephews in Clonfert. Later in life she began to crochet and produced beautiful bed covers.

Bridget always retained her strong West of Ireland accent and when anyone asked, 'How are you, Biddy?' she replied, 'The finesht.' While she loved fashion and style, she didn't like make-up. She used to say, 'Sure doesn't God and man know that a woman wasn't born with pink and blue and different-coloured eyelids?'

When Bill came in from work in the evenings they would sit at the table and catch up on the day's events. They liked listening to music and were both fans of Irish traditional music, as well as Frank Sinatra, Dean Martin and Josef Locke. In later life, Bridget became a fan of Shane McGowan and The Pogues. Anna smiles to remember it: 'My aunt used to say to her, "How could you like that fella and the gob of rotten teeth on him?" And my mother used to say, "Feck off, he's great, just listen to his music, he'd rise ya."'

Bridget loved politics and always had her opinions about the politicians of the day. Anna tells how 'one time Charlie Haughey had a cut on his head, it was supposed to be from a horse-riding accident, but my mother said his wife probably hit him with the brush for womanising. She used to talk about the Blue Shirts and how there were some locals in Clonfert who were sympathisers. Somebody painted their donkey blue and dyed a pair of knickers blue and left them on the gate-post when people were going to mass. I heard they all had a great laugh about that.'

Anna attended North William Street school, close to her home. The school had an orphanage attached to it. Unknown to Anna at the time, her aunt Mary Corrigan, Bill's younger sister, who had died in Loughrea Industrial School, had been due to be placed in that orphanage; the application was withdrawn. Anna said: 'It doesn't make sense, her father lived in Mountjoy Square, which was five minutes up the road, so why was she sent to Galway? It shocked me when I found out this information later on because it was the same school I went to.'

The head nun in Anna's school during her early years there was Sister Monica, who was the same nun who had worked in the boys' school when playwright Brendan Behan attended there. In *Brendan Behan, A Life* by Michael O'Sullivan (2000), Sister Monica is described as:

> the most dominant influence on Brendan's early school life. After his grandmother and mother, she was the most loved figure in his childhood. Sister Louise, who arrived at the school as a postulant two years before Brendan left, remembers Sr Monica as a tall and stately figure, yet she could appear very frail.
>
> Sr Monica had told Brendan to sleep at night with his arms folded so that if he died in his sleep he would have the sign of the cross on him. When in Borstal, Brendan, a self-confessed atheist, acted on Sr Monica's advice.

The *Irish Independent*, in an article on 17 January 2016, reported that Sister Monica was believed to have told Behan's mother she was 'rearing a genius':

When he was a little boy, it was Sister Monica, the head of William Street School, who taught Brendan his prayers in Irish and first set him off on poetry and the love of the language. She told his mother that 'she was rearing a genius'. In his last hours in the Meath Hospital when a visiting nun mopped his fevered brow with a cold compress, Brendan muttered: 'God bless you, Sister, may you be the mother of a bishop'.

Anna was born into the tenements, so it was the only life she'd ever known. To her, it was all normal and she enjoyed her childhood there with Bridget and Bill:

The boys in the school only stayed until they were seven years old.

I would go off to school every day and my mother gave me a flask with soup in it that I could keep warm in the winters, the school was freezing. There was little heating there. I remember one child tried to grab my flask and it fell on the floor and we got beaten for it by the nuns.

My father would go off to work and my mother would walk me to school and collect me at 3 p.m. She would stay at home, clean up and make lunch for my father who always came home with a friend between 1 and 2 p.m. She would only see him off when she would be getting ready to collect me.

Sr Joan taught me in the early years, and Sr Marie Louise had been in America before she came to the school. She became Head Nun. She was absolutely beautiful. She set up a little tuck shop in the school. Sr Joan left and I found out years later she married a Christian Brother.

Sister Marie Louise later let Anna run the school tuck shop because she was good with money and accounting. Anna also spent a lot of time in the Corporation Library, Charleville Mall, which was opposite the school: 'We had a teacher called Ms Brereton from second to sixth class and she instilled a great love of learning in me. She could answer any question you asked.'

Anna, who has a beautiful singing voice to this day, sang in the church choir in primary school, under the musical guidance of Sister Kevin, a nun who she says 'wouldn't impress on you'. Religion pervaded every part of daily life:

You had to learn your catechism and the fear of God was put into you all the time. The nuns would often talk about the original sin and how you could suffer in the fires of hell. When you made your Confirmation, you had to know it all off by heart in case the Bishop asked you a question. You would be terrified if you got anything wrong. You didn't start a class without blessing yourself.

Bridget devoted a lot of time to preparing Anna for school when she started in Junior Infants on her fourth birthday, on 1 September 1960:

My mother cut the dates out of the calendar and taught me how to add, I knew all the alphabet and the numbers, and I knew the clock by the time I was four years old. She would walk me to school and collect me. I was never allowed to play out on the street, but I remember my dad let me out and when I came back in I used the word 'fuck' and my mother went mad, she said, 'See, I told you, you can't rear a child on the streets'.

When the holidays came, Anna and her mother would go to Clonfert to see Bridget's family. At some stage they must have mended their broken relationship, but Anna isn't sure exactly when this occurred. The letter from Bill to Bridget while she was on holiday in Clonfert in 1957, is the only evidence Anna has of the reconciliation. At the end of June each year, just after school closed for the summer holidays, Anna and her mother would pack up and take the bus to Galway for two months. Having become a 'legitimate' mother after marrying Bill, it was now acceptable for Bridget to go home.

I went to Galway every summer, Christmas and Easter when I was young with my mother. People would laugh at me and call me a Jackeen when I went to Clonfert, and when I came back to Dublin I was a culchie. And on the days we were home and had free time we went to the Museums and the Art Gallery and the Natural History Museum. I went to the book shops with my father. I don't remember any bad feeling towards my mother when we went to Galway, but I did always feel a sense of alienation. I can't quite put my finger on it. I'd be dying to go home sometimes, but you had to stay. My father would come down for his holidays for two weeks to visit, but we stayed there myself and my mother for the full summer. Days were usually busy as there was lots to do on the small farms. I worked at the hay and the turf. I collected eggs and fed animals and milked cows.

When I was off school in Dublin we used to go to the outdoor baths in Blackrock. My father was a great swimmer. We used to go to Killiney and Dalkey on the train. My mother made great picnics. We used to go to the parks and listen to the bands playing on the bandstands.

As I got into my teenage years, I didn't bother going to Galway anymore. I preferred to be in Dublin. I remember when my mother's mother died in her home on the Three Road in Clonfert. We had to get the bus from Dublin and it was a long journey then. The bus went into every little town and stopped. It took ages. We got the bus to Banagher and then a hackney cab to Clonfert. Granny died on 7

March 1967 and my grandfather had died three years earlier, on 19 May 1964.

I can only imagine now what my mother was thinking, maybe it was how much time she had missed with them and why what happened, happened.

Growing up, Anna doesn't recall her mother being physically affectionate towards her:

My mother loved me of course, and I have no doubt about that. She wasn't one for kissing and hugging me, that was the way it was for most mothers at the time. It's only now that she's gone and I'm looking back over her life that many things she did make sense now.

We had angst between us, me and my mother. It was just this feeling I had. If we had a row, we never sat down and sorted it out, we just moved on.

I never, ever said sorry to her when we fought, and I only remember us laughing together when I was small. She was quiet enough, my mother, but she would tell you if she was angry and when she was angry, she was bossy. I was very sulky, and I gave a lot of back-chat. I just didn't want to hear any rules out of them. My dad never said anything to me, but I had more of a difficult relationship with my mother. I told her to feck off loads of times. We were both strong-willed, so we clashed. We only lived in one room, so there wasn't much you could do if you had a row. As I got older I'd just leave the room and go out. But when I was younger you just carried on as it was hard to give the silent treatment when we all lived in one room. My dad would say 'leave the child alone' all the time, I'd say it drove my mother mad.

Anna was very close to her father growing up and she was the apple of his eye:

He was a lovely man. We had no television when I was young, so we used to sit and listen to the radio. My father loved opera and there was an opera programme on once a week and we always listened to it. There was a story, or a book read on Sunday night on RTÉ and we would listen to that. Years later my father got a big radio with fourteen wave bands and we could pick up the shipping and the gardaí. You would hear, 'call out to Summerhill' and it would be the gardaí and you would be wondering who they were coming for.

We went to the Banba book shop a lot, which was in Tara Street, and there was another shop in Summerhill that was a second-hand book shop and my dad would buy me second-hand comics and books.

Dad worked as a driver for Water Brothers in O'Connell Street and they were a Tea & Wine Merchants. They supplied all the hotels around the country and they shipped it from the 'Depot' in East Wall and they distributed stuff on the trains. I went sometimes on the truck with him.

Bridget remained a devout Catholic, and the family of three went off to Gardiner Street church every Sunday for mass. By the time Anna was 13, however, she didn't want to go to church anymore:

I just stopped going and that was it. I had no interest in going, my mother was saying, 'You have to go and that's that', but my father was saying, 'Leave the child alone'. He always called me 'the child'. Now I'm wondering if that was from his time in the Industrial Schools, where nobody knew or cared about your name?

Every Sunday we went to Gardiner Street and later we would go to the church on Portland Row known as 'the Old Maids Home'. I didn't realise it at the time but the women were flocking in there from Seán McDermott Street Magdalene Laundry for mass.

Renault dealer and former *Apprentice* TV star Bill Cullen lived on Portland Row at the time and my mother knew his mother very well. My ma used to buy her fruit from his mother. People could get their bags of fruit in Moore Street, but my parents only had me, so my mam would buy two apples or an orange from her, her fruit was always the best quality and we would be delighted with that because we were not a huge family so you got to eat it all up. Mrs Cullen had a pram and I remember her selling outside Roche's Stores, she wasn't up Moore Street.

As a teenager, Anna was listening to all different types of music and her first boyfriend was her friend's brother: 'I went through loads of phases. I was a skinhead, then a hippie and then I got into the motorbikes, I tried every look. I was into all types of music too. I would have cousins up from the country and I would be going to the National Ballroom in Parnell Square to listen to Big Tom with them, then I'd leave and go to a have a Chinese meal somewhere else.'

While Anna and her parents were getting on with life in North Great Charles Street, the Mother and Baby Homes were still in operation all over the country. The last one only closed in 1996. Bridget may have been far away from the horrors of the Tuam Mother and Baby Home, but the Seán McDermott Street Magdalene Laundry was located less than 1km from her home, on. Bridget often had to pass by it to go to Busaras to get the bus to Galway. We can only imagine what she was thinking as she walked by its high walls, knowing first-hand what went on behind them. No doubt she felt for the girls and women imprisoned there, and probably also thanked her lucky stars that she had escaped. It's easy to imagine her vowing that her own Anna would never, ever end up in a place like that.

As Anna approached the end of her time in St Vincent's Girls' National School North William Street, she sat an entrance exam for and was accepted into the Dominican College on Eccles Street, which was a private school with boarders and day pupils. They also took in non-fee-paying students who passed the entrance exam. Anna remembers the moment they heard the news: 'The school rang my mam and dad at the corner shop, they would come up and get you for the phonecall, and we were asked to come into the school. I remember the smell of the polished floors and polished leather sofas, it was a school where people with money went.'

The school was offering Anna a place, but a 'voluntary' donation of around £50 was required to secure it. That was equivalent to five weeks' wages for her father, so that ended the matter immediately. Instead, she went to the Presentation Convent, Georges Hill, in the fruit markets in Dublin 7. The large school was considered modern at the time and was run by the Presentation nuns – the same order whose Head of Novices had offered Bridget a job in Loughrea looking after her mother.

Anna loved secondary school and excelled at all subjects, especially Geography, Maths and Bookkeeping. She was in the top streams for Irish, English and Maths:

My mother was brilliant with money and numbers, she said there was never a day that went by when she didn't have a penny in her purse and I obviously got it from her. I'm a bit like that myself. My mother was always good with housekeeping and money.

I loved school to start with, and back then I started wanting to do my own thing. I started smoking at 12 and drinking [alcohol] at 13. We would buy one cigarette and we got one match for free with it and we would be terrified if we were caught going to school with it because we were in our uniforms and would get into so much trouble. But I never got caught. When I was 13 we would buy a big bottle of cider and we would drink a few mouthfuls and be really drunk. We would get someone to buy it for us in the Off Licence, a girl who had her own room in the tenement, we would go to her bedroom and drink it there. She had a lock on her door. There could be six of us, we would have maybe two flagons of cider and then we would go off to see Thin Lizzy or Skid Row and it would start at 8 and we would be finished at 11. I loved Phil Lynott. It was only years later that I realised his own mother, Philomena, was in a workhouse with him because she wasn't married when he was born, and she gave up two other children after him. So many people were going through this pain behind closed doors. Phil was just so talented, a one off. I saw him when he was only starting off and he blew me away. He was unique, he stood out a mile, he was just a fantastic singer and musician. I used to see him in O'Connell's school and in the CYC in Fairview.

I remember Dickie Rock was popular when I was young, and Elvis. Later on, we listened to Radio Caroline.

I was good at bookkeeping and began to start thinking I'd like to leave school. It wasn't a big deal to leave school early in those days. If you got the Intermediate Certificate, you would be doing OK. We were taught by the nuns, so we were trained in bookkeeping and typing. If you left school after the Intermediate Certificate, you were guaranteed a job in those areas.

I had a bit of a laugh at school, but I wasn't keen on it. My parents wanted better for me. They argued as I got older that I should get a job in the civil service, a state job with a pension was a big thing then. A job with the nuns or the gardaí or the state and you were made for life.

When I left school I was 15 and I went straight to work in an office. No one ever tried to stop me, there was expectation, my father would have wanted me to stay on and my mother would have been the same, but I didn't care, I just wanted to do my own thing.

As Anna got older, Bill and Bridget started socialising more often. As a child Anna doesn't remember being babysat: 'I don't think they went out much, we just went out together and on Sundays we went on Mystery Tours and maybe to the beach.' But as she grew in independence, so did her parents start to enjoy some of the things they'd been missing:

When I got older they would go out for a ramble and lunch and maybe a drink, on Sundays they would go to see a band in the Phoenix Park and Fairview Park. I would go with them sometimes.

My father would drink a Guinness and my mother liked port, sherry maybe a glass of Guinness. He loved his cigarettes too and smoked Players non-tipped.

My mother was always a very energetic person and a morning person and when they would go out she walked very straight and slowly and she would give out to my father for walking fast.

At the age of 17 Anna secured a job in Hamburg, Germany, and left home for six months:

My dad loaned me the money to go. They would have preferred I stayed at home, but I wanted to see the world. I was nervous and excited. I often wonder would I have been better off to keep going on my travels and not come home, but I did.

I always worked in offices, I lived a double life and was into all sorts of partying. I would have ordered a pint back then no problem. I remember my friend Isabella waiting for me outside the pub, she wouldn't go in alone. I had to come get her.

I eventually got a job in the Post Office and I remember going to Clery's pub on Amiens Street with a couple of men I worked with after we came back from a hard day's working, loading and unloading vans and trains. I was around 22 or 23. I walked in and said, 'A pint of Carlsberg' and the barman said, 'You won't have one here'. I said I was working with the men but he said, 'If you want to drink here, go down to the snug there, love'.

It was funny back then. The way it was, if you were a woman, you couldn't just order a drink. Some pubs did not allow women at all. I've always gone into pubs on my own no problem and ordered pints, I didn't care back then. I just did it. I always worked, but I liked to have a few pints too. I always believed it didn't matter if you were a woman or a man, your money was a good as anybody's and I deserved to do exactly as I wanted.

When Anna was 19, her father got sick. He was 72 years old. He had been working for his employer for 10 years, but had lied to them about his age because he didn't want to give up work at retirement age. As far as his employers knew, he was 62. But he was now in his seventies and a smoker, and he was starting to feel the effects of a long, hard life:

He got some kind of a chest infection and the policy back then was that anyone over 65 was not taken into the Mater Hospital, so he went to St Mary's Old Folks Home in the Phoenix Park.

I used to drive a Honda 50 at that stage, I used to go visit on my bike. Getting there was difficult as it was very out of the way and isolated. My cousins came and brought my mother to visit by car. It wasn't until later in the years that my cousin told me one time my mother and herself went to visit my dad, and he freaked out and ran out in his pyjamas saying, 'Please take me out of here'. All the beds were lined up against the wall and along the middle of the floor. Thinking back, it was an old building like the Home, he must have got some sort of flashback. My mother did take him home, it was all a blur.

He eventually went back into hospital and he stopped eating and stopped taking his tablets. I remember the day he died very well. It was 25 May 1976 and a phone call came in to the local shop, Benny's, down the road. They sent up the girl from the shop. I went and took the call and was told my father was dead. I had to walk back up the road and tell my mother, who was sitting at home.

I just remember I was in bits and my mother was devastated. Then we got another phone call and had to go back down again to the shop and they wanted to do an autopsy on him. I said, 'No, leave him alone, that's enough.'

I had to go to the hospital and identify him. I couldn't let my mother do it, even though it was very hard.

I remember he wanted to be buried in a suit, back then only Protestants got buried in suits, or so the family said. Catholics were buried in brown 'habits'.

Male members of my mother's family came to organise his funeral, but I was having none of it. That was the usual thing, of men coming to take over the jobs, but I organised the funeral, I ordered the coffin and made all the arrangements.

I was devastated, he was the only man in my life I ever truly loved. I was spoiled, and no man could stand up to him or rate up to him. He never gave out to me. The house was my mother's domain, he never got involved in the house or the running of me. But he always stood up for me.

He didn't have a wake and he was brought from the Lourdes Church Parish to Glasnevin cemetery. I remember my mother was dressed in black and she was crying a lot. I never remember my mother crying until then. If she was down, she kept it to herself, but after my dad died we were both devastated. We were in our own space.

She was very lonely after he died. She never met anyone else after that and always said there was no one like him. It was like she lost a bit of her spark.

It wasn't until a year later – when Anna was 20 and came home and told her mother she was pregnant and had no partner – that the life in Bridget started to come back.

# 9

# Kicking Down Doors

It probably wasn't what Bridget had envisaged for her daughter, but when Anna came home and confessed that she was pregnant and single, her mother wasn't angry or upset. Bridget accepted this new development calmly and immediately set about helping her daughter to prepare for the birth. No doubt she worried about the effects of this on Anna's life, but she never let that show. She was a solid rock for Anna, reliable, constant and unmoving. It took Anna a long time to understand how incredible her mother's reaction was to this life-changing news:

When I think back now, I can put it into perspective. If she hadn't been around, I could have been in a Home myself. I was pregnant at 20 in 1977 when the Mother and Baby Homes were very much in full operation. My friend had a baby at the same time as me and she went into a Home. And if I had not had the support of my mother, I would have been in a Home too.

My mother never batted an eyelid at my pregnancy. When I told my mother I was pregnant, my friend Teresa was there too. I just blurted out, 'I'm pregnant' and ran out. My mother said, 'What just happened there?' My friend Teresa was left to pick up the pieces. My father had died by then, so it was just me and my mother.

My mother never once commented, never asked questions she shouldn't have and certainly never castigated me for anything. She made no remark about it except, 'Oh, OK.' I was able to walk up the street in 1977 with a bump and no ring on my finger and I didn't care.

It was thanks to Bridget's quiet support that Anna was able to cope with her pregnancy and face her neighbours without shame:

> I remember there was a group of my neighbours having a conversation in the doorway as I went by one day when I was about seven months pregnant. I could tell by the way the women were looking at me that the conversation was obviously about me being pregnant. And one of them said: 'Anna, you're getting very fat.' I turned around and said, 'So would you if you were seven months' pregnant.' They said, 'You're not, you're never, go away, seriously?'
>
> I never put that into perspective at the time, but it would have been a massive deal. It was still very shameful for women then.

Attitudes to pregnancy outside marriage had shifted to an extent by the 1970s and women who fell pregnant outside marriage were no longer facing destitution and forced to rely on the Catholic Church and its institutions for support. In 1973, the Social Welfare Act made provision for the payment of a deserted wives' benefit and an unmarried mother's allowance. A high-profile support group to represent the interests of single mothers, called Cherish, was formed at the same time. Mary Robinson, then a senator, was its first president. This group played a key role in the public debate and in helping to inform single mothers of their rights.

These changes were very welcome, but nonetheless being a single mother in Ireland in the 1970s was relatively rare and carried a huge social stigma. While this no longer meant social isolation, especially in inner-city Dublin, unmarried mothers still faced huge challenges, both from individuals and institutions. Landlords, for example, regularly refused to rent homes to unmarried women with children lest they be seen as condoning their 'behaviour', while getting a good job was almost impossible.

Bridget, who knew all too well what it was like to have a baby out of wedlock, protected Anna in the best way she knew how – by taking on some of the practical burdens that come with being a mother. She stepped in and took over some of the duties of motherhood when Anna's eldest daughter was born on 15 November 1977. Bridget took her role as grandmother very seriously. Anna describes how she and her eldest daughter wanted for nothing:

> I was very much a bit of a hippy and my mother was a great support with my daughter. I could go off and do my own thing and she would take care of her. In a way, it brought life back into her after my dad died. My father left us a bit of money and I bought myself a bigger motorbike, so I was still off being a biker chick and working and my mother stepped in as childminder. She was absolutely fantastic.
>
> I moved on my own track, I moved around in a hippy era where if you got pregnant as a single mother, you got on with it, but my mother at home said nothing negative about it, so why should anyone else? That's what I thought about it all.
>
> Some people in my era were starting to live together and it was the opening up of a different time. I was in a relationship, it wasn't anything permanent, I didn't live with my daughter's father. That's just the way it was. I wasn't even in a proper relationship with him. I have always done my own thing and been an individual, but when I look back on it now, I wonder how my mother must have really felt about it all. We [the father and I] broke up in the end completely.
>
> Me and my mother battled a lot, for many reasons, but I never doubted she loved me. She really took my child under her wing and they ended up having a very close relationship where they confided a lot in each other. I think now, with the arguments or the disagreements we had over the years, my mother must have really felt the pangs in her heart about me doing my own thing and having my daughter and being a single mother. There was no question in the world of my child being given up or taken off me.

And yet my mother didn't have that choice and I was completely unaware of how she was feeling because I knew nothing about my brothers. She must have felt some sort of jealousy towards me, how could she not? She didn't have the choices I had, and I didn't care what she thought because I didn't know what was underneath it all. So we argued, but now I realise it must have been so difficult for my mother. When I look at it now, she must have felt it was so unfair. And yet she never, ever judged me, but there were tough times between us. I was off doing my own thing. I had left school, I didn't care about anything. And my mother had lost her two boys because she couldn't do what I was doing.

Anna describes her young self as a 'biker chick', and she revelled in that whole scene. She was a rare sight on the Irish roads when she first starting driving motorbikes at the age of 18. At a time when Irish women were much likelier to be in the passenger seat of cars, she was happy to go her own way, under her own powerful bike.

If you met her in a pub for the first time, within a few minutes she would be giving you honest, straightforward and unvarnished opinions about any topic – including herself. She is a tough-talker, always straightforward and never afraid of a row – especially in defence of others. She is unfailingly loyal, afraid of nobody and a passionate defender of her family and friends. Put simply, Anna is not the crying type. She cries when deeply hurt, but not easily or quickly. But the discoveries she was to make about Bridget and her hidden life broke through that tough exterior. When she found out the truth about her mother's past – and her own – she cried and cried.

The first discovery came from Bridget herself, who told Anna that she had two miscarriages after Anna was born. Anna didn't know it then, but this meant her mother had lost four children altogether. Together with the family tragedies experienced by Bill and the losses experienced by Bridget, the couple had suffered incredible traumas during their lives.

Back then, there were no support groups, no organisations and no counselling for anyone who suffered the loss of a child. Bridget had no choice but to keep going.

> My mother told me she had two miscarriages after me. She was heartbroken over them, but she had my dad, and she got on with it. I never knew if she was suffering or not, she was generally a quiet person, but she was always doing something. I could never tell if she was sad. I'm sure my dad was a great comfort to her. I saw how badly she was affected after he died. Her best friend was gone.

Learning about her mother's miscarriages was difficult for Anna because she had always longed for a sibling in her life. Nothing could have prepared her for the news that she had two missing brothers.

In 1982 Anna became pregnant again, and gave birth to a second daughter, Sarah. As before, Bridget was an ever-present source of care and support. As time went on, the little family grew close and the girls depended on their grandmother, and she adored them. So it was a hard time for all of them when Bridget suffered a stroke in December 2000 and her health started to fail.

Bridget suffered a second stroke in March 2001 and was taken to the Mater Hospital in Dublin's north inner city, close to her home. It was clear she wasn't long for this world.

The night before Bridget passed away, Anna, her daughters and her partner, Paddy, were all by her bedside. Even then, Bridget didn't share her secret past with her family. She chose to take the story of John and William to the grave with her. This is something Anna has had to come to terms with over time:

> As she lay dying, we didn't have any final words, there were no exchanges that could change anything. I look back on it now and I understand the difficulties we had between us. My mother was

suffering and she wanted to protect me by not telling me anything. I just wish she had said something because so many things could have been different. She had an awful life before she met my father. I think they saved each other in many ways. I am really glad she had him. I think he knew what happened to her and her to him.

Bridget's three girls stayed by her bedside as her time drew near. She had endured much in her lifetime, but at the hour of her death she was attended with love, care and tenderness:

We were all in the hospital the night before she died and the Doctor told us to go home. He said she would not pass that night, but we would have a rough 24 hours or more and we should get some sleep, as it may be a long day and night next day. My daughter refused to leave and she stayed. My mother died with my eldest daughter by her side.

I was at home when my eldest daughter rang early in the morning and said she had passed away. I believe she was meant to be there, they were extremely close, my mother confided in her and the same went for my daughter.

I think her granddaughter was a blessing for my mother after she had lost so much. I can only see that now.

Just as she had done for her father, Anna had the sorrowful task of organising the funeral. Although they had battled and fought at times during her life, Anna and her mother had never really spent much time apart from each other. Their lives had been so closely intertwined for so long that Anna was left bereft at her loss.

I had to pick out the coffin and it reminded me so much of my dad's death. My friend Isabella brought me to the funeral home. I organised everything, the flowers and the meal afterwards and the music for the ceremony and the readings at the mass.

I spent some time with her after she passed, on the morning of the funeral. I watched her as she was laid out and wondered about her and her life and what was I going to do now. My children loved her and her them. But things would never be the same again. I realised she had the wrong rosary beads and I asked the undertaker if he could open the coffin. He said no. But he relented and allowed me change her rosary beads on her hands for ones I had. I am really grateful for that. I had won them in a school competition when I was young and they were her favourite. So maybe in a way I got to show my love before she was gone forever.

Bridget's funeral took place on Gardiner Street, in Dublin's city centre.

Now that she was left alone, without the warm shelter of her parents, Anna's mind often turned to their lives and to the things she still didn't know. Finally, in 2012 she took a step towards finding some answers. Like many people who wished to discover the truth about their relatives' lives in the Mother and Baby Homes, Anna turned to Barnardos Children's Charity for help. She requested the assistance of Clodagh Donnelly, Head of the Origins Information and Tracing Service, in tracing her father's background in the Kilkenny and Glin industrial schools. Through Barnados, Anna learned about her aunt Mary, who had died while in the care of the nuns in Loughrea.

The research into Bill Corrigan and his siblings was well underway when, out of curiosity, Anna asked Clodagh Donnelly if she could look up her mother's history, too. Anna knew nothing of Bridget's past in the Tuam Home, but on impulse she asked Clodagh to look up her mother because of a small, half-remembered comment she had heard during her childhood, which had made no sense to her. Anna had a very faint childhood recollection of her uncle shouting at her mother before turning to young Anna and saying, "Did you know your mother had two baby boys?" She had never heard another word about it again after that and had always doubted that the memory was accurate. It was just one sentence and Anna was very young, maybe seven or eight years old at the time. So when she gave Clodagh her mother's name, she didn't expect anything to come of it – except, maybe, to be told that her faint recollection of a conversation as a child was wrong. 'I never in a million years expected to hear it was all true and that my mother was in a Mother and Baby Home,' Anna says. 'I knew absolutely nothing about it all.'

Anna was washing the dishes at her home in Dublin when the call came, in early December 2012. She remembers Clodagh's soft voice on the other end of the phone telling her, 'I'd like you to come into us, before we give you any news.' But Anna could not wait, she knew Barnados had unearthed something important and she wanted to know everything. Now.

Clodagh eventually relented and gently told her the truth she had never even imagined: 'You have two brothers, Anna, and they were born before you in the Tuam Mother and Baby Home in Galway. Their names are John Desmond and William Joseph Dolan.'

It was a complete and utter bombshell.

She had my brothers' names, dates of birth and certificates. I thought my feet were going to come out from under me. I was on my own and I sat down at the kitchen table in absolute shock. I just sobbed my heart out. The tears and hurt actually came from the belly. I don't know if I have ever cried that hard. It was like I couldn't cry hard enough. I was broken-hearted. It was a very hard thing to take in, it was an awful shock. My body was shaking with the fright I got.

Not alone was I finding out about my brothers, I was finding out about myself, finding out about my mother and finding out about my father, it was just everything. The life I had lived and the life I believed was not the life that actually was. It was like nothing was real. I didn't know what to feel, but I know I was distressed.

Despite all the years they had lived together, Bridget had never even hinted at the darkness that lay in her past. Anna had to come to terms with her mother's silence on top of everything else:

> So many things were going through my mind. I felt as though I had been deprived of a family. I grew up an only child and I had no one except my parents. I could have done with two big brothers to mind me and protect me and things might have been a bit different.
>
> I actually had to do a 360-degree turn on my mother. There was often tension between us because we were two women in a house and we were both alpha females.
>
> I never cared what my parents thought, I just did my own thing. They knew there was no point in trying to make me see things their way or do what they wanted. I was never going to listen to them.

Suddenly, it felt like her treasured memories of her mother and her happy childhood were a lie. After being an only child for 56 years, as far as she was concerned, she discovered she was actually the youngest of three:

> I don't know anyone else who knows what that's like. It's like your whole life wasn't real, nothing will ever be the same again and the people I want answers from are dead.
>
> I can only surmise why my mother didn't tell me. I know she wouldn't have expected me to find out, and she certainly wouldn't have thought it was me who would bring the story of the Tuam grave to the media.
>
> I think if she saw how the story erupted after 25 May 2014, that she would be OK with it all. I do think she would speak out now if she saw how the story went global. My brothers were at the heart of that first big story. I believe somehow they were a driving force behind it all.

Clodagh followed up that phone call with a letter, setting out the information that had been unearthed by Barnardos. Anna received a letter, dated 7 December 2012, which explained that records uncovered from the HSE in Galway stated that John Desmond was born on 22 February 1946 and William Joseph was born on 21 May 1950. Clodagh's letter laid bare the Dolan family secret:

> Further to your letter dated 13th November 2012, requesting information in respect of the above-named siblings of Anne Marie Corrigan, I am writing to inform you that we have now completed a search of the records of the Children's Home Tuam, Co. Galway. I enclose below details of records in respect of Bridget Dolan, John Desmond Dolan and William Joseph Dolan.

Bridget was admitted into the Children's home Tuam on 26 January 1946 aged 26 years. Her residence previous to admission is given as Clonfert, Eyrecourt, Co. Galway. Bridget's marital status is recorded as 'single' and her occupation described as 'working from home'. The maternity records show that Bridget was admitted to the maternity ward on 21 February 1946 'in labour'.

The letter went on to explain that, according to the records uncovered, John and William had both sadly passed away. It also stated that there was no death certificate for William. Barnados had made enquiries as to the whereabouts of the boys' graves and advised Anna that 'The Children's home in Tuam is no longer there, however, I did make some enquiries with the caretaker of the graveyard in Tuam regarding the burial site for children who had died in the Tuam Home. The caretaker informed me that there is a small burial plot on the site where the Children's Home once stood. It is marked by a small grotto.'

The fact that Anna's brothers had a final resting place where she could go and pay her respects provided her with some comfort. It was the only tangible link she had to a past she would never know. Instantly,

Anna began to make plans to visit the site in Tuam and lay flowers and maybe put a plaque there to remember her two brothers. Or if there was a headstone, she could have John and William's names inscribed on it, if they weren't already there. She wanted a real, physical link to the brothers she had never seen or touched during their lives.

It crossed Anna's mind that her brothers may not have been baptised and therefore could be in a *cillín* grave, or children's burial ground, where unbaptised children were laid to rest. At the time of their deaths, the Catholic Church made a distinction between babies who had been baptised before dying and those who passed away without baptism. The souls of children who died without receiving the sacrament were believed to be sent to Limbo. They could not enter Heaven, but they would not suffer in Hell for eternity either. They existed in an in-between state, forever suspended in a nowhere because they weren't fit for Heaven.

After getting the news from Barnardos, Anna decided to learn everything she possibly could about her brothers and about what her mother had gone through. She requested baptismal certificates for her brothers, one from Galway University Hospital, where William was born, and John's from the Archdiocese of Tuam. She hoped these documents, which would be stored by the Church, would hold some more clues as to what had happened.

At this point, in early 2013, she had opened personal files on her computer for her mother and father, her two brothers and her aunt Mary, so that she had a safe place to store any information she came across. Even at that early stage, Anna knew she had a long, hard road ahead of her in uncovering the truth about her family. But she was determined to persevere.

In October 2013 Anna was forced to take time off work after falling ill. She was diagnosed with post-traumatic stress disorder and depression, as well as agoraphobia. Unable to work, she suddenly had more time on her hands. Despite being ill, she attacked the job of finding out about her family's past with relentless gusto and it filled her days and her mind.

Anna is a highly organised woman. Her kitchen in West Dublin is like a well-run office. She has a printer set up in the corner of her kitchen, sitting on a small cabinet with two drawers. The drawers are full of stationery, paper-clips, scissors, Blu-Tack and Sellotape. Her laptop is always open on her large kitchen table, and Anna is usually to be seen there, updating her filing system, typing emails and researching online from early morning until late at night. When people call to visit, she is often overhead saying, 'Hold on, I'm just in the middle of sending this email to the Taoiseach.' There is probably not a major politician in Ireland who has not received correspondence from Anna at some stage.

As an executive officer with the Revenue Commissioners for more than eleven years and a clerical officer in the Department of Employment Affairs and Social Protection for the previous ten years, Anna has a civil servant's respect for proper record-keeping. She has copies of every email, letter or note she has sent and received regarding her brothers' cases, and she knows exactly where everything is. But as she opened up her documents and filing system on her family in late 2012, Anna had no idea she was working towards exposing one of the biggest stories to come out of Ireland in the last decade. As far as she was concerned, this was a personal story, a piece of her life, and so she meticulously gathered as much information as she could and kept every scrap of paper she ever received on her brothers.

At first, she tried to avoid grieving for John and William, keeping busy and pulling her research together to keep her mind off it. But there were always the quiet moments, and the story would hit her like a ton of bricks every single time. Her only way to work through her grief was to find answers and hold her brothers' lives up to the light, so that their lost voices could be heard. She was their only way to be remembered now.

In 2015 the Irish government established the Mother and Baby Homes Commission of Investigation. Before the Commission was in place, survivors and their relatives were working alone, seeking out documents and information as individuals. In 2014, Anna applied for documents relating to her mother from the AIRR (Access to Institutional and Related Records) project in the Department of Health and also from a number of HSE (Health Service Executive) departments. Her requests were answered and she gathered valuable information. Once the Commission began its work, the flow of paperwork and personal files slowed down because all of the institutions involved sent their files to the Commission and it made things harder to access. However, by then Anna had retrieved several explosive documents regarding her brothers.

These were the documents that showed both John and William had been baptised, which meant they should have received a Catholic burial in a graveyard or cemetery. The documents Anna received showed clearly that there was no burial record for either child. This omission seemed inexplicable, and indeed no one could give Anna a reasonable explanation for it. Why were there no burial records for two Catholic children born and raised in a Catholic institution, who had both received the sacrament of baptism? It was this pressing question that started Anna's campaign for justice.

Back in December 2012, when Barnardos researcher Clodagh Donnelly had a follow-up meeting with Anna about her mother, she said to her that the story 'could easily become a national scandal and would probably end up in a book'. Anna recalls: 'I remember looking at her like she had two heads. My mother's story in a book? A national scandal? I never knew when I brought the story to the media that it would explode the way it did, never mind have the story made into a book.' At that time, there was no public statement or correspondence in the public domain that suggested the nuns knew about the unmarked grave in Tuam. Anna, however, had already received written confirmation from the police that there was local knowledge of the grave in Tuam.

In 2014, on St Patrick's weekend, Anna travelled to Tuam to give a donation to amateur historian Catherine Corless towards plaques for the children's names. At this stage, Catherine had launched an appeal to raise funds to mark the spot where she believed children who had been in the

Home were buried in a mass, unmarked grave. It was a small gesture, but one Anna felt was important to make: 'I was very ill, but it was something I really needed to do. I was staying with my friend, Dave Sweeney, who lives in Tuam. He took me for a pint and we met his brother, Barry, in Brown's Bar. Barry asked me why I was down in Tuam and Dave told him I had two brothers born in the Home. Dave's family lived across the road from the Home when he [was growing] up.'

When Barry discovered the reason for Anna's visit, he revealed his own terrifying ordeal with regard to the Tuam grave. When he was ten years old, Barry had been playing around the grounds of the old Home, which would have been long after it had closed down. He told Anna that he and his friend, Frances, had:

> found a concrete slab and broke it open. Inside were hundreds of bones and he said, 'It was like something out of a National Geographic film' and he hadn't slept since. Later Dave told me one evening a child was at the door of his house and he said he heard children crying. They believed the crying was coming from the Home, despite the fact that the Home had been closed for a number of years. Dave said that was a story the locals had reported many times. It was quite eerie.

The Bon Secours order had closed the Home in 1961 and then later, in 2001, had closed the Grove Hospital and moved out of Tuam. It has since emerged, in early 2017, that the Grove Hospital also has an unmarked babies' plot; it has yet to be examined.

By the time Barry Sweeney and Frances Hopkins had discovered the bones of the buried children, plans were underway to build the Dublin Road Housing Estate that surrounds the Tuam grave site today.

Around the same time Anna spoke to Barry Sweeney, another woman had uncovered details about the Tuam grave. Catherine Corless, a housewife and mother from Tuam with an interest in genealogy, had decided to research local rumours about an unmarked grave used by the

Home. While Catherine was unearthing information in Galway in 2012, Anna was uncovering explosive material in Dublin. The two women had never met or heard of each other, let alone spoken, but were working in parallel and slowly coming to the same conclusion about the burial site. Catherine was looking for the names of the forgotten children; Anna was looking for her missing, almost forgotten brothers. When the women finally became aware of each other, lots more pieces of the puzzle fell into place:

> I spent a lot of time in touch with people from Tuam, making connections about the Home and what went on there. I was put in contact with Catherine Corless by a police woman. Catherine had uncovered the names of the 796 children and my brother, John, was one of those names. I spoke to Catherine and I gave her all my research. I told Barry Sweeney about Catherine's work and asked could I put her in contact with him. He said fine and I passed his details on. It turned out that my friend Dave was in the same class as Catherine in school. Catherine didn't know about him and what had happened, so they connected and that story began to unfold. Catherine told me she had maps that suggested the children were buried in a septic tank. I reviewed what she had and began to realise that I could not sit on this story.

In 2012 Catherine Corless wrote an essay about the story of the Tuam Mother and Baby Home in the *Journal of the Old Tuam Society*, a local history periodical. She did not have the names or the number of children who had died in the Home at that time, but she was aware of the grave because of local memory and information. It was the first time any information about what was believed to be a small grave had appeared in print.

During her research, it became apparent to Catherine that there was a discrepancy between the number of death certificates and burial records for children in the Home, so she decided to try to quantify exactly what she was dealing with. Like any Irish citizen, Catherine Corless has the right to access a public register of birth, death and marriage certificates.

Catherine asked a woman in the Galway Births, Deaths and Marriages Registry for help in finding the names of the children who died in the Home. One by one, Ann Glennon checked all of the children whose place of birth on their death certificate was listed as: Tuam Mother and Baby Home. On her own time, this woman, Ann Glennon – who remains an unsung hero in the Tuam story – spent hours after she finished her day's work compiling the list of names and their details. Ann uncovered 798 children's names. Catherine was able to confirm that two of them had been buried in their family plot, leaving 796 unaccounted for. (It was reported that Catherine paid for each individual certificate, however, she later clarified that she instead had purchased a list of names and a selection of certificates.)

After getting a sense of the number of children who had died in the Home, Catherine, along with a number of residents from the Dublin Road Housing Estate, set up the children's home graveyard committee in the hope of raising money to fund plaques to record the names of the children who had died in the Home, so they could be remembered. The Committee reached out to the local newspapers, which published the story about the fundraising campaign. The story did not focus on the potential existence of a mass grave with up to 796 children buried in a septic tank. The report was read locally and helped raised a small amount of funds, but otherwise did not make an impact.

Following this, Teresa Kelly, chairperson of the committee, collected money outside the local churches to go towards the remembrance plaque, while Catherine contacted the Bon Secours order. Following a meeting with the nuns, who travelled from Cork to Galway to talk to Catherine, the order decided to donate €2,000 towards the committee's fund. Between donations and a local fundraising campaign, the committee raised around €6,000.

Meanwhile, Anna continued to make Freedom of Information (FOI) requests to several government departments in her attempts to uncover further information about her family. The further she probed, the less sense she could make of it all. The AIRR, which was set up to provide index records of people formerly in the care of the state, sent her copies of the ledgers returns kept by the nuns at Tuam. From these, Anna saw that her brother William's date of birth was not recorded correctly in other paperwork and didn't correspond with his birth certificate; her mother's date of birth was not correct either. This made Anna deeply suspicious and anxious to learn more.

It was also through the AIRR project that Anna secured the health inspection report of 1947, which gave a clear picture of the health and condition of the children in the care of the Bon Secours nuns at that time:

> Things really began to bother me when I received that document in the post, I think that was the turning point for me. I had not given a lot of my time to the Mother and Baby Homes or the Magdalene Laundries around the time of the Ryan Commission. [The Ryan Report, published in 2009, contained the findings of the Commission to Inquire into Child Abuse.] I had read it, yes, but unless you are personally affected, which I believed I wasn't, it didn't hit home as hard as it does now. It appeared to me that these children were neglected, my brother John was definitely neglected.

On 5 July 2013, Anna wrote to then Minister for Justice Alan Shatter, then Minister for Children and Youth Affairs Frances Fitzgerald and then Taoiseach Enda Kenny. 'My letters started with, *Please Help Me Find my brother (William)*'. In November 2013, Anna wrote to Independent TD Clare Daly, who went on to raise a number of questions in the Dáil regarding her missing brothers in December that year and again in January 2014. Unlike the other institutions around the country, Tuam was owned by Galway County Council. By law, the council had to be notified whenever a child died in the Home.

When Barnardos contacted the council on Anna's behalf, they were told that all records had been sent to the HSE Western Area Adoption Committee, Merlin Park, Galway, which later became part of Tusla – Child and Family Agency. Anna became increasingly frustrated at the lack of paperwork being made available to her and the incomplete, casual answers she was receiving. As she gazed at all her paperwork, spread out across her kitchen table, two documents stood out the most: one was the 1947 health inspection report, which described 13-month-old John as a 'miserable emaciated child who had no control over his bodily functions'; the other was the note in the nuns' ledgers stating that William was dead.

In August 2013 Anna had had enough. She decided the only place to go was to An Garda Síochána. She got on her motorbike, strapped on her helmet and drove to Ronanstown Garda Station, near her West Dublin home. She arrived into the station and said she wanted to file a missing persons report. The garda on duty offered to take Anna's statement. 'What is the name of the person who is missing?' she asked. 'And when did they go missing?' Anna replied: 'William Dolan is my brother and he's missing since 1951.'

The garda looked at Anna for a moment and then asked if she would come inside to discuss the matter further. Anna did so, and the garda listened and took her statement, telling Anna she had never dealt with a case like this before.

She was very nice and took my details and told me she would forward it on to the Superintendent in Lucan, to see if it was a valid complaint. She rang me the following week and asked me to come in and make a formal statement. I did return to the garda station and made my statement on 3 September 2013.

This was then forwarded to Tuam Garda Station, where a garda was given specific charge of enquiries. If my local garda station had not treated my statement with the seriousness it deserved and forwarded it on to Tuam, I don't know where I would be today with my enquiries.

Anna continued to request information from the government, and from anyone who could tell her anything about William and John. But she was struggling to move ahead with her investigations. Her visit to Tuam in March 2014 was a turning point. Anna began to see the bigger picture of the situation she was facing:

I decided I didn't want any more involvement with the fundraiser for the plaque over a grave. Because it wasn't a grave, it was a septic tank. The thoughts of my brothers being buried in a septic tank began to keep me awake at night. I began to understand how Barry Sweeney felt.

I couldn't get my head around the septic tank bit. Or the fact that this grave was known about since the seventies. It was extremely gut-wrenching stuff. The idea that you have a brother you never knew existed and he could be walking around America right now, totally oblivious to the fact that he has a family here, is really hard to deal with. And then the thoughts of my other brother, John, shoved into a cesspit with hundreds of other babies. I couldn't cope with it anymore.

Hundreds of children were buried in a septic tank and the world needed to know about it. I was getting nowhere fast and I was really anxious. My blood was boiling over it the more I thought about it, and no one could give me a straight answer.

On 11 May 2014, Anna went to her local shop and picked up a copy of the *Irish Mail on Sunday*, a paper she doesn't remember buying before this day. But for some reason, she picked it up and bought it. In it, there was an article about a woman called Lorraine Jackson, who was born on 17 March 1948 at the Royal Jubilee Hospital, Belfast, but sent to Bethany Home in Rathgar, Dublin (operational between 1934 and 1972), after her mother gave her up for adoption. Now 69 years old, Lorraine, who worked in the kitchen of the residence of the President of Ireland, Áras an Uachtaráin, was still trying to find her birth mother. The article described how Lorraine had attended a recent memorial service for the 222 neglected children who died at the Bethany Home between 1922 and 1949. Their graves in Mount Jerome Cemetery, in Harold's Cross, Dublin, had only been discovered in 2010.

Just like at the other Mother and Baby Homes, the Bethany Home children were subjected to physical abuse and serious neglect, which contributed to the high mortality rate there. A sculpture unveiled in Mount Jerome Cemetery marked the end of a campaign by survivors of the Home for recognition.

In the article Anna read that day, Lorraine Jackson was calling for legislation that would allow adoptees to access information about their identity, such as their birth certs. In Ireland, the law favours the rights of the birth mother, which means that adoptees like Lorraine could not access their information because of the right to privacy of their mothers. As Lorraine explained: 'I would like to have my medical records at least. I have been officially searching since 1990 and getting nowhere. It's ridiculous you can't find your information, yet in England [it's] no problem.'

A softly spoken, kind-hearted woman who didn't wish to ruffle any feathers, Lorraine Jackson was gently asking for what was rightly hers. 'I am still trying to find [my mother]. I have a social worker and we have been trying. The law provides for my mother's privacy, it doesn't provide for me.'

Something about this short article and the story of Lorraine Jackson struck a chord with Anna. She confided her frustration to her son-in-law, Paddy, and he suggested she take her story to the media. Anna had great faith in his opinion. He had advised her previously to make the missing person's report on William. Now he told her that there was only one way to get the story out there, and that was through the newspapers.

Anna sat down at her laptop and set in motion a newspaper article that would go on to reverberate around the world.

# 10

# Chasing the Truth

When the story of the final resting place of the children who died in the Tuam Mother and Baby Home was first told, it was laid bare in a stark and brutal manner. The headline read: '800 Babies Buried in a Mass Grave'. It was written by this author and published in the *Irish Mail on Sunday* on 25 May 2014. In unflinching terms, the article described how there were no burial records for hundreds of 'illegitimate' children who died in the Home, and how locals believed the remains had been deposited in an underground septic tank. It described Anna's story and it described the documentary evidence uncovered by Catherine Corless, which showed that the dead children were not buried in a graveyard. This fact was incontrovertible, and it lent weight to the local rumours that they had been deposited in a mass grave.

On the morning of the publication of the article, Anna waited for the grim reality of a mass grave filled with the bodies of innocent children, which had been built within the living memory of many of Ireland's leading politicians, to have an impact. But the wave of shock and horror did not come. There was no public outcry, no national scandal and no mention of the story in the Dáil. The story of the Tuam Babies buried in a septic tank ran on the same weekend as the local elections, which turned out to be the only story in town. The reaction of what is sometimes termed 'Official Ireland' to a story in a mid-market tabloid newspaper that referenced the work of an amateur historian and a campaigner was … disinterest. Instead, the swings-and-roundabouts of Ireland's local politics dominated the newspapers in the following days as Ireland's centrist political parties swapped a few percentage points of support in the latest chapter of their endless struggle.

Nevertheless, Anna Corrigan and Catherine Corless were happy because the shocking burials at Tuam had been given prominence in a national newspaper for the first time, which was an important achievement for two women unused to working with the media. Anna might not have enjoyed the public exposure, but she felt she had done the right thing:

> I felt very happy with it. It upset my eldest daughter because she was so close to my mam and it was very hard for her to see her granny and her two secret sons in a national paper. She is very like my mother in many ways. Personally, I wanted to find my brothers and I wanted the country to see what happened to my mother.
>
> Sarah, my other daughter, was supportive. It still breaks our hearts what happened to my mam. This story was too important to be ignored. I did stay in the background for as long as I could bear it.

The day after the story made the front page of the *Irish Mail on Sunday*, Catherine Corless was contacted by *Nuacht* – Ireland's Irish-language news service – and asked to do an interview on RTÉ. While Anna was very much the catalyst in bringing the story to the attention of the national media – which would eventually go on to make international headlines – she could not cope with putting herself at the heart of the story. Instead, for almost three years she preferred to be known as 'the sister of the Dolan brothers' and insisted her name not be made public.

> I could not come forward. I was dealing with a number of issues and I was very, very sick. I am also still coming to terms with my mother's story and William and John are always in the back of my mind. I wonder if they are alive, I wonder is John in the grave. I often think William is walking around America or Canada without a clue of what went on or who he is. I have found myself putting his name into the

search engine of Facebook and looking at dozens of William Dolans in America.

I've looked up many John Dolans, too. I have found myself saying, he looks a bit like me. He could have been sent to America under the same name, who knows? I have Googled his name many times. I have made a number of pleas in the *Irish Central* online paper for help in finding him. I have talked to genealogists. I've done DNA tests over the internet and on genealogy websites. But I have had no luck whatsoever. I can't find any living soul who could be him or know him.

I have even sent out random messages to several William and John Dolans in the US, asking them as politely and as sensitively as I can if they have any connection to the Dolans in Clonfert in Galway, or if they ever heard of the name Bridget Dolan. It is not something I would have ever thought about doing before.

The more I learn about the grave, the more doubts I have that John is in there too. I have no clue where they are for certain.

There was a William Dolan listed as a passenger going out on a Mauretania ship [RMS *Mauretania*] to America in 1951, but there was no age or address. My heart skipped a beat when I first read this information online on the passenger list. I really thought I was on to something. William would have been a year old and the right age for adoption. When I looked further, I learned there were two nuns and a priest on that manifest, that's when it really got tense for me. I thought I had him, there couldn't be that many William Dolans going to America. But then I discovered the travel for William was withdrawn and that's as far as I got. There is no record of a passport application form for him in the Department of Foreign Affairs either. According to the author of *Banished Babies*, Mike Milotte, records only started to be kept in the 1950s.

I have been digging for four years, reaching out to anyone who will listen. I have even gone to fortune-tellers and mediums. I would try anything at this stage if I thought it could shed light on the mystery. You can become obsessed with it, but I try and stay as calm as I can about it. I cannot allow my mental health to deteriorate further.

While the initial reaction to the story of the Tuam Babies in a national newspaper was slow, Nicky Ryan with *TheJournal.ie* covered the story on 27 May 2014 and by Wednesday, 28 May the momentum had started to gather speed. RTÉ broadcaster Philip Boucher-Hayes, who would become a champion of the story over the next few years, interviewed Teresa Killeen Kelly, Chairperson of the Chldren's Home Graveyard Committee, and Catherine Corless on *Liveline*, a popular daytime programme on RTÉ Radio 1. He gave the topic plenty of air-time and asked Catherine dozens of questions about her research. Teresa Killeen Kelly outlined plans for a memorial garden and plaques for the children's names, saying the committee hoped to raise €50,000 to achieve this.

Meanwhile, Anna sat at home with one ear on the radio and two eyes on her laptop. She was only interested in moving forward. 'Where to next?' was, and still is, her mantra.

On the following Thursday, 29 May 2014, Broadcaster Jonathan Healy, who was presenting the lunchtime programme on Newstalk, discussed the story and invited members of the Adoption Rights Alliance onto the programme for their reaction. On Saturday, 31 May Donal O'Keeffe wrote an opinion piece on the Tuam Babies, which had grabbed his attention since the story broke in 2014. Donal is one of the journalists who has championed the story since the beginning and has a deep understanding of the plight of all those who suffered in the home and who wrote about the story. He has gone on himself to write several sensitive and emotive opinion pieces as the story has evolved. On Sunday, 1 June Carol Hunt wrote an opinion piece in the *Sunday Independent*.

While there was some reaction on Twitter, by that weekend, sadly, the story of Anna's two brothers, and the 796 children buried in a septic tank, had gone off the radar. Anna found it difficult to come to terms with the lack of impact or consequence:

> I was disappointed because this was not a story that people didn't know about. The people of Tuam knew about it since the seventies, but we had more information about this grave and it needed to be given plenty of air-time.
>
> It's just the typical Irish way, find a pit full of bones, get the local parish priest to the site, cover it over, bless it and that's that. Not another word about it again. This was a burial site in the middle of a housing estate and the land was owned by the county council. Even they knew. They had the grave marked out on their maps. They built the houses all around that area and possibly on top of some remains.
>
> After that week and the lack of political interest, I believed the typical Irish way was going to happen again with this. But if you found a body in your garden today, the area would be sealed off and a technical examination would take place, it wouldn't be covered over and blessed.
>
> The story needed a big push. So, I decided to bring out the story of Mary Corrigan, my 13-year-old aunt who had died in Loughrea. I thought her story would wake people up to the seriousness of the situation.

On 1 June, the *Irish Mail on Sunday* ran a follow-up to the Tuam story that had run the week before, under the headline: 'The mass graves in Tuam are only the tip of the iceberg'. The story concentrated on how little Mary Corrigan, Anna's aunt, had died as a teenager in the Industrial School in Loughrea, Co. Galway, and that she too had no burial record. Anna was sure this was an unignorable story: 'I myself believe I have a unique story in the sense that I have no burial records for three missing relatives and this was strong enough to push the story without using my name. But that second story went nowhere either.'

However, this depressing pattern of reveal-and-ignore was about to change for good.

On 2 June 2014, thanks to Mailonline, the global news website published by the *Irish Mail*'s parent company, the story of the Tuam Babies got all the exposure it needed and deserved, and much more. The next day, a story by Terrence McCoy in *The Washington Post* was headlined: 'Historian believes bodies of 800 babies, long-dead, are in a tank at Irish home for unwed mothers'. After this, the story spread like wildfire across social media and could be seen on dozens of Facebook and Twitter pages. For the next six weeks the story continued to spill out over major global networks, such as Sky News, Al Jazeera, CBC News, National Public Radio in the USA and dozens of international TV and radio stations – the list was endless. It was the only thing people were talking about. Social media bloggers such as Donal O'Keefe, Liam Hogan, Izzy Kamikazee, Shame of Ireland and Fintan O'Toolbox continued to write about it. Philip Boucher-Hayes set up a media blog with regular updates and he brought Catherine Corless back onto the airwaves.

That same week, the stories of other institutions and their survivors began to receive a lot of coverage. On 6 June 2014 Conall Ó Fátharta, in the *Irish Examiner*, wrote how 'The mother and baby scandal was hidden in plain sight'. On Cork 96FM, just as he has always done over the years, presenter PJ Coogan devoted lots of air-time to the story of Bessborough, the Mother and Baby Home in Cork, while 4FM broadcaster Niall Boylan, who was born in the country's largest home, St Patrick's on the Navan Road in Dublin, also gave the story the attention it needed. Claire Ronan on Ocean FM in Sligo ran with the story, too, focusing on locals who were affected by the grave at Tuam or who had family buried there. Scott Williams and Venetia Quick on Q102 featured regular updates on the Tuam Babies story, while Teena Gates in Newstalk put the story on the news agenda at every given opportunity. *TheJournal.ie* reported how some state files from the National Archives had been recalled by the Department of Health following the Tuam Babies scandal. Every national and local media organisation in Ireland, from Galway Bay FM to 98FM in Dublin and Live 95 in Limerick, featured the item on their daily agenda. Suddenly, everyone was gripped by the story of the Tuam Babies.

As a result of this detailed and ongoing coverage, the government, finally, had to listen. Former Taoiseach Enda Kenny, who was on a trade mission in the USA at the time the story broke, was questioned about it by reporters over there. He said a government investigation would be carried out into the graves of the Tuam Babies by the end of that month.

During a Sunday morning discussion on 15 June 2014 on RTÉ Radio 1's *Marian Finucane Show*, Minister Leo Varadkar, who became Taoiseach in 2017, implied that everyone needed to calm down, that this was not a 'Holocaust' as had been suggested by some parts of the media. He went on to state, however, that a Commission of Investigation was going to be established.

The religious order that had run the scandal-hit Tuam Babies Home showed no public remorse for the 796 babies buried in a mass grave – until after it became international news. On 23 May, Sr Marie Ryan, the head of the Bon Secours order in Ireland, told the *Irish Mail on Sunday* that she 'couldn't put the matter forward' because the nuns in charge of Tuam were 'now deceased'.

Two weeks later, however, questions to the order by the *Irish Daily Mail* were responded to by a representative of top PR firm The Communications Clinic, which replied to queries with a far more sympathetic statement, saying the order was 'shocked and deeply saddened' after the *Mail*'s revelations about the appalling treatment of babies in the order's care.

While Catherine gave interview after interview, Anna followed the story on its many platforms, wrote emails and letters and helped to keep the story firmly in the public eye. Although unwilling to be identified publicly, Anna also conducted several interviews anonymously and provided record after record from her extensive research. She published the name of her newly established group on Twitter, Tuam

Babies Family Group (@tuambabiesfami1), and set up an email address (tuambabiesfamilygroup@yahoo.co.uk) so that other families with relatives in the grave and survivors of the Home could contact her.

Anna corresponded with several family members, sharing stories and information. Some were willing to tell their story publicly, such as Annette McKay, who has a sister in the Tuam grave, and Professor Thomas Garavan, whose aunt is believed to be buried there, while others wished to add their voices and stories anonymously. Their stories touched the hearts of millions of people all over the world, and the fundraising campaign by the children's home graveyard committee in Tuam took off. Following their appeal for donations towards building a memorial garden, the group began to receive large donations from all over the world. Within six weeks of the story making international headlines, €35,000, including €10,000 from a Canadian doctor, had been raised towards a memorial garden for the Tuam Babies.

Teresa Killeen Kelly recalled how she had addressed a congregation at the Cathedral of the Assumption in Tuam and asked for donations earlier that year, but had not made anything close to the flood of contributions that poured in from all over the world after the story broke. The designs for the memorial garden were drawn up and a crowdfunding page was put in place. Once enough money had been raised, a sculptor based in County Mayo was asked to undertake the work of designing the plaques that would bear the children's names. The sculptor was Mark Rode, who was based in Swinford, and this unusual commission was a first for him:

> I didn't know at first that there was institutional neglect. That didn't alter my approach to it, but after I thought about it, it's the most significant work I've done. There are four plaques with the names and dates of the deaths of the [796] children and a fifth pictorial plaque. It's a woman letting go of a child's hand. The mothers would stay on and rear the children in the Home for one year. I thought that must have been very sad.

Mark Rode finished the work, but the establishment of the Commission of Investigation into the Mother and Baby Homes in 2015 meant the erection of the plaques had to be put on hold. As Mark explains: 'Until the inquiry is complete, the plaques will be kept in storage. I don't want to put them up and then for them to have to add to the names.'

Anna travelled to Mark's studio in Mayo to see the plaques, and when she was there she broke down in tears, after weeks of holding back and listening to gut-wrenching stories from survivors on the airwaves:

> I just saw all the names on the plaques and it was very surreal. I didn't know what to think, but when I saw John Desmond's name I sobbed my heart out. It was a very moving experience and it was so sad to see it there. It was so real. I left some flowers by his name and thanked Mark for his work. They have not been shown to the public yet, but they are stunning, he has done a great job.
>
> John is a little boy I have no photo of, I don't know if anyone has a photo of him. I don't have a clue what he looked like. And when I see his name on that death list it hurts my heart so much.
>
> On one hand, it is of small, and I mean very small, consolation that his name is on the list. But what about William? There's nothing about him. He is a just a lost boy to me, they are both lost, but William isn't recognised in any way.

Given all that she had learned to this point, and given the fact that the plaques could not be hung at the burial site, Anna decided that the Pope should be called on to intervene. On 13 July 2014, she wrote to the Vatican, telling Pope Francis that he was her 'last hope' in a situation 'where there does not seem to be any hope of truth and justice'. She wrote simply: 'I NEED YOUR HELP.' The letter described the terrible legacy of the Tuam Mother and Baby Home to the pontiff:

As you can imagine I am totally distraught by the stance taken by these nuns and their refusal to come forward with the truth. What they saw fit to do was to employ a PR company. I was always led to believe that truth was one of the cornerstones of Catholic teachings along with kindness and caring for your fellow man. I believe that you are a good person and I beseech you to speak to this order of nuns and ask them to reveal all that they know and let there be some closure to these matters for me and for others that have been so affected. There are 796 children buried in the plot I have mentioned and until they are heard and recognised as having existed they may never find peace.

She ended her lengthy letter with the words: 'Please respond to me as a matter of urgency.' Sadly, Anna received no reply.

As momentum towards truth and justice was building, Dr James Reilly, then Minister for Children, said an investigation needed to be carried out before any memorial could be erected for the babies. He also officially informed the the children's home graveyard committee to tell its donors that the memorial would not be going ahead in the near future.

This was something Anna came to agree with, and as time went on she began to think more and more about bringing her brother's remains home to Dublin, to be buried beside her mother in Glasnevin. In a letter to Dr James Reilly on 19 April 2015, Anna said she was disappointed that he could not meet her, explaining that she wanted to 'discuss very important issues in respect of the Tuam Mother and Child Home and their implications for the Commission'. She again requested a meeting between the Minister and her new group, the Tuam Babies Family Group.

In a response sent on 29 May 2015, the Minister made it clear he could not meet with her, citing the Commission's ongoing work as the reason.

The Commission's Terms of Reference were agreed by government on 17 February 2015. The Commission was established because of the global reaction to the story of the Tuam Babies. Three people were appointed to oversee the investigation, which was tasked with examining the operation

Happiest day of their lives: Bridget and Bill signing the register on 7 September 1955. Bridget always described Bill as 'the love of her life'.

Cutting the wedding cake.

Bridget and Bill on their wedding day, 7 September 1955.

Bridget Corrigan dancing at her wedding with a guest (unknown) on 7 September 1955, which was held in Ballybough in Dublin 3.

Bill Corrigan, Bridget's husband and Anna's father.

Bill Corrigan (centre) with a group of friends on a day out before he got married at age 40. He had been a bachelor for many years and enjoyed travelling and socialising with his friends after a hard day's work.

Anna's grandmother (Bill's mother), Annie Corrigan, sadly succumbed to TB and died in a hospice in Harold's Cross on 11 February 1911. Her death sparked a split in her family, which tragically saw her three young children, Bill, John and Mary, sentenced to Industrial Schools.

Anna's house in North Great Charles Street, where she lived with her parents in a tenement building.

Bridget proudly cradles Anna in her arms on her christening day on 11 February 1956, with Anna's godmother, Bridie McEvoy. Bridget and Bill held a party in their back garden on 32 North Great Charles Street. This wasn't the first time Bridget had christened a baby. Both John and William, her secret Tuam babies, were also christened by the Bon Secours nuns. Anna believes they would have been on her mother's mind that day.

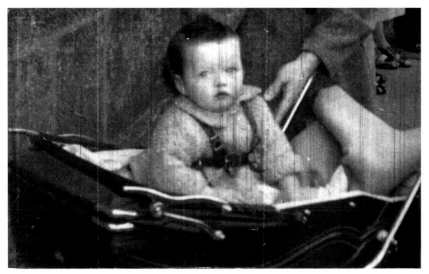

Anna at the age of nine months.

Bridget, Bill, Anna and her godmother, Bridie McEvoy, in the back garden of
32 North Great Charles Street at Anna's Christening in 1956.

Anna (aged two-and-a-half years) and her mother in the tenement house. Anna
lived with her mother in their one-bedroom flat until her twenties.

Anna's cot in the tenement in
32 North Great Charles Street.

Bridget, Bill and Anna meet
Santa in Christmas 1957.

Bridget lovingly holding Anna's hand (aged four) on a day out on one of their regular mystery tours.

Anna (aged three) on a picnic with her mother and father. Anna said her mother would make delicious lunches for their days out and Bill, who loved photography, captured most of their outings on film.

Family fun: the Corrigans waiting at the train station for one of their many weekend mystery tours around the country.

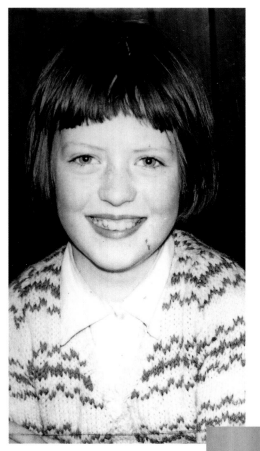

A school photo of Anna (aged seven) in North Williams Street.

Photo of Anna's First Holy Communion (aged seven) on 2 May 1964.

Close bond: after their sister, Mary, died in the Loughrea Industrial School, John and Bill Corrigan forged a strong relationship. Bill (seated) was best man at his brother John's wedding on 14 November 1934. John is linked by his wife, Nancy Darmody, who went on to be great friends with Bridget.

Little Maura Mollie Corrigan (aged three) from Dominick Street in Dublin's north inner city. After her mother's death, she was charged with 'want of proper guardianship' and, on 3 June 1911, sentenced to ten years in St Brigid's in Loughrea, Co. Galway. She died of pneumonia in the school on 1 November 1918. The Mercy nuns have told Anna that they have no record of her burial, even though she died in the school.

Anna (aged eight) enjoys a sunny afternoon with her parents, Bridget and Bill, in her uncle John Corrigan's house in Mount Brown, Dublin.

Bridget poses with a friend outside the Bon Secours hospital in Glasnevin, where she worked.

Bridget and Anna standing outside Clonfert Cathedral in her hometown in Co. Galway.

Anna (far right, aged six) with her cousins outside her grandmother's home in Clonfert, Co. Galway during her school summer holidays. Anna said she felt a sense of isolation during her visits there.

Bridget and Bill on a day out together. Anna said that as she got older, her parents had more free time to spend together and often went on day trips.

Anna celebrates her sixth birthday in North Great Charles Street with her cousin, Tommy Dolan, and parents, Bridget and Bill.

Bridget holding a child (unknown), with Bill, Anna and cousin Tommy on a day out in the park.

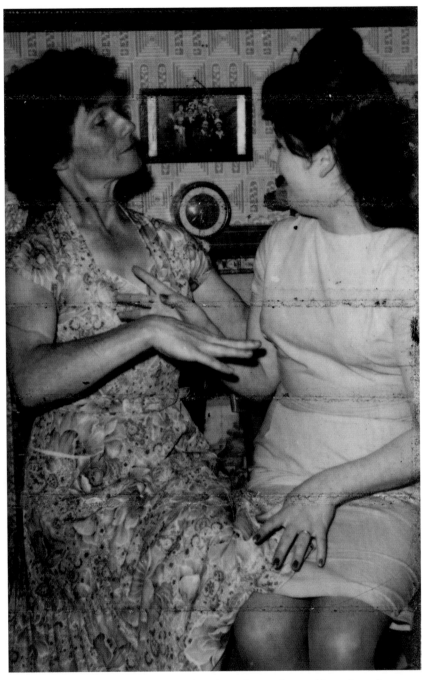

Bridget (aged 43) was a trusted friend to those close to her and here she enjoys a chat in her flat with her next door neighbor, Valerie. This is one of Anna's favourite photographs of her mother.

of fourteen institutions and four county homes operating between 1922 and 1998. Judge Yvonne Murphy was joined by commissioners Professor Mary Daly, a social historian, and Dr William Duncan, a family law expert. The Commission is examining the pathways of single women into and out of the institutions, as well as the burial arrangements.

The fourteen Mother and Baby Homes included in the Commission of Investigation are:

1. Ard Mhuire, Dunboyne, County Meath
2. Belmont (Flatlets), Belmont Avenue, Dublin 4
3. Bessborough House, Blackrock, Cork
4. Bethany Home, originally Blackhall Place, Dublin 7, and then from 1934 at Orwell Road, Rathgar, Dublin 6
5. Bon Secours Mother and Baby Home, Tuam, County Galway
6. Denny House, Eglinton Road, Dublin 4, originally Magdalen Home, 8 Lower Leeson Street, Dublin 2
7. Kilrush, Cooraclare Road, County Clare
8. Manor House, Castlepollard, County Westmeath
9. Ms Carr's (Flatlets), 16 Northbrook Road, Dublin 6
10. Regina Coeli Hostel, North Brunswick Street, Dublin 7
11. Seán Ross Abbey, Roscrea, County Tipperary
12. St Gerard's, originally 39 Mountjoy Square, Dublin 1
13. St Patrick's, Navan Road, Dublin 7, originally known as Pelletstown and subsequently transferred to Eglinton House, Eglinton Road, Dublin 4
14. The Castle, Newtowncunningham, County Donegal

The county homes included in the investigation are:

15. St Kevin's Institution (Dublin Union)
16. Stranorlar County Home, County Donegal (St Joseph's)
17. Cork City County Home (St Finbarr's)
18. Thomastown County Home, County Kilkenny (St Columba's)

There is another strand to the Commission of Investigation that brings up a whole other issue with regard to these institutions. The Terms of Reference also include children who were allegedly used in vaccine trials. This distressing issue was highlighted by an important article in the *Irish Daily Mail* on 6 June 2014, in which Neil Michael reported that 2,000 children were believed to have been used for drug tests during the era of religious-run homes. The article described how:

> The tests were carried out over six years for international drugs giant Burroughs Wellcome. Yet astonishingly, research by an award-winning university lecturer could find no evidence in Ireland that the trials ever took place.
>
> Instead, Michael Dwyer, of Cork University's School of History, found the data by painstakingly poring over tens of thousands of medical journal articles and archive files.
>
> Neither is there evidence of consent being given for the children to be experimented on – or on how many suffered debilitating side-effects or may have died as a result. The trials – for a one-shot diphtheria vaccine – were carried out before the vaccine was made available for commercial use in the UK.
>
> The latest revelations emerge as Enda Kenny was forced to intervene – while on a trade mission to the US – over the growing baby homes scandals that have been revealed by the *Mail* in recent weeks.
>
> As a clamour grows for a comprehensive inquiry, the Taoiseach told reporters yesterday that he had asked Children's Minister Charlie Flanagan 'to draw together a number of senior officials from across the departments, till we see what the scale of this is'.
>
> Mr Dwyer found the data in just six medical journal reports which he eventually sourced after three years of going through more than 25,000 medical journal articles. He also went through 15,000 Wellcome archive documents.

It was by counting up the figures each medical report provided that he was able to establish that 2,051 children and babies in residential care homes had been vaccinated. The trials were held between 1930 and 1936.

Homes where children were secretly tested included Bessborough in Co. Cork and Seán Ross Abbey in Roscrea, Co. Tipperary.

Children in the care of nuns and priests tended to be vaccinated before more than 41,280 other children in the wider Irish population were tested. Mr Dwyer said: 'What I have found is just the tip of a very large and submerged iceberg.'

The fact that no record of these trials can be found in the files relating to the Department of Local Government and Public Health, the Municipal Health Reports relating to Cork and Dublin, or the Wellcome Archives in London, suggests that vaccine trials would not have been acceptable to government, municipal authorities, or the general public.

Survivor of St Patrick's Mother and Baby Home and long-term activist David Kinsella said his records show that he was used in at least one vaccine trial, and his record shows at least 23 injections were given to him over a four-year period in the home, and some were used three or four times, which would have been inappropriate. This is something that has never been properly investigated before.

Born on 2 August 1958 in St Patrick's on the Navan Road, David is the eldest of five siblings whom he only learned about years later. His mother, Elizabeth, who was known as Lily, was 31 years old and from Dublin. David is a well-known campaigner for survivors and for up to 30 years has been a familiar face outside Leinster House, where he has often had the lonely task of spending hours protesting alone. He is a small, slight man, softly spoken and easy to talk to. David was in St Patrick's from 1958 until 1962. His records show that he was hospitalised six times in St Kevin's Hospital over the course of his time at the Home and that he received the Sacrament of the Anointing of the Sick at the age of four months. David notes: 'I was given the basic BCG vaccines on 22 December 1958 and four days later I'm anointed and confirmed. So, I was dying it seems.'

David was a very sick little boy, but says he has very few memories of his time in St Patrick's: 'I have vague recollections of putting my hands through the cot.' He has spent years researching the vaccine trials, and from this research he has the names of one vaccine which he believes was tested on him. There has never been an explanation given as to why these vaccine trials were carried out.

I couldn't walk until I was around four or five. I was very sick and I was in and out of St Kevin's Hospital and my adoptive mother, who was working there, saw me. She asked to adopt me and that's how it happened.

When I was adopted a Dr Coffey, who was attached to St Patricks' home, she would call out to the house. It was very unusual to call to the actual adoptee's house. In my case, my mother was telling me as best she could, how her and my dad used to have to hold me down on the couch, and the doctor, she would give me a big plastic needle into the bum and drops into the eyes. There were a few adoptees that Dr Coffey called out to, and I believe they were trying to manage an error associated with a vaccine trial and side-effects, or from a general medical observation that went on in time or went sideways.

She said, 'We thought you had a vitamin deficiency', but I think they were trying to see how I had been in all these trials and they were saying they better make sure nothing goes wrong.

I was blessed with my adoptive mother, she was an angel. I didn't get on so well with my adoptive father, but I think it was more that I was not his birth son, that may have been hard for him.

David has spent more than three decades highlighting his story and how his adoption and not knowing who he was have affected him. It serves as a poignant testimony to the far-reaching effects of this harsh and unforgiving regime:

I left St Patrick's in June 1962 and I was adopted just two months shy of four years of age.

By living your life this way and not knowing who you are, it means that you are constantly wanting to know about that invisible loss, and that loss manifested itself into an addiction.

I became a drinker and when I was in the pub, I would observe women in their fifties and would think, could that be mother? The crunch of my alcoholism was when I found out Valium could control the shakes.

I didn't drink on a daily basis, it was only at the weekends. I had the Valium before going to work the next day. I didn't drink during the week until I felt battered and beaten. Emotionally, I was trying to reach out, I couldn't understand this genetic bewilderment, it was overtaking me. I couldn't comprehend it.

At one stage, when heroin was sweeping into the Dublin, I remember buying palf [Dextromoramide, a powerful opioid analgesic] off a drug-dealer in Inchicore. It was giving me the ultimate high. It is a medical narcotic used for eye operations and banned in some countries. It was a hard-core drug. I was getting down off that drug, then your metabolism creates a desert thirst.

I was drinking and had these ghost pains and it was all down to the drinking. I was drinking, taking Valium and alcohol, and I couldn't control it. Before I came into my morning shift, my shift was at 7.00 a.m. and I had to get up at 5.00 a.m., I would take a load of Valium to feel normal before I came into work.

One day I found myself on the Naas Road, jumping from bonnet to bonnet of the cars that were parked at [traffic-]lights, when I was 20. I had lost my mind. The gardaí took me to hospital.

I eventually went into a psychiatric unit, then into detox for two weeks. The detox and the withdrawal, to describe it now, I was like the girl in *The Exorcist* bouncing on the bed, the withdrawal was so severe. I was trying to hold the shakes, the doctor said, 'Don't hold it, let it go.'

After meeting with social workers, David discovered he had four siblings, and he finally met one of his sisters and they spent hours getting to know each other:

I was overwhelmed when I got the news, and after arrangements were made, I met my sister on 12 November 2005 at the Great Southern Hotel after she flew in from London. We spent hours that day talking about the type of woman my birth mother was. My mother sadly never mentioned me to them. She left Ireland on the boat to go to the UK.

I am convinced my mother was told I was dead, particularly when I was anointed. You have shamed your family out of wedlock, so it was very hard for these women.

My sister gave me the first photo of my mother.

However, the relationship wasn't meant to be, and his siblings cut contact with him:

The last point of contact was I got an email in February 2006, saying, David, there is no other way to say this, I have met with your other siblings over the Christmas period and because their life has resolved without you for the last forty years, they want to leave it that. It was really upsetting.

David has had to try to pick up the pieces and move on with his life. He is one of at least 23,000 babies were born in the institutions under investigation by the Commission. However, there are a lot more that are not within the Commission's remit.

As the Commission's Terms of Reference were being announced, Anna sat in her 'office', in her kitchen, and watched Dr James Reilly describe the parameters of the investigation. She thought about her mother and her brothers and wrote down several notes and points about the Commission. She came to the conclusion that, given her own research and the fact that she had two open Garda enquiries into her brothers' lives and deaths, she would not participate in the Commission, but she did send in a submission (a testimony as to what occurred):

> I believe it is a smokescreen. I feel it is only going to interview people and let them pour their hearts out and that it will be a fact-finding mission with no resolution and no apology.
>
> I want truth and justice for my mother and my brothers and for all those who passed on or through the homes. I have learned more and more about the Industrial Schools, the Magdalene Laundries and I just want everything out in the open.
>
> But most importantly I want my brothers found, I want a DNA database set up, an archaeologist to find my brother John and if he is in that grave, I want him exhumed and brought home to be laid to rest with my mother in Glasnevin.
>
> Everything needs to be brought out in the open properly, so we can move on and try and heal.

Several adoptees urged the Commission to recommend a wider trawl for illegal adoptions that did not directly implicate the homes. Minister Reilly agreed that the Adoption Authority of Ireland's admission in 2010, following an audit, that thousands of children may have been illegally adopted from Ireland could lead to Garda investigations. It is understood that the Authority has told the Department of Children that only 99 people were illegally adopted, but it is aware that the passage of time will make it difficult to secure prosecutions. A further 20 illegal adoptions were later identified.

A final report was due in February 2018, but following a third interim report by the Commission, an extra twelve months was added to their investigation. Dr James Reilly said the Commission might produce evidence on illegal adoptions that could warrant prosecutions. He also said it was a matter for the Commission to recommend, at any time during its three-year investigation, whether survivors of the Protestant Bethany Home should receive redress.

The Commission will investigate the circumstances in which single women entered and left homes, the living conditions and care arrangements in the institutions, their mortality rates and burial arrangements. It will also examine whether regulations were broken during vaccine trials on child residents. Adoption arrangements, including illegal adoptions and the concealment of children's parentage, will also be scrutinised.

The former Minister James Reilly stated that he expected full compliance, including access to government records, and that a failure to do so could result in a fine or imprisonment. Anna wonders about the tranche of files being held in the Galway offices of Tusla – Child and Family Agency, which were uncovered in 2012 during the inquiry into state involvement with the Magdalene Laundries and which are still being held under lock and key. She is eager to find out what information they contain, always wondering: 'Do they hold the answers to the mystery of the Tuam site and illegal adoptions?'

As for the present investigation into the Mother and Baby Homes, the Commission's confidential committee aims to speak to those who lived and worked in the homes, gathering as much evidence as possible. Its remit was to prepare the information as a report within three years, but that has now been extended by another 12 months and a report is now due in February 2019. It is unclear in what manner the Commission was advertised in other countries, places to where Irish children may have been illegally adopted and may never know what is taking place here.

Certainly, many people have high hopes for the Commission of Investigation. Former Minister James Reilly said that he believed it would be critically important in coming to terms with the country's history. But there was mixed reaction to its Terms of Reference and how it proposed to move forward. One important clause, though, was the guarantee to investigate the burials – something that had not happened in the Ryan Report.

Investigating the burials of those children who died in religious-run institutions is a primary concern for their families and survivors, and there are key sources of information in that regard. Under the Registration of Maternity Homes Act 1934, all Mother and Baby Homes were obliged to notify the local council by registered post when a child died in their care. There is a set of ledgers from the Tuam Mother and Baby Home that marked a child called William Joseph Dolan as 'dead', and these ledgers are held by Tusla. But there is no death certificate for William. Are there other entries like this one in other ledgers? Galway County Council also holds records in its archives, but Anna has been unable to confirm what information they contain. She has received some paperwork, but not the notifications of the deaths of her brothers. The Home was obliged by law to inform the county council when a child died, and while such records have not yet been uncovered, the Home did register the deaths of the children in the General Register of Births, Deaths and Marriages.

Despite this promise by the Commission to investigate the burials, Anna was not happy with the set-up: 'By then I had already reported the cases of my two brothers to the gardaí and I didn't feel the Commission was going to do anything for my situation. So I decided just to keep at my own cases in the background and to keep working on anything else I could come up with.'

Anna had experienced a series of let-downs in the previous year, when requests for information were ignored, which only added to her frustration. On 21 July 2014 her solicitor wrote to the then Attorney General, Máire Whelan, calling on her to exercise her powers under the Coroner's Act 1962, section 24, in relation to what happened to John Desmond Dolan. At the time Anna said:

> I want justice and I want closure for my brother and my mother, who didn't get it when they were alive. I need John's body found, identified and taken out of the ground, which is going to be difficult because that means all the other babies' bodies will have to be taken out.
>
> I've already gone to the gardaí to make a report about my brother and how I believe his death was due to neglect and malnutrition and that this is criminal behaviour. They took my complaint and logged it and sent it to Tuam Garda Station in June 2014.
>
> I want all the relevant autopsies carried out in order that we can establish whether he died of the measles, like it says on his death certificate along with being called a congenital idiot, or did he die from neglect and malnutrition, as I'm led to believe. He was born normal and by 13 months he was emaciated with a voracious appetite …
>
> If in the findings of digging up the grave there are two boys with the same DNA who are associated with me, then that's the end of my search. But at the moment he, like his brother William, is a missing person.

Following the organ retention scandal in Ireland, which revealed that children's organs had been kept after post-mortem examination in hospitals without the consent of parents – and which prompted the setting up of an Inquiry in 2005, looking at cases since the 1970s – Anna decided that, even though John had died in 1947, she needed to know if her brother's remains could have been experimented on. On 28 July 2014 she wrote to the National University of Galway (NUI) to ask them for information.

On 8 January 2015, Professor Peter Dockery of the Anatomy Department, School of Medicine, replied to her request:

> I realise that you have waited for a significant period of time for this response. This was due to the comprehensive nature of the enquiries which had to be made.
>
> Following a thorough examination of the records held here in the University and after consultation with the authorities in University College Hospital, Galway (UCHG) who examined their own records at our request I can inform you that no evidence exists to indicate that the remains of an infant, the subject of your enquiry were received by the Anatomy Department.

The letter signed off with, 'I would like to take this opportunity to offer our condolences'. This letter, for now at least, gave Anna some comfort.

On 5 September 2015, Anna decided to apply to Galway County Council for two exhumation licences to try to locate and identify John's and William's remains; she had been informed that they were both dead, and in order to clear up the matter she wanted both children's deaths investigated and their remains found. According to the county council in its first response to Anna's exhumation application, on 7 January 2016: 'In the circumstances where an individual burial plot cannot be sufficiently identified it is not permissible for the council to issue an exhumation licence.'

Another setback. But despite the delays, bureaucratic complications and disagreements, the momentum created by the investigation conducted by the Commission was unstoppable. The truth was slowly emerging.

# 11

# The Right to Rest in Peace

S ince the 1990s, Ireland has experienced wave after wave of stories about child abuse in institutions run by the Catholic Church. Initially, these tales came to light when brave survivors of clerical sexual abuse gave evidence in open court about the horrors they had experienced in schools and care homes at the hands of men and women of the cloth. Their evidence started a process of reassessment of the legacy of the Catholic Church's social programmes that would see the country's view of the Church changed forever.

By the time the details of the existence of a mass grave at the Tuam Mother and Baby Home had been uncovered, Ireland was regularly being described as a 'post-Catholic' country. The grip on power the Church had enjoyed in Irish society had long been broken and, in the aftermath, fatigue at the never-ending series of scandals connected with Church had set in. When it came to the sins of the Church, much of the public had become disconnected and had largely tuned out.

However, the visceral and unforgettable image of the remains of children lying in a septic tank still had the power to shock. As the story of the Tuam Babies continued to unfold in the public arena over the course of 2014 and 2015, Catherine Corless revealed that she believed the mass grave could contain the remains of more than just the children. She went public with the names of nine women she believed had also died in the

Home during the period 1925–1961. Of those nine women, Catherine could find burial records for only four.

Using the same research methods that had helped her to locate the names of the children, she looked for the death certificate of any women who had 'Tuam Mother and Baby Home' recorded as her place of death. After drawing up a list of names, she investigated where the women were from and began to look for their burial records in their home towns by checking with local cemeteries and undertakers. The women, who were aged between 24 and 42 years, were all inmates in the Home and had given birth there.

By law, all burials must be registered with the local authority, with the location of the grave noted. Catherine undertook to search the townlands of origin of all nine women. The nine woman whose burial records could not be located were: Kathleen Tully (29), Dunmore, County Galway; Annie Reilly (39), Loughrea, County Galway; Mary Anne Rock (42), Ballina, County Mayo; Margaret Henry (24), Bushfield, County Mayo; Mary McLoughlin (27), Belfast, County Antrim; Mary Joyce (age unknown), Connemara, County Galway; Annie Roughneen (42), Claremorris, County Mayo; Bridget O'Reilly (32), Ballina, County Mayo; and Mary Hickey (36), Loughrea, County Galway.

Of these nine women, two of them – Annie Roughneen and Margaret Henry – both had children who died in the Home and are among the 796 children believed to be in the mass grave. Annie's child was a girl, also Annie, and Margaret's child was a son, James.

Annie Roughneen was from Ballyglass, Claremorris, and is recorded as having died in the Home on 13 August 1941 from pulmonary tuberculosis. Her baby, Annie, died at three weeks old on 29 July 1941. No burial records have been found for mother or baby. Catherine suspected baby Annie's remains never left the Home and then began to suspect that her mother may have been buried along with her.

Similarly, Margaret Henry from Bushfield in County Mayo died shortly after her child, on 4 April 1940, from cardiac failure. Her baby,

James, had died on 11 March, aged five weeks. Catherine told the *Irish Mail on Sunday* at the time that she could not find burial records for Margaret. These two cases helped form part of a picture that led Catherine to suspect that a number of women who had no families had been buried in unmarked graves on the Tuam site.

Mary Hickey, who had an address in Loughrea, County Galway, was 36 when she died on 3 June 1961. Her baby, Patricia, was born on the same day. There is no death certificate for Patricia, meaning she was either adopted or fostered. The baby's birth certificate said she was from Ranamacken, Loughrea.

Bridget O'Reilly gave birth to her son, Martin Joseph, on 10 July 1946. She died from measles in the Home on 20 May 1947. Catherine Corless could find no burial record for her either. There was an address for Cloghans, but Catherine went to nearby Ballina and could find no records there for her.

Unlike a number of the other children, Mary Joyce's daughter had survived. Mary Joyce died on 25 August 1948, of whooping cough and cardiac failure. There is no burial record for her. She had a baby, Mary. Catherine said: 'Mary Bridget Joyce was born to Mary Joyce in June 1946. Mary Bridget is probably alive, there is no death cert for her.'

However, after Catherine publicised her findings, she was later contacted by the families of Margaret Henry and Mary Hickey and they told her that the women were not in the Tuam grave because their families had buried them in family plots.

A third family contacted Catherine to say a woman called Annie Donoghue, who was believed to be in the Home at Tuam, had died in 1951 and they could not locate her burial records. That research is currently ongoing by Catherine.

This means there are four women, at least, whose remains and burials remain unaccounted for according to Catherine's research. Tragically, the stigma surrounding unmarried mothers was so great that even after they died, these women's remains were often not claimed by their families because they did not want to be associated with the shame of an unwed pregnancy. In some cases, the body was claimed and buried privately by the families, out of sight of the neighbours, and sometimes their names were not inscribed on the headstone for the family.

This was the case for Kathleen Tully, who had given birth to her daughter, Catherine, in the Home at Tuam on 24 February 1944. Sadly, Kathleen died four months later, on 19 June, from septicaemia. She was 29 years old. Catherine, who remained in the Home until she was five years old, was later fostered out to a family in Oranmore, County Galway. When she left that foster home in her teens she, like many survivors of the homes, moved to the UK to start a new life. Catherine has since died, but in the 1980s she travelled on a pilgrimage to Galway in search of her mother Kathleen's grave and her long-lost family. Catherine knelt down at her family's grave in Shanballymore cemetery in Dunmore, County Galway, not realising that her mother was under her feet. Smiling for the camera, Catherine was oblivious to the fact she was actually at her mother's grave. She didn't know because Kathleen's name was not inscribed on the headstone.

Catherine Tully's daughter, Teresa McHugh Waldron, who lives in London, only learned in 2014 that her mother had, in fact, been to her mother's grave. She said she was 'shocked and saddened to learn the truth':

> That was such a bittersweet moment, learning that my mother was there at her mother's final resting place and had no idea. We were only children and we didn't know how to go about finding places in a country we didn't know.
>
> My mother wanted to try and retrace her steps, so all we could find was her family grave. When Kathleen, my grandmother's name, was not on the headstone, we just accepted that she was not there. It is so bittersweet, but it is also hugely important that my mother was there. She knows now she was at the right grave.

Teresa said she met some of her mother's family in Dunmore and they had taken her to the cemetery:

> I remember the day well. My mother sat there in silence, saying her goodbyes, we all said our goodbyes, but we didn't know my granny was buried there. Her name was not on the headstone and no one could tell us anything. Back then you wouldn't even think she's in there with her family because of her name not being there, but thank God she is.
>
> There was an old gravestone on it with Julia and Thomas, my great-grandparents, then another two family members went in there too. My mum kind of lost touch with her family, I think that's the way it worked in those days, it was such a stigma that she was in a Mother and Baby Home and fostered out, so it would have been hard for her to maintain any kind of relationship with the family she didn't know.
>
> It was a relief to learn that my mother was actually at the right grave, even if she didn't know it. Someone did say at the time she's probably down there, but there was no name so we never knew. We took a lot of photos of the day and now they mean more to me than ever. We are happy to contribute to have our grandmother's name being put on the headstone.
>
> It is the idea of all those babies in a septic tank and other mothers who died there lying in a mass grave which is not marked that is very distressing. Thank God, Kathleen was in the [family] grave and not missing, at least her family brought her home.
>
> My mother felt very alone at times and often thought, Do I have a sister out there, do I have a mother? It must be awful not knowing these things. My mother was such a kind and caring person, she went through a lot, I probably don't know the half of it.
>
> We were asking people about our family in Galway when we were there and it's sad because you feel like a nuisance. I think my mother

and all she went through and everyone involved in that Home deserves recognition and an apology for what they went through. So many people were separated so unnecessarily.

My mother was … wonderful. No one has ever made her real or my grandmother, they were just women put into a home and forgotten about, but I am glad my grandmother was not forgotten about in her family and buried properly. We can be grateful for that.

Kathleen's daughter eventually left the Home at the age of five, but even this event is not properly accounted for, according to Teresa:

My mother wasn't officially adopted. She just went to live with a family in Oranmore, like a foster child. This lady went to the Home in Tuam and said she wanted a little girl for this other little girl she was fostering, so they could be friends. My mum was five, she lived in that place until she was fostered.

It was like she didn't have a history, she never spoke about her childhood. She never wanted to talk about it. Mum was lucky to be brought up in a family unit, but always wondered where her own family were because nobody talked about personal situations then. My mum went and trained as an auxiliary nurse in the Galway Hospital and she saved up her money and wanted to come to England, I think to escape. Jobs were quite rare and there were a lot of jobs in London. She came over on her own, went to Islington and settled.

When she used to go back to Ireland, she used to hate it. Her friends would say, 'Oh, I'm going home this year,' but my mother didn't feel like that.

In London, Catherine, who was not married, fell pregnant and, like her mother, ended up in a Mother and Baby Home. In 1967, she gave birth to her daughter, Christina, who was to be given up for adoption. At the

183

last minute, Catherine told the nuns she was not letting her daughter go and refused to sign the papers. Teresa said: 'I think she realised what her mum had gone through and she was going to be adopted and everything and at the last minute, my mum said, "I'm not giving you the baby," and wouldn't sign the papers. So, I have a lovely older sister because of her.' Catherine raised Christina in a flat with a friend who helped her with the baby while she worked in hotels as a chambermaid. Teresa is grateful that her mother had the courage to keep her baby: 'I'm so happy my mum held on to my older sister, good on her. It was amazing she did that.'

Catherine went on to meet and fall in love with Vincent McHugh and the couple, who were together for 30 years, had three children, Teresa, Margaret and Vincent:

They didn't get married for years, but they were together a long time. Dad was a civil engineer and Mum eventually went back to work in the hospitals and worked with people who had dementia.

They did well for themselves. They owned their own home and worked very hard. My dad was lovely and so was my mother. Dad never got stroppy or lost it. He was quiet. He worked for years but he got cancer from the asbestos and died 21 years ago.

Then my older sister, Christina, wanted to find her real dad, so they went back to the same place my mum met him and he was still there. So then my mother decided, 'I want to find my mum.' I think, for all those years, she thought she wasn't allowed to look for her.

My mum was only 61 when she died, she got cancer. I think she got it because she was always worried and stressed about what people thought of her. She was such a lovely person, you wouldn't think she had a strict background. She hardly learned anything at school. She was always afraid of getting things wrong in school and getting slapped. My mum had real trouble reading. She couldn't grasp it at all.

I felt sorry for my mum. It was like she had no identity, no background. She never spoke about her past. I think she believed she was not allowed to.

Catherine Tully had died before the story about the Tuam Babies made headlines around the world. 'I panicked when I heard about it over here in the UK,' Teresa admits. 'I had thought my grandmother died and was in that grave. I wondered about my mother and felt so sorry for my poor mum. I wondered how she would feel if she knew the truth, because she was born in there and her mum died when she was a baby. My mother didn't even know she died in there but they are together now, bless them.'

It is not just unmarried mothers who were put into the Mother and Baby Homes. Professor Thomas Garavan's 88-year-old mother, Mary, from the West of Ireland, was born in November 1928 and spent four years in the Home. She was the eldest of seven, all from the same parents, who went to live in the Home. Shockingly, nobody ever told her or her siblings that they were related to each other. Mary's first sister was born in 1932 and was placed in the Home in 1934, while Mary was there. In 1937, Mary went to live with a foster family and a Child Officer brought her sister to live with them. Mary remembers:

That was the very first time I knew I had a sister. I believed I was an only child up until then. My parents went on to have five more children right up until 1940, when the last boy was born. All of us were placed in the Tuam Home, but none of us knew each other and were never told.

I remember going into the Home, I was around four years old. There was a big massive hall in it and it was full of young kids running around and they were dirty and cold. There was well over one hundred children in there, and there were three or four nuns who minded us.

I made my Holy Communion in the Home, that was a big do and off we went up to the cathedral and we were all lined out for the communion, more effort went into that than into rearing us.

I also remember sometimes there was visitors, I assumed they were from the department coming to visit the homes and we would be spruced up, a big effort was made to clean us all up.

Mary said she was shocked when she discovered she had a second sister when she was fostered into a family in her local town: 'I didn't know until someone in the town told me that there is a girl above the town and she has the same surname and she must be your sister. The minute I saw her, I knew she was my sister. I was delighted to get out of the Home. I do remember hearing that babies were dying, but I never saw the dead children.'

Mary has since found records showing she had another sister and three other brothers. One of her siblings, Teresa Angela, came into the Home on 9 September 1936 and died on 10 October 1936.

She was born in 1935. I knew nothing about her until my nephew found the birth and death certs. My sister is in that mass grave with all those poor unfortunates.

I'm upset and angry over things, but I can laugh it off and talk about it sometimes, my sisters are not the same.

We found my brothers eventually, they were fostered out and then moved abroad to the UK and America. They didn't know about us and have not met yet. It's very sad. One brother is in America, and I've two brothers in England.

After the initial publication of the Tuam story and the establishment of the Commission of Investigation, Anna and the families and survivors were delighted and expected the excavation of the site to begin almost immediately. When this did not happen, however, some of the optimism surrounding the investigation began to fade, replaced by a concern that it would not happen. For many of the families impacted by Tuam, the excavation of the site was always the most important job that the Commission could carry out.

So when, on 30 September 2016, the Commission of Investigation announced that it was to carry out test excavations at the site of the Tuam grave, the news was greeted with great relief by those affected. A notice on its website said the excavation would 'begin on 1st October and last for approximately 5 weeks'. The Commission explained that the 'purpose of the excavation is to resolve a number of queries that the Mother and Baby Homes Commission has in relation to the interment of human remains at this location'.

It would not be the first time the ground had been scanned.

In the weeks after the publication of the first story in May 2014, the *Irish Mail on Sunday* decided to carry out a preliminary scan of the area in an attempt to see if the local rumours of a mass grave had a basis in fact. The ground scan was carried out in 2014 by a top engineering company on behalf of the newspaper, and it found two anomalies at the site of the grave. Kevin Bright, Director with TST Engineering, said:

At the time we found two anomalies on the site of the Tuam grave but they were not natural and they were not normal, we knew the area needed further investigation, it was very clear that something had happened.

[We] found the first anomaly on the left of the site and we could only describe it as a box type structure, the measurements of that structure was five metres by five metres and this was all underground.

We found to the right of the site, where there is the large wall, there is a larger anomaly, which is an area of ground which measures 12 metres in length and three to four metres wide.

It was like something had been put in the ground and covered up with soil or stones or whatever was there, but the results show this area is not natural.

We believe the next step is to dig the area or carry out slit trenches, which is a lot more sensitive, you could go four to five feet deep into the ground without upsetting the land. Bones could be spread out there … but they would need to be all together to determine straight away that it was bones. You could do four or five slit trenches along them at 50cm, that was our conclusion and recommendation at that time.

The second anomaly area is almost 36 metres squared. We were not able to tell you where the bottom of the anomaly area is from a surface scan, it could go very deep down.

The news that the Commission was to excavate the area was welcomed by Anna, who had never wavered in her belief that there were human remains on the site. At the time Anna said: 'I know that some or all of the children are in there. I know what Barry Sweeney said and what he saw, so something is there and any excavation of the site is welcome, but we want the whole site investigated.'

Following the exploratory work carried out at the grave by the Commission, a second notice appeared on its website on 30 January 2017 stating that the excavation would be 'continued for a further two or three weeks starting 30th January 2017'. It was then that Anna knew they had found something of importance underneath the ground.

I was reading about human remains being found on the site on Twitter. I know nothing was confirmed, but as family members of the children in the graves this information is important to us. You wouldn't announce any details of anyone else's death to the world without informing families first.

One woman who is highly experienced in this field is forensic anthropologist Professor Dame Sue Black. The Scottish academic is a leading expert worldwide and she confirmed that there is nothing more complicated than excavating a mass grave of child remains. Professor Black became the head forensic anthropologist to the British Forensic Team in Kosovo, Sierra Leone and Grenada. She also worked on the Thai Tsunami Victim Identification Operation in 2005. Speaking to the *Irish Daily Mail* in April 2016, before the excavation was undertaken, she said:

Children's remains are very challenging, so the people who are doing the excavations need to have a really good understanding of the developing skeleton because sometimes you're looking at bones that look nothing more like stones in the ground and so it is a very skilled operation.

If these children were mass buried, then as the body decomposes all the different body parts and bones end up mixing up with each other because the ground is never static, it's always turning over, so you'll get a filtering down of different bones at different levels. It is not as easy as a mass grave of adults, it's much more complicated. If the children are wrapped or in a container, then that is better. The DNA analysis can be carried out easier, but you have to match it with someone.

You couldn't think of a more complicated grave than a mass grave of children.

Whatever they do with this grave it will set a precedent for what happens to the others [Mother and Baby Home graves], that's why they have to get this one right. It needs pragmatism and empathy. You meet the needs of everyone as best you can. The children who died in the homes have rights including the right to an identity. There is one law, an international law, which is the right of an identity and only children have the right to an identity. Whether that extends to after their death is another matter, but in terms of international law, once you are 18 you don't have a legal right to an identity but you do if you are 17, so a child has a legal right to an identity.

The scan was carried out on behalf of the Commission and on 3 March 2017 it was announced that human remains had been discovered at the Tuam site. The story of the Tuam Babies was once again all over the front pages. The families were never notified of the discovery, instead Minister Zappone telephoned Catherine Corless on the morning of 3 March, who in turn contacted Anna. Minister Zappone later announced that she was going to update her Department's website on the first Friday of every month with regard to the Commission, and she held events in Dublin and Cork to meet with survivors.

This was the moment so many people had worked so tirelessly to achieve: proof that residents of the Tuam Mother and Baby Home had been buried at the site. All those who had denied the story or dismissed it as a hoax now had to deal with the truth of the situation. There could be no dismissing of scientific evidence.

However, Anna's quest to find out what had happened to her brothers was proving fruitless. In a letter from An Garda Síochána on 18 November 2015, a number of questions posed by Anna were answered following a meeting in her home with the Detective Inspector of Tuam Garda Station and two other gardaí. In a follow-up letter, she asked if a criminal investigation had been launched into the disappearance of her brother, William. An Garda Síochána responded: 'William Joseph is being treated as a missing person enquiry. It is not being treated as a criminal investigation, aspects of criminality have been alluded to, but due to the passage of time, evidence as regards same is not forthcoming.'

Anna asked if her brother's missing persons case had been put on the Garda Missing Person's web page, to which An Garda Síochána replied: 'William Joseph Dolan is not on the missing person web page. Investigators have decided not to put him on same as there is insufficient detail about William Joseph Dolan available to record it accurately. It is also believed that recording William Joseph Dolan on the web page will not benefit the enquiry.'

On 6 December 2017, Anna decided to attend the annual Missing Persons Day at Farmleigh, in Dublin, which is organised by RTÉ journalist Barry Cummins. The emotional event was attended by the Minister for Justice Charlie Flanagan, as well as the Deputy Garda Commissioner John Twomey, and by dozens of families of missing people. Each year, families are invited to speak about their loss, share their stories and speak to the media. Afterwards the families lay roses in the lake outside Farmleigh, in memory of their loved ones.

At Farmleigh, Anna met high-profile campaigner Alice Cairns, whose 13-year-old son Philip vanished on his walk back to school after his lunch break on 23 October 1986 and was never seen again. The father of Deirdre Jacobs, who went missing on 28 July 1998, also spoke about the impact of losing his daughter. Michael Jacobs called on the government to implement a group of specialised officers to look for people who have disappeared, saying the current Garda set-up was 'hit and miss'.

Anna was glad to be part of the event: 'It was very moving to be there and to meet people who feel the same as me. I could relate to them in many ways. I have never forgotten the story of Philip Cairns and to meet his mother and be able to share my story about William meant a lot to me. I never thought I would have something in common with families like these. They are a true inspiration, how they keep fighting and keep campaigning to highlight their stories.'

Anna also wanted to pay special tribute to the late Josephine Pender, who tirelessly campaigned to find her missing pregnant daughter Fiona for 21 years, before she sadly passed away on 13 September 2017. In her lifetime, Josephine had paid tribute to the Tuam Babies publicly by saying they were 'just as important' as her Fiona and unborn grandchild saying, 'They are babies that are missing, it's the same thing. My Fiona was pregnant too – her baby means just as much to me as her.'

Addressing the event, Barry Cummins spoke about the Tuam Mother and Baby Home and the current investigation to try to establish the truth of what happened all those years ago. He welcomed Anna to the event saying: 'There is a woman here today who is missing her brother, Anna Corrigan, and her brother William Joseph Dolan missing since 1951. There are so many families missing somebody and searching for answers.'

Anna was moved to tears by this recognition of William and her campaign for him: 'That's the first time I ever felt William was respected and real. He was acknowledged for the first time.'

Only a month earlier she had written a letter to Galway County Council, dated 2 November 2017, saying she wished to revisit an exhumation application she had made on 1 July 2015. Anna had been denied an exhumation licence in 2015, but since then the grave had been excavated twice by the Commission of Investigation, so she decided to lodge a second application.

Her application was turned down again. They said, 'The site remains under the control of the Commission and the Council is not therefore in a position to address the matter of exhumation licences pertaining to this site at this time. You are, of course, free to raise this matter directly with the Commission and a copy of your letters and this response will be forwarded to the Commission.' Anna responded, 'The Commission cannot interfere with the Laws of the Land or my rights.'

On 5 December 2017 the government agreed to a request from the Commission for a one-year extension to its report. The announcement of the delay was met with fury from survivors and relatives of those buried in Tuam. A number of members of the Coalition of Mother and Baby Home Survivors (CMABS, founded 2013) have released statements about the latest report, saying they were 'outraged' at yet another delay in the investigation. Clodagh Malone, of Beyond Adoption Ireland (founded 2010), also expressed outrage at the news, saying: 'This is utterly shameful. Our community is heartbroken and devastated. Tears are flowing.' Clodagh has worked tirelessly to remember survivors of St

Patrick's Mother and Baby Home, where she was born, and in 2017 she organised the first memorial for the children who died in the home and who are buried at Glasnevin Cemetery in Dublin.

On 12 December 2017, a week after the publication of the Commission's third interim report, Minister Zappone published a technical report on the Tuam Mother and Baby Home. This gave the government five options regarding what the next steps for the grave could be:

Option 1: Build a memorial and not disturb the site any further, but identify the bodies by research of archives for the memorial. Cost: €100,000–€500,000.

Option 2: Removing human remains from sub-surface chambers. It wouldn't include forensic examination or DNA testing of bodies and they would be taken to a more suitable location. Three months for engineering works/ground preparation, plus eight weeks for onsite excavation. Cost: €300,000–€800,000.

Option 3: Forensic examination and recovery of known human remains in the specific area known as the memorial garden where the underground chambers are. DNA testing could be considered. It would take six to eight months. Cost: €500,000–€1.2 million.

Option 4: To extend that forensic examination to recover bodies in large areas in parts of the ground which have already been deemed of interest. It would include mortuary facilities, a full-time Garda presence and DNA testing – and would take six to 12 months. Cost: €2million–€2.5million.

Option 5: Full excavation of the whole site of the Mother and Baby Home which would take up to two years. It would include the removal and identification of the remains. Cost: €3 million– €5 million, depending on findings as work proceeds.

The report also stated that Ireland's Special Rapporteur on Child Protection, Dr Geoffrey Shannon, will carry out a detailed study on the Tuam Mother and Baby Home in order to identify any breaches of human rights.

Option 5, to excavate the site and carry out DNA tests on the remains, is estimated to cost up to €5 million. However, the report also notes 'the impossibility of achieving positive DNA identification of infants and young juveniles without samples from living relatives'. It adds that 'identification will be extremely difficult, and will depend on the quality of the remains recovered'. The report states that infants' remains are less likely to be usable for DNA tests because the best source of DNA is usually teeth, including the root. These are not sufficiently formed until the age of two years.

It should be noted that there is a counter-argument to this, however, put forward by other experts, such as Dr Kathryn Charleton, Dentist with Yew Tree Dental Clinic, Newry, County Down. The opposing view, as put forward by Dr Charleton, is that:

> We have eruption from six months onwards, and by the age of two we have a full set of 20 deciduous teeth. Their adult teeth don't come up until they're six years old, but there are 20 teeth in the mouth at two years old.
>
> A tooth can help identify anyone, there is a full set, there are still traces of DNA on teeth. You would need to match it, but you can take a definite sample.
>
> When they are buried remains, it would be like bone material, it depends on how much is left and how long it is there, but it is definitely worth checking. When you see skulls they still have their teeth, obviously baby teeth are weaker, but it is not impossible.

The families of the children buried at Tuam assert that they are the only ones entitled to decide on the grave's future. As Anna pointed out:

There is only one answer to this, and that is to take DNA from us, the families, because we want our relatives back. There is no other option. They were separated from their family in life through no fault of their own, and they are not going to be separated in death.

The expert group are wrong in what they are saying in relation to finding it hard to identify bodies, especially the children under two, like John. We've consulted with a number of experts ourselves and have been told you can go in on [the] petrous bone of the skull, and that even infant bones should yield plenty of good quality DNA.

The families are the only ones who can decide on the future of the grave – no one else. I don't know why anyone else is even being asked.

When published, the outcome of the report by Dr Geoffrey Shannon is likely to influence the government's decision on what to do with the remains found in Tuam. A document issued by Minister Zappone stated that 'any investigation proposed here may benefit from a consideration of the human rights norms prevailing at the relevant time'.

In the Technical Report on the Tuam Site published on 12 December 2017 it states that: 'The memorial garden at the site had been registered in 2016 as an archaeological monument, i.e. a children's burial ground (SMR GA043-141----), but subsequent to the excavations carried out by the Mother and Baby Home Commission of Investigation, the classification was made "a redundant record" (see section 1.3.1).' However, it was Anna Corrigan who had the grave delisted as a monument in 2016 when she wrote to Margaret Keane, Senior Archaeologist with the National Monuments Service (NMS), on 8 August that year. Anna had submitted a lengthy document to the NMS, outlining how the grave could not be a national monument because it was not a *cillíní* as listed. The children buried there had been baptised. Anna wants this matter clarified: 'The Independent Technical Group are completely incorrect in what they say in their report, it was me who had the monument delisted and I have the paperwork to confirm this.'

On Tuesday, 30 January 2018, a notification arrived from Michael Owens of Galway County Council to the Tuam Babies Family Group (and other interested parties) with the subject heading: 'Consultation on the Options and Appropriate Courses of Actions available to Government at the site of the former Mother & Baby Home, Tuam'. The notification read:

I refer to the above and attach herewith for your information a copy of the notice and guidance template for submissions in relation to the public consultation process.

The notice will be published in both national and local print media, tomorrow, 31st January 2018, with a closing date for submissions of 4 pm on Friday, 16th March 2018. In addition, you will note that facilitated consultation events will be held in Tuam and Dublin during the period 1st–9th March 2018 with registration for same by the 2nd March 2018.

It is currently proposed to hold the consultation events in Tuam on Thursday, 8th & Friday, 9th March 2018. The consultation event on the 8th March is to facilitate former residents and relatives of former residents of the Mother & Baby Home. It is proposed to hold a consultation event for local residents and members of the public on the 9th March 2018. In addition, a consultation event will be held in Dublin earlier in the week to afford the option of an alternative location.

Attached to the form was a list of five options, for the respondent to cast their vote:

Please indicate your preferred option by placing an X in the appropriate box
i)   Memorialisation.
ii)  Exhumation of known human remains.
iii) Forensic excavation and recovery of known human remains.

iv) Forensic excavation and recovery of known human remains with further evaluation/excavation of other areas of interest.

v) Forensic excavation of the total available area.

A further box-ticking exercise allowed the respondent to identify him/herself as:

Former resident of the Mother & Baby Home, Tuam.
Relative of a former resident of the Mother & Baby Home, Tuam.
Local resident (Dublin Road Estate, Athenry Road, Tober Jarlath Road, Tuam).
Member of the Public.

Anna and the Tuam Babies Family Group were horrified. On behalf of the Group, Anna sent out a group email to Ministers Zappone and Flanagan, and cc'd every Galway County Councillor. The email, sent on 2 February 2018, read as follows:

Vox Pop on Human beings. These are our families. How would you feel if this was your sibling, Mother or Aunt or Wife??

There are 796 children buried there, foetal remains and 4 adults according to the research of Catherine Corless and already known by the Galway County Council and the Bon Secour Nuns.

Consultative process on appropriate courses of Actions? This is a Mass Grave site containing human remains and we the members of this group have a combined 8 family members in this Septic Tank. You have not spoken to us directly but you can afford the public at large a chance to put an X in the appropriate Box as to what should happen. This is a national scandal, not a popularity contest for who wants the tidiest cover-up. This can't be the same as in the 70s.

How dare you.

Anna Corrigan P.R.

Tuam Babies Family Group

Anna initially reacted with scepticism when the Commission of Investigation was set up. She feared, as did many families and survivors, that the Commission was merely a way to kill the controversy, to kick an uncomfortable past further into the future. But the announcement by Minister Zappone that remains had been found at the site changed everything for the families. Hope replaced scepticism that day, and the families felt the answers they had waited so long to hear were just around the corner. As a result, the delay of the final report until 2019 has been hard on the families and survivors all over the country – even though they retain faith that the Commission does want to get to the long-buried truth of the Tuam Home. The reality for those affected by the Tuam Babies story is that they will never be fully at peace until they know for certain if their lost ones are in the cold ground under the Home, and if they can then decide how best to honour and remember those lost souls. They say that peace comes dropping slow, and that is certainly the case at Tuam. It has been a long, slow process, but no one is giving up until it has been completed, and completed properly.

# 12

# Resistance and Persistence

As Anna's search for her missing brother William continued, she began to look further into the cases of illegal adoptions to the USA, as well as cases around the world where death certificates may have been falsified in order to cover the tracks of babies who may have been sold abroad.

On 3 June 2015, Conall Ó Fátharta in the *Irish Examiner* wrote about the McAleese investigation and its aftermath. The investigation had been established to examine the state's involvement in the Magdalene Laundries. It was an interdepartmental group, chaired by Senator Martin McAleese. It had no remit to investigate any allegations of criminal offences that occurred in the Laundries. In his article Ó Fátharta reported that:

> In 2012, while preparing material for the McAleese investigation into Magdalene laundries, two separate HSE reports noted the issue of infant deaths at both Tuam and Bessborough. One noted that almost 500 children died in Bessborough in less than 20 years.
>
> Both reports mentioned the possibility that children had been trafficked for adoption with one speculating that it was possible that death certificates were falsified so children could be 'brokered' for adoption.

Both mentioned that these issues needed to be investigated as a matter of urgency; one was so concerned about the implications of what was located at Tuam that it recommended the minister be informed immediately so that a State inquiry could be launched.

It also noted the possibility that up to 1,000 children may have been trafficked from the Tuam Mother and Baby Home, which could 'prove to be a scandal that dwarfs other, more recent issues with the Church and State'.

None of the concerns are mentioned in the McAleese report. However, the issue of Mother and Baby Homes was outside of its terms of remit.

This thought haunted Anna. Had William been sold to a family in the USA for money, as Mike Milotte claimed many children had in his book *Banished Babies* all those years ago? Or had John's death certificate been falsified by the nuns in their ledgers?

Dr Declan McKeown is a consultant public health physician and a medical epidemiologist with the Medical Intelligence Unit, which operates within the HSE. The article in the *Irish Examiner* on 3 June 2015 revealed that a FOI request highlighted 'Concerns that up to 1,000 children may have been "trafficked" to the US from the Tuam Mother and Baby Home' in "a scandal that dwarfs other, more recent issues with the Church and State", and that these concerns had been raised by the HSE in 2012.

Declan McKeown and his team had raised pressing questions after uncovering information about the Tuam and Bessborough homes while carrying out research for the McAleese report. The *Irish Examiner* reported:

The note relays the concerns raised by the principal social worker for adoption in HSE West who had found 'a large archive of photographs, documentation and correspondence relating to children sent for adoption to the USA' and 'documentation in relation to discharges and admissions to psychiatric institutions in the Western area'.

It also uncovered letters to parents asking for money for the upkeep of some children that had already been discharged or had died. The social worker, 'working in her own time and on her own dollar', had compiled a list of 'up to 1,000 names', but said it was 'not clear yet whether all of these relate to the ongoing examination of the Magdalene system, or whether they relate to the adoption of children by parents, possibly in the USA'.

This may prove to be a scandal that dwarfs other, more recent issues with the Church and State, because of the very emotive sensitivities around adoption of babies, with or without the will of the mother.

A concern is that, if there is evidence of trafficking babies, that it must have been facilitated by doctors, social workers etc., and a number of these health professionals may still be working in the system.

In a follow-up article in the *Irish Examiner* on 9 November 2015, Conall Ó Fátharta asked: 'Why was the order informing the State of higher numbers of infant deaths in Bessborough than it was recording in its own death register?' He went on to report:

> The figures are worth repeating. An inspection report from Department of Local Government and Public Health (DLGPH) by inspector Alice Litster in late 1944 revealed that between March 31, 1938, and December 5, 1944, a total of 353 infants died in Bessborough (out of 610 births).
>
> Ms Litster stated that the figures for 1939 to 1941 'were furnished by the superioress', while those for 1943 and 1944 had been 'checked and verified and their accuracy can be vouched for'.
>
> However, the order's own death register – supplied by the Registrar General for Ireland 'for the purpose of facilitating the accurate registration of deaths' in Bessborough – for the exact same time

period, records just 273 deaths. That is a discrepancy of 80 deaths.

New material released under FOI reveals that not only was the report seen by two departments, its contents compelled Dr Declan McKeown … to write to principal officer at the DCYA and member of the McAleese Committee Denis O'Sullivan on November 1, 2012, to warn that 'adoption, birth and registration and the recording of infant mortality' were issues that may require 'deeper investigation'.

Could the claims by Declan McKeown and his team in the HSE Intelligence Unit have been possible? With her brother still 'missing' and the story that he may have been adopted to the USA passed to a family member by her mother, Anna tried to gather every bit of information she could.

As part of the research for this book, two requests were put to the New York City Mayor's office on 11 and 20 March 2017 regarding Irish children trafficked to the States, but went answered. In addition, four requests were made to the Vatican on 7, 10, 23 and 27 March 2017; those requests were received, but not responded to. Two requests for access to the Tuam Archdiocese, on 11 October 2017 and 31 January 2018, also went unanswered. This is a familiar occurrence for survivors, family members and researchers. There has been huge resistance to delivering the information that could tell the truth, huge resistance to looking squarely at what happened and admitting it.

Michael Byrne, who discovered in November 2017 that he was born in the Tuam Mother and Baby Home and later adopted through St Patrick's Guild in Dublin, uncovered further documentation about his adoption in January 2018, which he has provided for this book. These letters are important because they show what could have happened to William Dolan, whom Anna believes was illegally adopted. This may be the path he took. And this was the thinking of the nuns. Perhaps somewhere in the Dublin orphanages, William's paperwork is there, and the mystery will be one day solved.

Addressing Michael Byrne's adoptive family on 13 October 1960, the Sister in Charge at St Patrick's Guild Adoption Society wrote:

I delayed writing to you until I had some definite news about Patrick [this was Michael's birth name, by which he was known in the Home]. We have consulted with the American Embassy here and they are willing to let him go to you subject to him passing his medical tests here provided you state in your affidavit you are aware of his handicap and are willing to take him in spite of that.

We cannot of course make any definite promise about him until you have been approved by His Grace, our Archbishop, and we can take him to the clinic for the medical.

Just in case things do not work out it would be better if Catholic Charities, when sending their report and recommendation, did not mention him at all, just to do their report in the ordinary way, without any reference to any specific child.

This also on account of the regulation of His Grace our Archbishop that no specific child be promised to any couple until they have been approved by him!

As soon as your Patrick is legally adopted, you could start proceedings immediately. We enclose herewith a list of requirements for a second child which you could keep in a safe place until required.

We are, needless to say, delighted at the prospect of little Patrick's going to you. It is an answer to prayer. To feel that there is such a wonderful future for the little fellow – we all love him so much. He is so sweet natured and has such a lovely background. We will miss him very much when he leaves us. But we will be simply compensated in the knowledge that he is with such wonderful parents. God grant that our dreams come true!

NB be sure to see that no reference is made to Patrick in any of your papers this will only be concerned with the visa affidavit which will come later.

In a follow-up letter by the Catholic Charities Bureau in the USA on 4 June 1961, Rev. Edward T. O'Connell wrote to Michael's adoptive family saying: 'We at Catholic Charities are very grateful for your generosity and thoughtfulness. It is only through the fees we receive from our adoptive couples that we are able to carry on our work here.'

Michael's letters do not refer to how much money his parents gave for this particular adoption, but it is widely accepted that families in the USA paid large fees to adopt children from Ireland. Michael said he was shocked to read the letters, particularly the part about the financial angle and asked drily, 'How much did I go for?' He also recalled how his parish priest, Fr McCall, lived with his adoptive parents while the rectory of his local church of St Jeremiah's was being built in 1957, the same year as Michael was born in Tuam. Michael said: 'My parents were obviously quite religious, it looks like the payments they made were paid locally too.' Upon receipt of Michael Byrne's letters, correspondence was sent to Catholic Charities in Boston on 28 January 2018 regarding the possibility of William Joseph Dolan's adoption also passing through this agency. A response was received the next day on 29 January 2016 saying:

> Unfortunately, we do not have any record of a William Dolan being adopted through this branch of Catholic Charities which is in the Archdiocese of Boston. It is interesting that someone referred you to us as to my knowledge we did not place any babies that were born in Ireland in any of our adoptive homes. Could it have been another Catholic Charities? Please let me know if I can be of further assistance. Best of luck in your research.

When pressed further in follow-up emails from this author on 29 January and again on 12 February 2018, a reply was received from a spokesperson on 14 February 2018 saying:

Our official name back then was the Catholic Charitable Bureau. Do you have any idea when he would have come over here, as the only possible way to see if he in fact came into our custody was to look at the ledgers which list every baby coming and going? In my fifteen years of doing this work though I have not come across one case where the child came from Ireland, though have seen children coming from other areas.

On 14 February 2018, copies of Michael Byrne's correspondence regarding his own adoption through the Catholic Charitable Bureau were forwarded to the Archdiocese of Boston to confirm that his adoption did, in fact, go through this organisation. A spokesperson responded on 26 February 2018 saying:

While it appears now we were involved in at least a few adoptions from Ireland, there is no way to know how many and how much people were charged. The fees/'contributions' tended to be very low by today's standards and depended greatly on the year that they took place. I wish I could shed more light on the topic. Please let me know if you have any other specific questions. Any children who were adopted through our agency from another country are usually found only under the names of their adoptive parents, which makes any search for children without that information difficult.

Again, the search for William hit a brick wall. With the passage of time and new staff employed in the Archdiocese, it seems that any hope of finding William is fading.

While requests made to the Tuam Archdiocese to view their records received no reply, the letters cited below were provided for this book with the kind permission of the Dublin Diocesan Archives. These valuable documents help shine some light on foreign adoptions out of Ireland in the mid-twentieth century.

Many of the letters refer to the foreign adoptions organised by St Patrick's Guild, the place where Michael Byrne's files were dealt with because he had been transferred to a Dublin orphanage from Tuam due to his disabilities. St Patrick's Guild Adoption Society is believed to have organised up to 2,000 unregistered adoptions.

Catriona Crowe, Head of Special Projects at the National Archives of Ireland, discovered a tranche of files showing that 2,000 Irish children were adopted to the USA between 1948 and 1974. Her work led to the setting up of a national register for adopted children and birth parents.

In the letters provided by the Dublin Diocesan Archives, a clear image of foreign adoptions emerges. In a letter dated 10 May 1951, the Sister in Charge of St Patrick's Guild, Sr Elizabeth, wrote to the Rev. C. Mangan stating:

The following is an account, as requested by you, of the present position in the Guild with regard to cases and adoptions. It is indeed a truly desperate situation. I have already told you that we have twelve cases of extreme urgency at this moment and we are helpless, we cannot assist them. The babies are born some time, the mothers are paying big fees (in some cases exorbitant ones) in Nursing Homes and each case has some special feature which makes it imperative that speedy relief should be given. Yet we have not a single vacancy either at Temple Hill or with a foster mother. These twelve girls were promised help long ago, their reputation and the reputation of their families is at stake. I hate to think of their anxiety and disappointment. I have now booked cases up to and including next November. Girls are flocking here daily, some of them in great distress and the best I can do for them is to hold out hope that they might be relieved in December or the New Year. Many of them will become disheartened, no doubt and who can be sure that the children will be safe.

Since the 'Legal Adoption' proposals were turned down in the Dáil there has been a noticeable falling off in applicants for babies.

Hitherto intending adopters – and those who had already adopted – hoped that there would be some form of legal adoption which would make the position of the child and themselves more secure. Now that they know this is out of the question they seem to have lost heart in the matter. We even have had some children returned to us when the adopting couple saw that the child would have to know later on that he or she did not really belong to them. They had not the courage to face the ordeal. Added to that was the fear that perhaps in later years the child could be claimed by the natural mother. We have tried every possible way to allay their fears but without result. The Americans have been a sad loss to our children. For almost twelve months no child has gone to the USA and we think with longing of those grand Catholic homes which offered such love and security to our little babes.

We have done everything we possibly could to get foster mothers from personal requests and enquiries to advertising, not only in the big Dailies and Weeklies, but in many of the provincial papers even down to Cork. The result has been most disappointing.

On 23 March 1950, Sr Frances Elizabeth wrote again to Fr Mangan saying she had:

seven adoptions already arranged for the USA. Three of the children have been issued with visas and four have their passports. All transport has been arranged. In one case the adopter is on his way over to take the baby back with him. One of these intending adopters is a personal friend of his Eminence, Cardinal Spelman and His Lordship, Doctor O'Leary, both of whom have recommended him. I beg His Grace to allow us to send these little children. It would be such a bitter blow to the adopters to be denied their little child just when their hopes were about to be realised. Also, I would be very grateful if you would advise me what to say to the many others whose applications I have already received.

Lest there should be any confusion I would like His Grace to know that the six children whose picture was in the paper recently before they embarked to the USA were not from St. Patricks' Guild. We have always been most careful to avoid publicity.

And the letters continued in a desperate bid to have children adopted. On 5 April 1951, Sr Monica of the Sisters of Charity, writing from St Patrick's Mother and Baby Home, wrote to Father Mangan saying:

> Subject to my telephone conversation this morning. I shall be very grateful if you will ask His Grace the Archbishop if I may proceed with a few adoptions I have on hands since May last year. Since then I have sent no children to America and I have refused all the applications with the exception of these few.
>
> His Grace kindly gave me permission a few weeks ago to send children to a [name redacted] family. Owing to the long delay in hearing from me, this family took children from their own country and so withdrew their application.
>
> From time to time the mothers write to me to get their children adopted. I am enclosing letters from a couple of these. Indeed nearly every mother admitted to the Home asks me to get their child adopted, if possible. I have very little opportunity of doing this as we scarcely get an adoption in Ireland.
>
> At the moment, I have nine American families on hands whom I consider suitable, their papers are not quite complete except in the cases of three. We have the permission of the Chief Executive officer, Dublin Board of Assistance, to proceed with them provided I have the permission of His Grace the Archbishop.

In a nine-page letter from the Pro Cathedral in Dublin on 29 May 1951 to Fr Mangan, Monsignor Cecil Barret, Director of the Catholic

Social Welfare Bureau from 1954 to 1964, reacted to a letter from St Patrick's Guild and the position it 'finds itself in with regard to cases and adoptions'. He wrote: 'In view of the large number of illegitimate births which occur annually in Ireland (1,557 in 1950) each rescue agency must be prepared always to receive very many applications for assistance.' He said the first aim of the Guild and the Catholic Protection and Rescue Society was to 'avoid separating mother and baby' and that parents should be 'prevailed upon to look after their daughter themselves'. He described how difficult it was to find foster mothers and 'their scarcity has for many years been the greatest worry of all rescue workers' and that the 'Archbishop of Birmingham had appealed to the Catholics of his Diocese to act as foster mothers'.

He said there was a low figure for adoptions in 1950, which was 'solely due to a change in the Secretaryship' saying 'The Secretary had resigned on marriage in April 1950 and the new Secretary had to be trained in this branch of work as she was not familiar with it. She is now getting into her stride and already in the five months of 1951 we have arranged 31 adoptions.' He gave a break-down of adoptions from 1937 to 1950, and that the adoptions went from 15 to 76 each year over those years. He said that 'Whilst experiencing the same difficulties as the Guild in finding suitable foster mothers, I find it somewhat easier to find good adoptive parents.' He explained how there was a 'fairly constant demand for girls over one year (for adoptions). For boys over one year is more irregular but nevertheless workable. It is not easy to arrange the adoption of any child under one year but it is more difficult with a boy than a girl.' He explained: 'We obtain our adoptive parents through advertising in the Dublin newspapers and I am convinced that prospective applicants are attracted by the Priest's name in the advertisement.'

On the subject of Legal Adoption, Monsignor Barret wrote:

The recent agitation in favour of legal adoption has made some people postpone taking a child in the hope that legal adoption will come. Some of those who had already taken a child were upset by the publicity given to what are called the disabilities of the present position in regard to the mother's right to reclaim her child etc. I have noticed recently that some mothers specifically ask us to arrange for the legal adoption of the child as they think that the child would get a better home in that way. There is one serious error into which very many people fall in connection with legal adoption. Legal adoption does not necessarily hide the child's illegitimacy and the adoption certificates make it clear that the child is an adopted child. Consequently, even with legal adoption the child must learn that his adopters are not his natural parents and his conclusion must be that he is illegitimate.

He advised that all adoptive parents tell their children they are adopted when they are young. He went on to say that he had 'never been in favour of sending Irish children to America for adoption' and 'that the biggest problem faced by the Catholic Protection and Rescue Society' at that time was 'finance'. He said: 'the cost of maintaining over 250 children has been increasing annually in recent years and we are finding it most difficult to meet it. Our deficit in 1950 was £4,100 and our reserves merely amount to £5000.'

Back then, a lone applicant adopting a child was something that did not happen. Lone applicants have only been permitted to adopt children since the early 1990s in Ireland. The following letter, dated 13 September 1951 from the Pro Cathedral in Dublin, shows how Monsignor Cecil Barrett felt towards one single man hoping to adopt a child:

Dear Father Mangan, I have been asked to reply to you by Father Martin in connection with an unusual adoption application recently received by Sister Francis Elizabeth.

Frankly, I would not approve of a single man adopting any child, and nowhere is it considered good adoption practise. The adoption of a child by a single man has none of the qualities required of a good adoption.

The main consideration in any adoption must be the interests of the child and it is easy to envisage the dangers to which a child would be exposed who was given over to the complete control of a single man. Any adoption is fraught with risk, but in the case before us the risks are considerably increased. May I add, that on a number of occasions I have received such applications, but on investigation I always found that the applicants were to say the least 'odd and peculiar'.

I also hold the view that a young man would be unwise to adopt a child, especially in view of the likelihood of his marriage at some later date.

With every good wish, Yours very sincerely Cecil S Barret.

The resistance of the nuns to giving survivors information about their birth history is rooted in Irish law. Currently, the law states that a person who gives up a child has a right to privacy. However, much of the legal debate surrounds whether this right to privacy exists even after the birth parents die. The Catholic orders in Ireland have tended to stick extremely rigidly to a narrow interpretation of the law and therefore largely refuse to share any information with the survivors. The Commission of Investigation is currently investigating illegal adoptions that are believed to have occurred from nearly all the Mother and Baby Homes under its remit. Given the nature of illegal adoptions, comprehensive figures are not yet available regarding the Tuam Mother and Baby Home, but the HSE concerns, as well as anecdotes from hundreds of people, all point to the practice being widespread.

When Mother and Baby Homes were in operation, the idea that a survivor had the right to take a case against the state for neglect or abuse by the nuns was completely unheard of. It was unimaginable. But one brave survivor of Tuam, Peter Mulryan, is now Chairperson of the Tuam Home Survivors Network, which was officially launched in a poignant ceremony in December 2017.

Peter, who is 73 and from Ballinasloe, County Galway, brought a case against Tusla – Child and Family Agency on 5 December 2016. His sister, Marian Bridget Mulryan, is believed to be one of the 796 children who died in the Home. Mr Mulryan has been forced to take his case to the High Court to get the records of his little sister, who is recorded by the Bon Secours nuns as having died in the Home on 12 February 1955 when she was just nine months old. An order for a judicial review was granted in the High Court by Judge Richard Humphreys in March 2017. However, Mr Mulryan, who is suffering with cancer, has still not received any further documentation in relation to his search for his sister, and his case is unresolved and remains before the courts (February 2018).

At the time of his case Mr Mulryan said: 'It's far from over yet, but it is a step in the right direction. I hope I open the doors for everyone else. I hope my health improves in the meantime. It is significant, and it's been a battle, but I am pleased it's moving now.'

During a High Court hearing on 6 March 2017, a leading solicitor for Peter Mulryan's case accused the head of the Bon Secours order of 'lying through her teeth'. Solicitor Kevin Higgins was speaking up for Mr Mulryan and his baby sister, whom 'he never met'. The case took a dramatic turn after the court heard how on 15 February 2017, Sr Marie Ryan told Tusla's legal services that the Tuam Mother and Baby Home had closed in 1961 and that:

> all records maintained in respect of the Home were handed over to the Co. Galway Board of Health and no records were withheld by the congregation. As far as we understand all of these records are now held by your agency, Tusla. We are unaware of any burial records maintained by the congregation in respect of the children who died in St Mary's Mother and Baby Home. We cannot confirm

their location, we cannot furnish the records to the Child and Family Agency and we are unaware of the existence of any such records and therefore cannot know if they were subsequently destroyed.

However, Mr Higgins told the court that an affidavit from Tusla, dated 2 February 2017, said that it had records for Mother and Baby Homes in the west since 2011, not 1961. Mr Higgins said: 'So it was not 1961, as Sr Marie Ryan says. Sr Marie Ryan is lying through her teeth.' He added that another letter from Sr Ryan, dated 9 April 2013, demonstrated that the congregation knew more about what had happened to the children who died there than was now being claimed. That letter – addressed to Anna Corrigan – gave explicit details about John Desmond's burial. This, Mr Higgins asserted, meant that the Bon Secours order knew 'a lot more' in 2013 and knew 'where the babies are buried'.

Peter Mulryan has no memories of his time in the Home, but when he finally got to meet his mother, she filled in some of the gaps. His mother, who was from Addergoole, County Galway, was forced to leave the family home at seven or eight months' pregnant, when the local parish priest learned she was pregnant out of wedlock. Her father carried her 32km on his bicycle, under the cover of darkness, to hand her over to the nuns in Tuam:

It was at least 20 miles away and there was an awful hill. They left at midnight so they wouldn't be seen. She was about 33. Some complications set in about a week before the birth, so she was brought to the Regional Hospital in Galway and that's where I was born. I was there for six days and then we went to Tuam. My mother was there for a year working or, as I call it, slaving away. She left after a year and was sent to the Magdalene Laundry in Galway city.

Mr Mulryan was eventually fostered, at the age of four-and-a-half, by an elderly woman and her unmarried son. But even after his foster mother's death, when he was aged 19, he was too afraid to leave the only home he could remember: 'I stayed on until I was 33. I was afraid of the unknown, afraid to leave. Where would I go?' Luckily, his life changed when he was 27 and he met the woman who would become his wife, Kathleen. She has been by her husband's side throughout his court battle and his search for his sister.

Sr Marie Ryan has never agreed to an interview with regards to the Tuam Mother and Baby Home. The only reporter who managed to track her down was Patrick O'Connell of the *Sunday World*. On 12 March 2017, he revealed that, when approached, Sr Ryan refused to speak to him about the horror of the 796 children buried in a septic tank. Asked by the *Sunday World* to comment on allegations in the High Court that she 'is lying through her teeth' about what levels of knowledge the order has over the fate of the Tuam babies, Sr Ryan replied simply, 'No comment'.

While all attention has been focused on the remains at the Home, there is growing concern that the site of the nearby Grove Hospital, also run by the Bon Secours order, might also house burials. The order left the Grove Hospital in 2001, at which time the HSE bought the site. The HSE sought planning permission for the development of a mental health and disability facility on the site, but this was appealed to An Bord Pleanála by a group of people who believe they have family members who are buried on the site.

On 4 September 2017 the *Irish Daily Mail* revealed that an excavation will take place on the grounds of the Grove Hospital to determine if an unmarked children's grave is located at the site. The ground-penetrating scan will be similar to that carried out at the Home and the findings will be made public. In FOI documents released to the *Irish Daily Mail*, An Bord Pleanála has determined that the conditions for the granting of planning permission include an excavation at the site:

The developer shall facilitate the preservation, recording and protection of archaeological materials or features that may exist within the site.

Employ a suitably qualified archaeologist who shall monitor all site and other investigation works ... in order to conserve the archaeological heritage of the site and to secure the preservation and protection of any remains that may exist within the site.

A spokesperson for the HSE said it 'had intended and is now conditioned to carry out an archaeological assessment and site investigations prior to the commencement of the works. A suitably qualified archaeologist will be appointed to monitor and report on all site investigations and other excavations during the course of these works.'

A source told the *Irish Daily Mail* that 'The assessment's sole purpose is look for a children's grave', following a series of complaints to the HSE and Galway County Council. It's understood the highly specialised heat-penetrating scan will take place 'as soon as possible'. The source went on to say that:

There have been claims that a children's grave is on the site of the old Grove Hospital in Tuam since the names of the 796 children were confirmed in the Mother and Baby Home in the same town.

Officials are quite sure there isn't a grave on this particular site but the assessment needs to be carried out.

An archaeological exploration will help to do an extensive search as part of the planning for the new facility.

The assessment's sole purpose is look for a children's grave on the site.

The natural next step before any building work commences is to look for a children's grave. We know the nuns buried each other there and they exhumed their remains and reinterred them in Knock. So there was a grave there.

All findings will be made public and there is a commitment to investigate this matter and the examination will take place as soon as possible. The planning permission is there.

One woman has revealed how she believes the tiny remains of her baby sister, who died at birth, could be discovered when the grounds of the Grove Hospital are excavated. Helena Madden Feeney said she was devastated when she learned she had a sister called Maria, who was buried by the Bon Secours nuns in an unmarked grave after her stillbirth on 19 December 1969. Helena's heartbroken father told her he went to the Grove Hospital with a tiny white coffin so he could take his baby daughter's remains away to a family plot. However, when he got there, he claimed the nuns told him they had already buried his little girl at the back of the hospital. Helena said: 'He came home with an empty white coffin. I can't imagine what that was like for him and my parents never forgot that.'

Helena from Castlerea, County Roscommon, said the story of her sister had left a lasting wound in her family:

My parents never, ever got over Maria's burial and how the nuns took that decision to bury her away from them.

My mother was devastated when Maria died and was in no fit state to make any decisions, so when the nuns told her they were burying her in the hospital grounds, my mother must have said OK. But how could she have been in the right frame of mind for that?

My poor father went to the hospital with a white coffin to take Maria's remains away and the nuns told him she was already buried. They always spoke about Maria and even before my father passed away two years ago, he was still saying how much he was hurting over that.

If my parents were alive, I feel they would speak out now that all of this is out in the public domain as it is so horrible. They loved her so much that they engraved her name on the family headstone, even though her remains are not there.

Kathleen Madden, Helena's mother, died on 4 January 2013 when she was

70 from pancreatic cancer, and two years later her husband Paddy died from pneumonia. Helena still grieves for them:

> I miss them something terrible. I felt I needed to say something about how they suffered over Maria and how that decision was taken from them. If I could speak to the nuns responsible for this, I would like to know why they did what they did. It's about time someone came out and gave us some answers.

A spokesperson for the Bon Secours nuns said they had no comment to make about Helena's story.

'No comment.' Two words designed to frustrate and annoy when someone is searching for answers. The Bon Secours order has been approached many times with questions, requests for information have been sent to them, genuine questions that need to be answered, but again and again people seeking information come up against the brick wall of 'no comment'. This is very hurtful for those affected by the Tuam Babies story. They want to know the truth and to make reparation for past wrongs. But these past wrongs are being compounded by a current wrong – because it is wrong to withhold information that could bring peace and healing. By continually resisting, the order is forcing families and survivors to keep persisting, and it is an exhausting trial for them.

Hopefully, one day the order will be able to open up and give out the information it has, no matter how slight it may seem to be. Failing that, it seems that the ground might give up their secrets anyway, because whatever burials might be at the Home or at the Grove Hospital will be uncovered. It's only a matter of time.

# 13

# Snapshots of Stolen Lives

The stories from the families of women who were incarcerated in the Tuam Mother and Baby Home have received a huge amount of global attention, mostly because of the nature of burial of the children's bodies. However, their grim and brutal experiences are no worse and no different than the thousands of other 'sinful' women kept in other Catholic and Protestant institutions across the country. Thousands of these women and children have not been included in the Commission, which means their stories will not be heard as loudly. But the truth is that there are still a large number of unregistered and unconsecrated graves attached to old workhouses, psychiatric hospitals, Magdalene Laundries and Mother and Baby Homes all across Ireland.

In order to give a small number of the unheard a chance to be heard, what follows is a collection of stories from survivors and their families from other institutions across Ireland. Every person interviewed here could easily write their own book.

## Breda Tuite, adopted through St Patrick's Guild Agency in 1959

Breda Tuite stood over the grave of her birth mother for the first time and burst into tears. It was the end of an exhausting 30-year search and the closest she had come to her own flesh and blood since the day she was born. Breda had come to pay her respects to the woman who had given her up when she was born and had never wanted any contact with her again.

Bridget 'Babe' Leonard (*née* Stack) spent nearly 60 years keeping her only child a secret from the community she had settled into after she got married. She was determined not to be found, but Breda Tuite was equally determined to find her mother. Sadly, it was too late by the time she was finally given the information she had fought so hard to get. Under Irish law, adoptees are not legally entitled to their adoption file and birth-family details. This meant that Breda had to uncover her birth history alone.

Breda Tuite is a married grandmother from Skerries in north Dublin. She is a well-spoken, determined, successful and stylish businesswoman who is always impeccably turned out. When she speaks, she is honest, caring and straightforward. She has been co-managing a supermarket in Skerries for several years and has strong ties to her customers and community. But the love of her life is her family.

Breda was born Bridget Stack on 6 April 1959 at Holles Street Hospital in Dublin. Her mother, who had the same name, had travelled from north Kerry to give birth in secret and give up her baby for adoption. On 13 April little Bridget was transferred to St Patrick's Infant Hospital in Blackrock for nursery care. Her birth mother returned to Kerry and never uttered a word of her pregnancy or her daughter. She later married, but had no children. She moved to Glin, in County Limerick, with her husband, where she lived out the rest of her days.

Meanwhile, little Bridget was adopted on 5 July 1960. She had a happy childhood and adored her adoptive parents. She never thought much about her birth family until she suffered a serious medical condition in the 1980s and needed her medical history. The request was made, only to be told her birth mother would not provide this information. Legislation in Ireland favours the birth mother, and thus around 48,000 adoptees are not automatically entitled to these vital personal details.

As a result, Breda spent almost 30 years pleading with St Patrick's Guild, the adoption agency in Dublin that had organised her adoption. She wrote several letters and made countless phonecalls to Sr Frances Fahy at St Patrick's Guild. Given the seriousness of her medical complaint, the Adoption Authority of Ireland (AAI) intervened in her case and Breda was eventually given her birth certificate. However, she was still unable to track down her birth mother or get any medical information.

In October 2014, it was announced that St Patrick's Guild was closing down and that the files held there would be given to the AAI. Breda made a desperate plea to the Guild to release her files to help unlock the mystery around her identity and medical history, but, like thousands of others in her situation, she hit a brick wall.

I only ever wanted to get my medical records, I wasn't looking for a happy-ever-after.

I first tried to get my file in 1994 but they said no, then in 1997 I tried again to get information but I kept getting the brush off.

Ten years ago my daughter fell ill too and she had type 1 diabetes and very serious arthritis in her spine. I had no medical history to give her, the doctors at Beaumont Hospital were asking me all about the medical history, but I couldn't tell them anything.

For those reasons alone, I should have been given the details. I had to go up and meet Sr Frances Fahy to ask for my file and she contacted my birth mother, but my birth mother said no she shouldn't have it. My birth mother then wrote a letter saying she didn't want me to have anything.

I didn't want to upset her, all I wanted to do was say thank you. I've had a wonderful life but still, Frances Fahy kept giving me the brush off and my birth mother was having none of it.

I've been ringing every January for years to see if she is still alive.

In the end, Tusla – Child and Family Agency, contacted Breda in early 2017 and she was invited for a meeting.

I met a lovely social worker and I got the feeling I was going to get the help I had asked for. In a follow-up call from the same social worker, I was told to come in for another meeting and this time I had to bring someone – so I brought my daughter. My stomach was in knots when I went and that's when I was told my birth mother had died … I was devastated.

'Babe' had died in February 2015. In her online obituary there is no mention of her long-lost daughter. Breda is not surprised by this: 'She lived her life as though I did not exist and that was unfair to me. You read so many stories of devastated birth mothers cruelly separated from their children and they spend their lives looking for them, that did not happen to me. My birth mother did not want anyone to know about me. But I am thankful I was adopted because I had a great life. Maybe in her own way she was scared of what people would think of her if they found out about me.'

In August 2017 Breda and her daughter, Orlaigh, drove to Breda's birth mother's hometown to visit her grave, to help Breda find closure.

I needed to see the grave and I needed to say thank you. I made contact with her local priest through a friend who was completely astounded that I was Babe's secret child.

He contacted a friend of hers who nursed Babe as she was dying and was very close to her. This lady was also really, really shocked, but thank God I was welcomed with open arms.

I'd say I was the talk of the village, my birth mother was clearly held in high esteem. I think maybe that was why she didn't want to talk about me. Maybe in her own way she believed she would fall off her pedestal. But the reality was, it would not have been like that because her friends and relatives could not have been more understanding of my situation. You read about these stories of how people are rejected and almost blamed for stirring up trouble, when it wasn't like that at all. I spent the weekend there and I was treated so well.

But Breda was there to fulfil her lifelong journey: she needed to see her mother's grave.

I got to the grave and it was devastating, I sobbed my heart out and everyone around me was crying. It was a truly heartbreaking situation and everyone was so upset. Even the priest was upset. I can only imagine how they were feeling because they knew this woman all their lives and I was standing there crying for the woman I never knew and as the child they never knew about. I told my birth mother, thank you. And I meant it, but I also felt she really hurt me, by rejecting me. However, I forgive her and I have found a whole new group of friends and family because of her.

I got all the answers I wanted, I got a photograph and I got to hear all about her. My cousins said if they had known about me, they would have made her meet me one time, no matter how hard it would be for her and I do feel I was the lucky one, there but for the grace of God go I.

Everyone deserves to know who they are and it should not have taken this long and I should never have had to fight so hard for this information.

I had done everything I could to find out who I was, but I had to wait until Babe was dead before I could actually go to her hometown and meet her friends and family because I had hit a brick wall in my search. It has been a long time coming, but I've done what I set out to do.

## Desmond Lally, born in the Tuam Mother and Baby Home in 1951

Desmond Lally will never forget the first conversation he had with his long-lost brother on the telephone from America. It was 2013, and he had just found out his mother, who gave him up for adoption in 1946, had gone on to have four more children, one of whom had also been in the Tuam Mother and Baby Home. On the phone from Ireland, his brother Michael said, 'Dessie, how are you?' before explaining he also had three half-sisters. Desmond cried for days afterwards.

The soft-spoken dad-of-two was born on 13 July 1946 in the Tuam Mother and Baby Home, where he stayed for five years. He has little or no information about his past, but thanks to a relative he tracked down online and who carried out some enquires for him in Ireland, he discovered he had four siblings in Galway, which eventually led to the phone call from Michael.

Desmond has been living in America since 1982 and has never lost his Irish accent. He's desperate to return home, but he doesn't have the financial means to do so. Having found his birth family on Facebook, he learned his mother, who went on to become a nurse, had died in 1962, aged 46. Over the phone from his home in the States, Desmond says he has no memories of Tuam, except for the day he was taken away to live with a foster family.

My understanding is I was in the Home until I was four or five. Then I was fostered out, I don't have any track of the time from when I was born to the time until I was sent out to a foster home. I believe I was four or five at the time. I don't remember the home, but I got visions of someone walking me down the road to the foster family. And that is the only thing I remember. It's kinda creepy.

I was fostered by a family who owned a farm. Nobody there would give me support. I don't know what happened between the day I was born until the time I was four or five. I am missing that time right there.

I never got any records. I was fostered and I was moved from one home to another. I wish I had answers, it bugs me a lot. I don't understand what happened in the Home, but it could not have been easy for my mother who, like all the other mothers, ended up in there because they were pregnant.

Desmond went on to work on a farm as a child after he was 'boarded out'.

I was on a farm in Ballinsloe as a foster child and I was physically abused at the first home and abused in the second home. At 16 I walked out. I ended up walking to Dublin. Back in them days I walked and hitch-hiked and went on a donkey and cart. All I remember about Dublin, I was woken up at 4.00 a.m. by a police officer after I fell asleep in the window of a clothing store. I got a kick in the butt and he was saying, wake up son. That police officer was absolutely wonderful in the end and he gave me some pocket money for myself and guided me to a home. I eventually got on the boat to England. I lived in England for years and worked for Walls sausage meat factory in London. I lived in Cricklewood for years.

The abuse I suffered was unbearable. I was beaten so badly in foster care. I walked out at 16 and got away. In England, I met a lady, got married [had two children] and got divorced, and I was drinking a lot of the time. I was meeting the wrong kind of people. I think I came out of there with many a hangover. I still look back on the old days and know I drank too much.

I met another lady and she had family living in America, so I ended up moving to there with her so I could be close to her family, but I wanted to find out about my family in Galway.

Four years ago I went on Facebook, punched in my last name, Lally. I hooked up with a couple of Lallys. I had no information, but I always had a vision my mother's name was Margaret.

Three months later I got a call from my brother who was also in the Tuam Home and he said my poor mother had already gone to heaven and she had died young, she was only 46.

Then I hooked up with somebody else, Christine, and she lived in New Zealand and that time Christine was making a trip to Galway for a month's vacation she asked me if I had any information. She did make contact with me while she was there. She found my brother in Dublin and he contacted me. I cried for days afterwards.

My brother came out to meet me [in America] in October 2017 and my daughter made all the arrangements and I burst out crying when I laid eyes on him.

He told me our mother got married and had three girls. They know about us now and hopefully one day we'll meet them.

Desmond said that when the news about the 796 children buried in a mass grave in Tuam made headlines in America in 2014, it took time for him to fully take in the story.

When I realised what happened, I guess it was a living nightmare. I couldn't take it in. It struck me it wasn't so much me, it was the 796 babies who perished at the hands of the nuns, I have a soft spot for all them kids still. Hopefully I can come over and pay my respects.

In America they were stunned. I hadn't seen it on TV and I don't get the newspaper, but I found out about it eventually, there were a lot of the children in that place and some were fostered or adopted to America. It was big news.

As far as I know my brother was in the children's home, but I don't know how long. In a kind of a way I have cried many a night about what went on there. It was all them babies, that's the hardest part. All the ones who died. Nobody knows how some of us survived and hundreds didn't.

I survived, but life was terrible. I was abused growing up as a child, with my foster family I was beaten, whatever I did was never right. I was beaten all the time, by the dad. In one case I was taken to the hospital because one of my foster family broke my wrist with a shovel ...

I lived in Ballinsloe and Ballymoe in Galway. I was just a slave, I worked on the farm all day, from 4.00 a.m. when I was just five years old. If I spilled the milk I would get beaten up for it, and that happened a lot because the cow kicked the bucket all the time and spilled the milk.

Desmond wrote to the Commission of Investigation in April 2017 and explained he had 'only recently heard that a Commission of Investigation into Mother and Baby Homes has been set up'. He wrote: 'This was never notified in the US. I heard this through an Irish connection I have. They told me that survivors can come forward and give evidence about their time in the homes and what happened when they were fostered/ boarded out. Please advise as to how I can apply, and can you let me know how the funds [to travel to give evidence] will be made available.'

Desmond says the Commission never acknowledged his letter.

I would have liked to have told my story. But they never wrote back to me or contacted me. I am not the only Tuam survivor living in the States and should have been told about this.

One of my dreams is to go back to Tuam and go and pay my respects to my mom's grave and to the mothers and babies who died. I see pictures of it, I want to go out there. I don't understand why I survived, my brother survived, and I don't understand how we lived and they died.

I closed the book once we moved to the US, but it was reopened with the story in the *Irish Mail on Sunday*. Being a child you don't remember anything from the Home. All I remember about that was being walked down the boreen in Galway to a foster home, that is all I remember, by a nun. My mind is totally blank after that. I never got a thank you or I love you. I remember once getting a pair of socks for my birthday.

I am retired now and have undergone a hip operation recently. I would need someone to take care of me and help me if I moved to Ireland, but I don't know if that is possible. I hope to get home. Life has been very hard.

Des has set up a crowdfunding page in an effort to return home to live in Galway in Ireland (https://www.gofundme.com/yearningforhome).

## Sharon McGuigan, admitted to Dunboyne Mother and Baby Home in November 1985

Sharon McGuigan was 16 years old and five months' pregnant when she was dropped at a bus station in Monaghan town; from there a bus would take her to Dunboyne Mother and Baby Home in nearby County Meath. The pretty teenager had been groomed and raped by a married man twice her age who was known to her family. When she discovered she was pregnant, she had no choice but to take her bundle of shame and hide it with the nuns in Dunboyne.

Sharon had just completed her Intermediate Certificate exam (Junior Cert.) when she began to feel ill. A trip to her local GP soon confirmed her worst fears: she was pregnant. After her family learned the news, she was given a choice: stay at home and hide for the entire pregnancy, or go to a Mother and Baby Home – but her baby would be given up for adoption immediately no matter what choice she took.

Terrified and alone, with no job, money or roof over her head to call her own, she chose the latter. She packed her bags and was left at the bus stop on 25 November 1985. She said: 'I was as green as the grass, I hadn't a clue about sex, I hadn't a clue about anything like that, I didn't have a boyfriend. I discovered I was pregnant and was so frightened, I didn't know what I was going to do.'

The shy mother of three (her eldest was adopted) still suffers with depression and anxiety after being forced to give up her child. Sharon is now 48 years old but could pass for a woman in her thirties. Despite being an attractive, well-dressed woman, she suffers with extremely low self-esteem: 'People do give me compliments, but honestly I don't see it and never have. I suppose I've learned through counselling that the damage I suffered has a lot to do with how I see myself.'

Sharon's father, who has since died, suffered with alcoholism and a man known to her family saw the vulnerability in her when she needed a father figure most. He began grooming her, gaining her trust, until he eventually got his way and forced himself on her after taking her on a drive one day, and she became pregnant.

As an adult now and a mother I often look back and ask myself why I went with him that day. It only happened once, but I got pregnant. It is easy when you are an adult to blame yourself, but I was a child. I still give myself a hard time over it. I often ask myself why I didn't stop him.

People don't know enough about the grooming process. When you think of sexual abuse or rape, you think of violence. That didn't happen here. My father was an alcoholic and he saw that and took advantage. I was a very innocent 16-year-old and he was a married 35-year-old. I just went to the doctor because my periods had stopped. I found out then I was pregnant.

He did a test there and then. I remember the wee wheel which showed when my last period was and he worked it around from there.

There was no conversation of what I was going to do. I was in total shock. I thought, what am I going to do here, I can't tell my parents.

So I didn't tell them for ages. It was the teacher at school who noticed I was very withdrawn and asked me to go and talk to her. I went into her office. She kept asking me what was wrong. I was there for more than two hours and I wouldn't say because I was petrified.

She kept saying, 'Are you on drugs?' Eventually they got it out of me and I said I wanted to go home and they said, 'We will leave you home.' By then it was 7.30 in the evening. Her and a priest left me home. When I went home my parents weren't there so I went into automatic pilot, I cleaned the fire and did my jobs. I said [to the teacher and priest], 'There is no point staying, go ahead,' but they wouldn't go.

My parents came home to see a priest and a school teacher and they knew something was wrong. It was the priest who mentioned going to Dunboyne and that he would look into it. My teacher could see how scared I was, so she gave me her phone number discreetly and told me if there was any trouble to ring her and she would come get me. I am still in touch with her, she is my guardian angel.

Within two weeks, everything had been quietly organised for Sharon. 'I told my parents I was pregnant by some fella from England who I met at a disco. I was too afraid to say what had happened.'

Sharon remembers the walk up to Dunboyne Home.

There was big long lane up to it, it's still the same now except it's the Dunboyne Castle Hotel and you drive up a big car park out the front. I remembered the big red door and to the left of the door was a greeting room.

I didn't know the nun who collected me off the bus, but she drove me to the Home and when I got there she took me into this room and some girl came in and she asked for tea and toast and it was brought in. I was told there was no bed, I had to sleep on a camp bed for five weeks because it was full, there was no room, there was two floors and maybe around 40 girls from all over the country.

The girls there all gelled together, there was a great friendship and in a sense there was a bit of relief because you were all there in the same boat. I love all sorts of creative things, like knitting, sewing, crochet. I taught myself how to knit in Dunboyne and I absolutely love making things, that is something positive I took from that experience.

Sharon was brought to Holles Street Hospital in Dublin, where she gave birth to her daughter on 21 February 1986.

She was a month premature and was put in intensive care. I spent five days in the hospital. I spent every day in intensive care with her and that was the only time I had with her and after that I had to leave and I had to leave her in intensive care. For years I blocked that out. I didn't remember leaving the hospital, but ten years ago I went to counselling and I broke down. I remembered everything.

She was discharged from hospital on 10 March and the hospital sent me a letter. I have written to my daughter and she wrote back and I wrote back to her and there's been nothing since. She was placed in foster care with a family and they adopted her in January 1987.

Sharon returned home and never spoke about her daughter again.

I suffered with depression for 23 years. I didn't know where I was, I was numb, when it comes to my kids I'm not saying they done without, but I am a better parent now because of counselling. Only for my husband, I did the feeding and cleaning and anything else, but I couldn't give the emotion. I couldn't give the hugs or anything like that. I couldn't give the love, my husband gave that part to the kids.

My children are wonderful and we are the best of friends. I'd be lost without them.

The depression I went through was just terrible. I have lost 23 years of my life, I don't remember a lot of it.

I had no problem with the nuns, they treated us very well, you weren't abused, you weren't treated badly. I always compare it to the animals in the zoo, they are sheltered, fed and looked after, that's what they done. With regards to emotional counselling and support, there wasn't any of that. There was no explaining of what you went through.

I remember there was a girl whose baby died when I was there, but I don't know what happened or where the baby was buried. I don't remember hearing anything. I remember that we were all really scared it would happen to our baby.

Sharon remembers working hard in the Home and being given a list of jobs to carry out every day, which began at 6.00 a.m. The girls would be given breakfast before attending mass and then starting their chores.

I had to sweep and wash stairs from top to the bottom. That was tough work. There was a rota and it changed every week. I eventually developed high blood pressure, I had to rest and wasn't allowed to do chores. We had our dinner at 1 p.m. and we went to a Portakabin at the back for an hour. I remember we had packs of cards, we would pack them and seal them. I don't know if the nuns sold them or what they were for. Once a fortnight we would go to the nuns' office and get an allowance, which we had to sign for.

After 3 or 4 o'clock was our time, we could watch telly, knit, go for a walk. You were allowed to leave and go up the street. We went to Dublin one time, Christmas Eve, and it was so funny there was four of us walking around pregnant. One girl kept her baby and she remembers a lot about it. She told me I cried for ages when I gave up my daughter.

The sense of loss you feel, the abandonment and the depression about it all is horrific. I will never get those years back with my daughter, and she's not ready to meet me.

I always hope she will come back to me. We should not have been made to feel so ashamed and to be cast aside. I just want to tell my story and to not be mistreated because of something that wasn't my fault. That father of my child is still alive and I have thought about reporting him to the police for what he did, but I have to think about my own children. They mean so much to me, I just have to keep going and hoping.

I want an acknowledgement of what happened to women like me. The nuns, while they were good to me, they must accept that this was not the mistake of the fallen women, everyone involved needs to take responsibility. I was only 16.

All I have now is photos of my daughter in an incubator, her birth cert and some polaroid photos. I hope always that she will come back to me, she has a beautiful brother and sister and we would love to meet her.

## Finbarr O'Regan, born in Clonakilty County Home, County Cork, in 1952

Finbarr O'Regan was the youngest of three children his young, single mother gave birth to in the Clonakilty County Home. From his own research, he has discovered that he had a sister who died in the Home, but he has no idea where she is buried because he cannot find any records for her. He also has another sister who, like him, survived the Home, but she has since passed away.

Finbarr has been trying to get his story out in the open via the media for quite some time. He watched with interest the massive explosion surrounding the Tuam Mother and Baby Home, but felt the other, not so well-known homes were being ignored.

He was born on 28 March 1952 to a young, unmarried woman called Hannah O'Regan, in a Home run by the Sisters of Mercy. The Clonakilty County Home is not included in the Commission of Investigation, but Finbarr nonetheless sent a submission to the Commission for consideration. In records he has uncovered from his time there, he has discovered that his mother went into the Home in October 1951, before he was born. She had already been in and out of the Home twice before that, having given birth to two girls out of wedlock before she had Finbarr: 'She was harassed by the authorities and the gardaí because she had three children out of marriage. She was around 23 or 24 at the time. She was very good at having babies, but she was not able to keep them.'

In his research, Finbarr uncovered shocking letters from the sergeant's office at Clonakilty Garda Station, where several demands were made of his birth mother regarding 'parental monies'. In one letter, dated 1 March 1952, Garda P. Brogan wrote to Garda Thomas Finnerty in the office of the Collector Parental Money unit: 'Please interview Hannah O'Regan at the Co. Home Clonakilty and ascertain from her whether she is in a position to pay the arrears in this case and if not whether she would take steps to have an application made to the District Court at Clonakilty for a variation … If she is unwilling to make the application then you as a collector will have to take steps to have it done please.'

Garda Thomas Finnerty wrote back two days later, on 3 March 1953, to say he had 'interviewed Hanah O'Regan at the Co. Home Clonakilty and on this date and she informed me she is not in a position to pay arrears as she has no income of any description'. Ms O'Regan explained she would go to court regarding her position. At that time, Finbarr's mother was back in the Home pregnant with him, had already given up one child and her eldest child had died. Yet she was being pressured for maintenance payments when she was in a Mother and Baby Home. Ms O'Regan was pursued for maintenance payments again in letters from An Garda Síochána on 4 March 1952, and again on 17 May 1952.

Finbarr was never adopted, perhaps because his mother refused to sign adoption papers, but unfortunately he can't get the answers to many of his questions because of lack of paperwork. He married in 1976, and it was then he decided to look at his past and try to uncover the truth about his identity and his birth mother.

I was trying to trace a sister in UK around 30 years ago, and I discovered Teresa was the eldest and was born in 1944 and another sister, Kathleen, was born around 1947.

The records showed me I was boarded out from 1958, when I was five years old. When I was first boarded out it was to a sister and brother, but I think I was held there for six months to 12 months.

I was in the county home for five years. I don't remember a whole lot, but I do have flashbacks. I remember being in a room on a swing, I think they were tied up on tyres, and the child would be put on it and straw on the ground.

There was a mortuary in the county home. I remember we were let roam loose around the building and I went into the mortuary and saw the dead people. I would have been around four or five years of age. I think they would be elderly people hospitalised there. They would call it a nursing home. They could have been in there because they were very sick. I would be left wander off and find them. I was frightened to see the bodies, it did have an effect on me.

Looking back, I don't feel I was cared for. I know we weren't looked after properly.

I had no concept of time, but I do know I was fostered to a sister and brother and then I went to a family who were older, maybe in their fifties, and as far as I remember they had three boys and a girl. The state paid a certain amount of money to families who fostered kids from the Home and you were brought out to farm the land.

With that family it probably wasn't the right mix. I should have been with someone in their thirties. I was with them probably until I was 14. I remember them well. I can't say anything about the family, I didn't get abused or anything like that, but I was there strictly to work. Every day I sowed potatoes, corn, hay, anything at all and went to the bog to cut turf, it was a dairy farm so I would get up at 7.00 a.m. and would milk the cows before I went to school. It was really, really hard work.

I was only six or seven [years old] and I would go to school and fall asleep in class. When you came in from school you had to do it all again. It took away from you doing lessons and trying to keep your schooling up. I wasn't able to keep up with the rest of the class. I went to primary school in West Cork and I often think I did not get the chances I should have got. I was working too young and was exhausted as a child.

Finbarr left school at 14, which was common in those days, but as a foster child any financial payments to his foster family stopped once he finished at school: 'Once the money stopped many of [the families] didn't want to know any longer and you were moved.' He was one of those children who was moved and recalls how two women from the local Health Authority came to bring him to a new home. He was taken to 9 Frankfield Terrace, Summer Hill, South Cork City, which was run by the charity St Vincent de Paul.

It was a half-way house where fellas that were down on their luck lived. There was a man there, a well-known Peace Commissioner called Cornelius Curtin, who is dead now. He would show up in court and vouch for young men and take them in to live in the half-way house instead of them being put in an institution. It was a big house and there would be six or seven kept there.

Unfortunately, that man in charge was a sex pervert. He assaulted the boys that were coming in there. Curtin died in 1989, married with children, and he was abusing the boys. He sexually abused me once.

I was taken for a drive one evening with him and he started putting his hand inside my pants. I told him to stop and he told me it was OK.

I was in that house about two years, that only happened once, but it doesn't matter if it happened once or 2,000 times, it shouldn't happen at all. I tried to stop him, but he brushed me aside. I think when you are abused, it is very hard for you in later life, you have very little confidence. I always believed I would never become anything.

There are men now and they have said he abused them as well.

Curtin was the pillar of society at the time, but no one ever questioned why he was taking these boys into the home.

When I got out of that home after two years and got other lodgings, I went working in the woollen mills and in a garage for 12 months, and then I moved onto another job. I was a very hard worker. It was very difficult wages, we were very poor, and I had to pay for my lodgings too.

Around ten years ago, after he attended counselling, Finbarr made a complaint to St Vincent de Paul about the abuse he had suffered. He decided to take legal action and a settlement of €10,000 was given to him by the charity. He also made a complaint to An Garda Síochána around five years ago, even though Curtin had since died: 'It was something I had to do, he got away with it and he was there working like a saviour when he was doing it to access boys. The gardaí did investigate it, but he is dead now. I wonder if others ever came forward.'

Later in life, after he married, Finbarr and his wife began to look for his birth mother.

When I was in the second foster home, my mother came to visit me. She invited me to join their family in England and I went over there and lasted three or four days. She said, 'I'm your mother.' I felt OK, I suppose, being only 12 or 13 at the time, it didn't really mean that much, but I was torn between the people I was staying with who were like my family. There was lots of lies, I was led to believe some people were my aunts and uncles, when they weren't. It was all kind of very confusing.

My mother wanted me to go to the UK. I was only a boy from the country, I went, but it was all confusing. I came back again to the second foster home. It was after that then I was taken to this house in Cork City.

I really didn't fall in and mix.

When I did track my mother down later in the years, she had gone to the UK and got married and had four other children.

My wife and I got married in 1976 and after about a year my mother was supposed to come to the wedding and then didn't come and that was difficult for me. But I had an aunt who came to the wedding.

Finbarr decided to go over to see his mother a year after he married, but her tone towards him had changed and he found her to be 'very cold'.

Things had completely changed, I was an adult then. My mother told me I had a sister in the Industrial School in Clonakilty and she had a horrific time there, she died three or four years ago and she was badly abused and brain-washed and she was just 66 when she died.

My other sister, Teresa, only lived six months, she was a baby when she died, she had gastroenteritis. It was fatal in those days. She is believed to be buried on the grounds of the Home. I got no help in the finding of her other than Barnados told me that I have a sister who died.

My aunt won't tell me anything, it is very hard to get to the bottom of things. I put up a monument where her grandfather and mother were buried at their headstone, but I don't know for sure where her remains are. There are graves everywhere.

Finbarr never met his biological father, but he did ask his mother who he was. 'She just said in her words who the father was and he was a man who died of a heart attack at 65. I have a load of documentation that leads up to that [backs that up].'

Finbarr last saw his mother in 1989 and didn't see her before she died on 24 April 1996 in Leyton, in the UK.

I don't think she wanted to see me. I think myself when you are looking back over your life, the whole thing is very difficult and you do not get the recognition you deserve having gone through something like this.

When you were boarded out you were slave labour and you probably did not get a chance at better education and you weren't encouraged to go on in school and you didn't have the confidence to do well in life.

When I think of that home run by Curtin and he abusing kids under the smokescreen of a charity, it really makes my blood boil. We had no choice but to go to these places and he took advantage.

From the day those women dropped me off at that house there were no checks and balances made, I never heard from them or the state ever since. They never called back to see how I got on. They couldn't care less.

I think it is about time the state put that right. I have a lot of health issues, which have been attributed to when I was very young. These issues were not taken care of.

In terms of my identity, I know who I am, I know who my mother was, but I never found out who my father was. My mother told me some of it, I think she told the sister who died she had the same father, but I can't say I believe her. It was a statement of convenience.

I want some recognition for what people like me went through and for my two sisters who died, one sister only had six months of a life, the other died at 66 with no peace. All of these things need to be recognised, there are homes all over the country who took these women and children in, all of them deserved the same investigation as the Tuam Home.

## Eileen Macken, born in 1937 and raised in Kirwan House Mother and Baby Home on North Circular Road, north Dublin

Eileen Macken wrapped her arms around her long-lost family for the first time in 80 years. It was the moment she had waited all her life for, and now she had finally met someone she was related to. Her family looked like her, the records matched and on her death bed her late birth mother had told a family member she had a secret she would take with her to the grave. It all added up. Eileen believed she was the secret.

Eileen Macken, which is her married name, had been placed in a Mother and Baby Home called Kirwan House on North Circular Road in Dublin when she was two-and-a-half years old, and she lived there until she was a teenager, when she was moved to a doctor's home where she worked as a domestic. At the age of 18 she decided she wanted to go to the UK to become a nurse, which meant she needed her documents for identification. There were no records in the Home, so she received a birth certificate from the Department of Local Government & Public Health, which was housed in the Customs House at the time. The document said: 'baby Miller, born March 1937 at 37 Lower Leeson Street'.

For sixty years, Eileen believed these were her correct birth details. A few years ago she began tracing her own past, and her research led her to a family of Millers in Belfast:

When I was born, I know well my mother had me out of wedlock, God love her, and even though I never met her, I'm loving a woman I have never known or seen. I want to put my arms around her and tell her I have no anger or bitterness. I have no idea what happened to her. This is what is hurting me, I don't know if I was taken from her or if she died at the time, or if she lived, then when did she eventually die? I couldn't understand, being a mother myself, leaving your baby. But something happened, I don't know what, and I have been to every library, every archive, every Protestant building where you can look for birth certs because the orphanage was a Protestant orphanage, that must be why.

I think I may have been born in the Bethany Home in Rathgar, but I am not sure. There are no records for that Home, there is nothing to point me in the right direction. I remember one of the women who worked in the Home said to me, 'If you grow up to be anything like your mother, you will be a wonderful person.' But that is all I was ever told.

I did a genealogy course and I had found out about the Millers with all the searching I was doing and in between times I was searching, I got very sick and I had to give it up and I had to try again.

In 2016 Eileen plucked up the courage to contact the Miller family. The family were delighted to hear from her, telling her about the secret that the woman she believed to be her mother had mentioned on her death bed.

We all put it together and believed that I was the secret she couldn't tell anyone about. It all added up, except it didn't add up in the end at all.

I went and visited the family, I brought them out for dinner, they had said yes, they would love to meet me, they were absolutely wonderful, we all thought we looked like each other, it was a perfect match, so we all thought.

But my daughter kept saying, 'Mam, you don't have all the proof, you only have the certificate.'

Eileen stayed in touch with the Millers and decided to travel to Belfast again in 2017 to visit them.

We had a great time and they were dying to see me again. My daughter Hazel, she kept saying, 'Now Mam, you have no proof, try and not get too excited.' I was delighted with life, I was thinking, here is my mother's family, she has two girls and one boy, I have sisters and a brother. They were telling their family and brought people to meet me and I was telling my friends.

The Millers agreed to do a DNA test, and Eileen insisted on paying the €400 bill for it.

We had a great day with them and they gave us a good send-off, they said they were hoping for good news.

Three weeks later it all fell apart. The DNA [test results] said no connection whatsoever. I was devastated. I thought I was going to fall down and die.

So I don't know who I am, where I am, where I came from, all I know is the orphanage I was in for around 15 years. I was taken out after finishing school, I was taken out of there and brought to a doctor's house where I was told that's where I would stay.

I would love to know who I am or where I came from, I have nothing concrete at all. People say, what do you want to know for now, you're 80? But they don't know what it's like not to have a clue who you are.

I was always led to believe I was born in March 1937, but I can't find a single record that adds up and there seems to be nothing available to me to help me find my identity.

The birth cert I was given was 19 August 1937 for a Miller baby and this was the only one that made sense, but it's not my birth cert at all.

Eileen, who has been married to her devoted husband George for 58 years, said she would be lost without her two daughters and her son. Tragically, the couple lost their other son, Stephen, when he was six-and-a-half years old, having been born with a deformation in his heart.

> He died on the operating table and that was in 1969. You think life goes on and you get over these things. You don't. It is like it happened yesterday. I have lost my mother and my son and I have been an orphan all my life. I don't feel sorry for myself, but I would love, before I die, to know who exactly I am.

## Michael O'Flaherty, resident in Tuam Mother and Baby Home in 1948–1953

Michael O'Flaherty wanted to join the army, but to do that he needed to provide the Defence Forces with details of his birth mother and father – which he was unable to do. Having lived in the Tuam Mother and Baby Home for the first five years of his life, he didn't have this vital information. He had little or no details about his birth history. Desperate to get his life on track, having spent his childhood in difficult circumstances in foster care, he sat down in front of Sergeant Tom Coll from Donegal and laid his cards on the table in response to the query about his background:

> I don't have that information. And if I don't get in here, I will end up on the streets. I lived in the Tuam Mother and Baby Home for five years and I have no records and no birth history. I don't know who my mother or father are. All I can do is give you the little bit of information I have and hope that you will take me on anyway.

Impressed by his honesty, Sergeant Coll at Renmore Barracks in Galway told Michael to come back in four weeks. Sure enough, on 16 March 1972 Michael returned to the main gate and waited for Sergeant Coll with his heart in his mouth. Getting this job was his ticket to a new life, a fresh start and a chance to make something of himself. Michael was one of thousands of cruelly branded 'illegitimate children', which automatically left him at a disadvantage with regard to any future opportunities in life.

I was born out of wedlock and that made my application difficult because the army need to know who you are and where you came from. I could only answer so much.

I went away, and came back in four weeks and Sergeant Coll came to the main gate and brought me in for breakfast. He said, 'Michael, you're in.' It was the best news I ever got, and I will never forget that man. He gave me my start. I had no friends and no family, but the army gave me all of that and more.

Michael was born a healthy baby, weighing 7lbs 10oz, at 8.00 p.m. on 15 February 1948 in the Regional Hospital in Galway. After his birth he was taken to the Tuam Mother and Baby Home.

After he married in 1975, Michael and his wife looked for his records, which they got. His birth history showed his mother had a normal delivery and he was her first pregnancy. The day after he was born, he was taken back to Galway Regional Hospital, where he was baptised. He was then returned to the Home, where he stayed until he was five-and-a-half years old. In the records he uncovered years later, he learned that his mother was admitted into the Home on 5 February 1948 and that she was 20 years old. She was discharged a year later, on 15 February 1949, when Michael was one.

My mother came back to see me the next day and the nuns told her, 'Go on back and mind your own business, your baby is gone.' My mother didn't know what to do, and when she went home the parish priest heard about her return to the family home and came to her house straightaway.

He said, 'Ah Mr Flaherty, I see your daughter is home' and her father said he was so happy to have her back. But the priest said, 'I'm not happy, she brought shame on the family, so by this week or next, get her out of here.' The priest said that about my mother and so she had to go, how disgraceful is that?

Michael was approved for fostering on 16 November 1953, but he has no memories of his time in the Tuam institution.

I can't remember a thing, maybe that is trauma, I don't know, or maybe I shut it all out. All I remember is being moved out in the night under the radar, I remember being put into an ambulance and the car was going forward and the hedges were going backwards. I didn't know what being afraid was, and I remember being brought to a house and being told this is your mam and dad.

I remember the first family I went to, they were based in Galway and the woman of the house treated me like her son, she adored me, she really loved me. She was a treasure, and cooked and cleaned and she played with me, I was the apple of her eye. I was the youngest of [her] four daughters and two sons.

But the man of the house, he was not a nice person, she protected me from him, but in the end I had to go. He didn't want me there, I wasn't his son, he would have had a problem with that.

During his time with his first foster family, Michael ran away a lot, and he was also beaten regularly by the man of the house for answering back and giving cheek.

He was a cruel man, but my foster mother was an angel. They had a big farm and lived off the land. I had to work very hard. I had to pull the sugar-beet, I was working in the bog, I had to bring the sheep to Athenry Mart. I was up from four o'clock in the morning and I'd have to walk the sheep all the way. I was exhausted, and they worked me to the bone. Once I hit the bed, I was gone. I never had any nightmares because I was so deep in sleep from exhaustion. But I was wetting the bed all the time, a problem I suffered right up until I was 40 years old. I rarely got to school, only on a wet day when you couldn't do the work at home.

At the age of 13, Michael had to undergo surgery to remove two hernias, which were a direct result of hard labour. At 14, Michael's school records describe him as 'of low intelligence and very retarded', suggesting perhaps he 'should go to a special needs school'. He had little or no support from the state or school, and Michael feared retaliation at home if he complained.

I remember one Sunday evening I was out playing hurling with the lads. My foster father was reading the *Connaught Tribune*, and he says, 'Go on up to bed,' on a lovely summer's evening! I said, 'It's only 6 o'clock, Dad', He says, 'Go on up there or I'll give you a skelp.' He wanted me in bed at 6.00 p.m. It was horrible, but up I went.

And a half hour later I came down again I went down on all fours out the door then I got on the bike and went to the pictures. It was just great. I was really happy that day.

The next day my foster mother said, 'I called into you and you weren't there'. So, I told her what I did and she said, 'Don't worry, I won't tell him, I won't say a word.' She knew he would have beaten me and she was protecting me.

I ran away a lot, once I went away for three days. I couldn't take the beatings all the time. I would say most people who went into foster homes were beaten. I had no problem with the children, but the father was a bad article. So, he wrote to the social workers about me acting up over him and I had to go. My foster mother died three weeks later. She loved me very much. I think me going broke her heart.

A lot of the time I found it hard to get answers about my life. I remember looking for records about being in hospital and was told I was never sick a day in my life, I got the same answers all the time, but the truth was I was in hospital and had an operation for two hernias.

In a letter written by his foster family to social services on 17 August 1963 it says: 'Dear Miss, I think it is better for you to come yourself and take Michael as he is very troublesome for me and will not obey me. Going away and not coming back. I'm sure he would do better with this other family and he will not cry after a few days.' In a follow-up letter to the Department of Health dated 6 September 1964 it read: 'For some time past Michael's position in this household has been an uneasy one. The foster mother's son is married and is living in the foster home with his wife and family. The married son and his wife asked if Michael could be removed from the home. They have made it abundantly clear to Michael that he is not wanted there. Michael himself wished to leave the home.'

Any such letter received nowadays by an adult who had been in foster care would be devastating. Michael obviously needed support and his foster family needed help supporting him – clearly this did not happen and he was moved on.

When he was 15, Michael was taken by social workers to a new family who were big dairy farmers in Headford, County Galway, where he remained for eight-and-a-half years, working on the farm. He was badly neglected in that second family, too, he wasn't fed properly and was made live in a shed. 'The reason I lived in the shed was because I was wetting the bed and the mother of the home didn't want me to wet any of her beds.' It was when Michael left this foster family that he decided he wanted to join the army.

That is when Sergeant Coll gave me a job in the 1st Battalion, which is based in Renmore Barracks, County Galway. I was sent on a chef's course from Galway to Dublin in October 1972. My boss said to me, 'Flaherty, get your arse down here at 0700 and get down to the station.' Off he sent me to Dublin, to McKee Barracks, to do the course.

I went back down to Galway at Christmas and back to Dublin in January 1973. I met my future wife, Ann, and told her my story and she said, 'Don't worry, we'll find your mother.'

We got married on 5 April 1975 in Haddington Road and I moved to Dublin permanently two weeks after that. I had to wait for a transfer. We bought our house and settled down.

An issue arose the week before Michael's wedding when he could not locate his baptismal certificate from any official body. However, the army was able to recover it. Michael was stationed in the Fifth Battalion in Collins Barracks on Dublin's quays at that time, where he continued to work as a chef. He said: 'I didn't find it hard leaving Galway, you obey your orders, you go where you are sent, even though you're a chef, you are still a solider.'

Now retired, Michael still follows a strict regime from his days in the army. He wakes early, likes to keep a nice and tidy home and on cold days he will light his stove. Michael is a straight talker, and respect is a very important thing to him, he likes to be respected and to show respect. He is currently working as a volunteer steward in Croke Park and is involved in all types of sports.

It is a very important thing to me in life not to brush people off and to show them respect. I think as someone from the Tuam Home, there is a lot that happened and it needs to be acknowledged. I know I don't remember much of it, but what did my mother do that was so wrong? She loved me, she wanted me in her life, and she was deprived of that. She deserves an apology.

In 1998 Michael's wife suggested they look for his records and try again to find his birth mother. 'My wife said we could go to Lombard Street, to the GRO, and we looked for certificates, we got the addresses and details that we needed to start the search. We went down to Galway and started looking for my records, this was years before this Commission got underway.'

Michael and Ann tried from 1975 to 1995 to obtain his records, but had no success. When the Freedom of Information Act was passed in 1997, the couple applied for Michael's records again and this time they were successful. 'We went to Merlin Park [HSE West offices] and started looking for records. I got my mother's address and I wrote to her and she wrote back.'

In 1998, shortly after Michael wrote to his mother, she wrote back and asked if he would like to come and meet her. In a letter dated 11 November 1998 Patricia Flaherty wrote: 'Hello Michael, so delighted and happy you have got in contact with me. Michael, I have never forgotten you, you were always in my thoughts. I brought such shame on my family. I was treated like an outcast.'

> I had no doubts whatsoever about meeting her, she was the loveliest woman, she said she was delighted to have a daughter-in-law and two grandkids. I met her in 1988 at Christmas, when Galway won the All Ireland. I met her in Chester Road in Manchester.
>
> She was delighted, she was shaking, she was in hospital for a while, she had cancer, she was only 71 and she got my letters in hospital. Her son opened it, and he said, 'You have an adopted child', that was that. He wasn't happy. He never socialised with us.
>
> Her husband must have passed on, she never said and I never asked. My mother was the eldest of 16 in that family, so she said.
>
> When we first met, she told me that she couldn't go looking for me, that she had no authority. I said, 'It was my wish to meet you', and it worked out so well.

When she heard I was in the army she thought it was because I was in trouble, but I told her I didn't have time to be in trouble. I joined the army for a better life and to have money and to come and see my mother. She hugged me so much, she wouldn't let me go.

Patricia Flaherty sadly passed away in October 1999. She was cremated in Manchester, and Michael placed a plaque on the wall of the crematorium for her with a special inscription.

She was a lovely woman. She was delighted we met, she looked well. She had cancer and one morning she sat up and said, 'I am ready now', and they went downstairs and she died. I was over there for a week with her before that.

It was easy to be around her, and before she died she said to my wife, 'You look after him now, please.'

I told her I was in the Lebanon in 1980 with the army and I thought about her every day when I was over there for six months. I told her, 'When you are there, all you have is a rifle, you can't eat very well with the heat over there, you bring your rifle everywhere, it's your friend, so I used my time there to think about my mother.' I didn't care about my father and didn't want to ever know who he was.

When my mother left Galway in 1949, she only came back to Ireland three times, to bury her mother, and to bury her father and to spend a weekend with us.

It is 20 years since Michael lost his beloved mother and he says there is a lot of water under the bridge now.

I miss her. I drank a lot at the time, probably because of my past. But when I gave it all up my mother said she was delighted. I had money and didn't know what to be doing with it, except to drink. This country has a bad history, my mother was one of the women who had to leave the country because she was a fallen woman. But she died peacefully and I am happy now. I brought her over to Dublin and I called her Mother.

In terms of moving forward and what I want from the Commission, I want an apology for the way my mother was treated and the way I was treated in the foster home, it was all wrong. I want redress, too, for what I suffered.

My mother was working in the Home all the time, scrubbing the floors and feeding the babies. It was very hard work but we got to meet and have a good relationship.

I will be 70 on my next birthday, but I keep busy and do all I can to keep my mind busy. I have my own allotment and I grow my own veg, sprouts, carrots, parsnips, peas and potatoes. Nowadays, I am involved in hurling and coaching in St Mark's GAA club in Tallaght, and I work in Croke Park. I am also a referee for school matches and club matches. I umpire, and I meet people all the time, it is a nice life and a good laugh. I just keep going, but I hope the Commission do the right thing and give the survivors and families what they deserve.

## Niall Boylan, adopted from St Patrick's Home, Navan Road, Dublin

Niall Boylan spent most of his life living less than 500m from the sister he never knew he had, because no one thought to tell him she existed. Born just 13 months apart, Niall and his sister (who does not wish to be named) hung out at the same nightclubs and had similar friends. And even when Niall was finally reunited with his birth mother – she didn't tell Niall about his sister.

'We could have ended up going out with each other,' Niall says. 'That is how important it is to tell people they are adopted and that they have siblings. We were adopted to families who lived near each other. I can't remember meeting her, I could have passed her on the street, but either way we were both oblivious to each other's existence and that was wrong.'

Niall only discovered he had a biological sister in 2014, and as a presenter on 4FM he spoke out in the media about how the information was passed onto him 'casually' by the adoption agency he had contacted to help him search for his mother.

Born in St Patrick's Home on Dublin's Navan Road, Niall was later adopted by Frank and Lily Boylan and raised in Raheny in Dublin, along with the couple's biological daughter Geraldine and his younger brother Arthur, who was also adopted. Tragically, in 1987, at the age of 24, Arthur disappeared after his Christmas office party in the Henry Grattan pub. Afterwards he went on to a party in Ballyfermot. He disappeared and was missing for four days. Eventually, gardaí discovered his body at the bottom of the Lock in Crumlin, south Dublin, and Niall was left with the torturous task of identifying him: 'There's been a lot of heartache in my family and I still miss Arthur, he was a lovely guy, and my mother was devastated, she was never right after it.'

Niall's sister was adopted by another family in north Dublin. In 2014, after the adoption agency told Niall about the sister he hadn't known existed, he responded by reaching out to her through a social worker in the hope that she would like to meet him. The social worker passed on the information to his sister and said he had already made the information public. His sister contacted 4FM straightaway. The pair remained in regular contact and have met.

Niall got to meet his birth mother and also a third child, who was reared by his mother's sister-in-law. Their birth mother eventually got married and had another child, whom she raised with her husband. Niall said he feels very sorry for his birth mother, who, like thousands of women, had to keep her secrets to herself for fear of the Church. As Niall says:

> They never knew from one end of the day to the next if their babies would be gone when they came back from cleaning the church. You had no control over anything like that.

My birth mother said mothers would put notes about their babies into their nappies, in case they were gone when they returned to the Home that evening, and they hoped the adoptive parents would keep the details of them for when their children grew up.

Niall never found out the identity of his birth father, although he did ask his birth mother to tell him. 'She wouldn't really say, she just remained vague about it all.'

In June 2017, the *Niall Boylan Show* won Best Scheduled Talk Show at the world radio awards in New York. His entry included the story of the Tuam Mother and Baby Home and the coverage of the significant find of human remains at the site of the grave. Niall and his producer, Helena O'Toole, travelled to New York to collect their prize. It was a moment of healing for Niall, as he turned grief and loss into a story that resonated with listeners around the world.

## Bethany Home for Protestant Women, Rathgar, Dublin

It wasn't only Catholic orders that took on the role of dealing with 'fallen women' – there were also Protestant Mother and Baby Homes around the country. Perhaps the best-known of these is the Bethany Home, which operated from 1921 to 1972, first in Blackhall Place and then in Orwell Road in Rathgar, south Dublin.

Dr Niall Meehan, head of the Journalism & Media Faculty at Griffith College in Dublin, was conducting research into Protestants' lives during the War of Independence (1919–1921), and he was curious about the social controls that operated within the Protestant community in the new Irish state, a subject that seldom featured in media or academic accounts. As part of this wider research, he looked into Bethany Home after he came across a short interview with former resident Derek Leinster in *The Guardian* in 2009:

I reached out to Derek as there seemed to be little or no information on unmarried mothers in the Protestant community. Derek founded the Bethany Home Survivors Group and wanted to tell his story, but no one was listening. On the back of the *Guardian* profile I wrote an article for Derek which Peter Murtagh at the *Irish Times* published.

As I had never heard of the Bethany Home, I went through Derek's information. One thing he had was a document on sources of women's history that referred to the minutes of the Home in the Church of Ireland library. I rang the Representative Church Body Library (RCBL), and I asked to see the minutes. They said they would get back to me.

I got into the car and drove to the library, but there were no records. I then contacted Catriona Crowe in the National Archives to assess if the original record was incorrect. She thought not. Lo and behold, the minutes appeared. They listed unnamed children who arrived, were born and died at the home. That got me thinking, if children died, they must be buried somewhere.

The body that holds records of the Home, the Protestant Adoption and Counselling Trust (PACT), now known as Here2Help, was next on my list. I asked did they have records of children that died – they wrote back and said, 'it's private', but I said, 'It's not private, the children are dead and that's a matter of public record.'

Niall looked to the surrounding cemeteries close to Bethany Home, and his first port of call was the nineteenth-century Mount Jerome Cemetery, in Harold's Cross.

I walked around looking for any sort of orphanage headstone, or names of similar institutions. But there was no reference to Bethany. So, I spoke to one of the cemetery officials and asked did he ever hear about Bethany Home children being buried there, but he said no.

I then wrote to the official and gave him the details of the deaths I had in the mid to late 1930s, when there was a large number of deaths, so he took that list and checked the register and he found children in an unmarked plot at the graveyard from the Bethany Homes and gave me the list.

I spent some weeks going through the names and double-checking them. In May 2010, we had 40 graves from that 1930s period.

Niall then uncovered a further 179 deaths from the 1920s until the late 1940s.

Shockingly, the causes of death for these children was often starvation. The children, it seemed, were deliberately neglected: 'I think that is the hardest part, knowing how they were simply ignored and ill-treated, and left to starve. I went through the microfilm record, which is notoriously difficult to read. So I had to go over it again and again.'

Niall was with Derek Leinster when he and other survivors of the group unveiled the names of the children on a special headstone at the cemetery in April 2014. While he is extremely humble about his dedication and his shocking find, he believes the discovery of the Protestant children's remains never received the attention it deserved in comparison to the children in Tuam, simply because they were Protestant:

> Most southern Irish people have an emotional attachment to their Roman Catholic identity, even if that is increasingly negative. In the absence of knowledge of daily Protestant existence a Protestant stereotype substitutes. Many also worry about confusing the message about abuse in the Catholic Church if similar stories of abuse in a Protestant setting are included. The government is also keen to keep a sole focus on the Catholic Church, as it keeps attention away from state responsibility for failing to prevent abuse in institutions run by both denominations.

Niall admitted that the emotional impact of his work hit him at a much later stage:

It is kind of a gradual effect, it wasn't immediate, as we uncovered more and more names, it makes your outlook on life a bit depressed, but I had a determination to keep going. If I felt like that, how did survivors feel? They have been ignored all of their lives. They are looking at their colleagues who didn't make it, they see themselves as people who were destined to be forgotten if they lived or died.

I was committed to making sure their story was told. It affected me as I started meeting other survivors. The momentum kept me going.

The attitude of the state, however, is that this was a private institution and nothing to do with them. They don't want to take any responsibility for it.

My view is, if you were in a children's home, you were eligible to be part of a redress scheme. An inspectors' report into the Bethany Home in 1939 described it as a children's home.

Lack of attention is hurtful to the survivors: 220 Protestant babies didn't count in 2010, but 800 Catholics did in 2014. It's to do with the personal level of negative attachment most people have to the Catholic Church.

Catholics don't really know much about Protestants, they at one stage in history had different employments, different schools, so there is little or no connection. People lack information. When the Tuam Babies story broke, I knew that story was going to get more attention, I am realistic. While I don't differentiate between the children's religions, it is important to show that this is why the Bethany babies didn't get the same attention.

Because the Tuam Babies were Catholic, the government was forced into setting up the Commission. I do think I helped to unveil a story that otherwise would have remained hidden. I certainly think I helped make people aware of these children.

My research also showed that the state was indifferent to neglect and death in the home. In 1939 the Deputy Chief Medical Advisor reacted to internal and external reports of neglect in the Bethany Home. He entered Bethany on three occasions and said it was 'well recognised' that 'illegitimate children are delicate'. He wrote that negative attention on Bethany would go away if it stopped admitting Catholics into its 'Protestant atmosphere'. Between April 1939 and April 1940 no Bethany child died because, uniquely, they were hospitalised. When the Home passed a resolution in October 1939, at the medical advisor's request, stating that Catholics would no longer be admitted, public attention went away and children started dying again. The state was interested in a level sectarian playing field, not those who lay beneath it.

In January 2018, Derek Leinster announced that up to 60 additional 'nursed-out' Bethany children were buried in Mount Jerome Cemetery. He called on the government to 'act now' and provide the aging survivors with redress and an apology.

## Diane Croghan, Ireland's youngest Magdalene Home inmate

Diane Croghan became one of the youngest Magdalene women when she was sent to the Summerhill Laundry in Wexford at just eight years of age. That was in 1948, and she stayed in the Laundry until she escaped at the age of 13. She sneaked out in a laundry van with her friend and never looked back. She walked from Wexford to Dublin, a distance of around 130km, and was taken in by a worker in the Shelbourne Hotel, who got her a job as a domestic.

The mother of eight, who is now 77 years old, said she feels for the young mothers who were forced to give up their babies all those years ago, and for the children who suffered as a result. And while she's not angry with her mother for giving her up, she struggles to accept what happened to her sister. She believes her mother 'chose to abandon her little sister', and that is an act that has haunted Diane all her life:

My mother knew well when she left my sister in that awful home [the Regina Coeli], she knew damn well. I can't voice an opinion about all mothers, but my mother has an awful lot to answer for. I feel nothing for my mother. I am not angry, she had me and she was young and she had to give me up, I accept that. I can't feel anything for her. That's OK.

But six years later, she had my sister with another man and abandoned her completely. My mother dumped my sister at two years of age in the Regina Coeli home and she was then brought to the Dublin District Court where she was convicted of being destitute and sentenced to live in the Regina Coeli home until she was 14, which was appalling. I can't accept my mother did that. That was a horrible place. I can't get my head around that. She had already been through one pregnancy and that didn't work out, OK, but a second time? And then for my sister to be convicted of something like that and she only a toddler. No, that's not OK.

I can only voice my own situation, I am not speaking about other unmarried mothers, because I do believe hundreds of women were put under pressure by the state, but there are mothers, I believe, who didn't care and didn't want their children and my mother was one of them.

Diane was born in Enniscorthy County Home on 13 December 1940 to her then 16-year-old mother Gretta Hagan, who was from Rosslare, County Wexford. Both mother and daughter stayed together in the Home until Diane was three years old. At that point, Gretta escaped and ran away. She was 19 then, and she never came back for her daughter. Diane's grandparents paid money to the Home for Diane's upkeep and she was eventually boarded out with a foster family, where she stayed until she was eight.

However, Gretta went on to have a second baby girl in 1946 – the unfortunate child who was sentenced at two years of age to fourteen years in an industrial school in Cavan after she was left in the Regina Coeli. After that, Diane's grandparents stopped paying support money, which is how Diane ended up being taken away by a priest and moved into a Magdalene Laundry when she was just eight years old. She hated it there: 'It was a horrible place. I tried to escape once before and I got battered. When I planned the second escape, I made sure I didn't get caught.'

Diane got married in 1960 and went on to have eight children with her husband, from whom she is now separated. Two of her sons are accomplished writers – her eldest, Declan, is a renowned TV scriptwriter who has had huge success in the US with *The Walking Dead*, while her son Alan wrote the bestselling book *Disorganised Child*. For Diane, her children make everything worthwhile: 'I am very proud of my children as long as they are happy, that is all that matters. If they want to be milkmen or road sweepers I don't care, as long as they are happy.'

Diane eventually tracked down her mother to where she was living in Manchester, but Gretta didn't want to know her. By then, Gretta was married with two sons and a daughter, and she had never told them about Diane and her sister in Ireland.

She wouldn't have known about me only I went looking for her. She died in 2003 of dementia, but I went to see her and she said, 'Sorry, and find your sister.' My half-brother, who was trying to deal with the news about me, was very annoyed with our mother and said, 'Good God, how many skeletons does she have in the cupboard?'

I am glad all this news has come out about the Mother and Baby Homes. Everything needs to be out in the open.

I am proud of who I am, we didn't do anything wrong.

# Epilogue:
# Living with the Past

After the public and widespread outrage unleashed by the Tuam story in 2014, the backlash was as swift as it was inevitable. Within days of the story's initial publication, a range of different voices emerged to discredit the idea that there was a mass, unmarked grave on the Tuam site. While these critical voices included some of the expected pro-Catholic Church commentators, both in Ireland and abroad, more unexpectedly they also included among them a number of publications not known for sympathising with the Church.

Unlike previous investigations into institutional abuse, the Tuam Babies scandal had emerged – and had been driven forward – without the help of anyone from what is known as 'Official Ireland'. Instead of coming on the back of a publication in one of the main broadsheet newspapers or on the back of research carried out by a well-known historian, the story had emerged in a tabloid newspaper as a result of the work of an amateur historian and a woman looking for her brothers.

One week after the story was published across the world, the liberal-leaning *Irish Times* published an article entitled, 'The Trouble with the Septic Tank story'. The article claimed that not all of the children could be buried on the site in Tuam. The piece in *The Irish Times* also claimed that Catherine Corless had been misrepresented and that there was 'confusion' about a number of her claims. It stated that no more than 200 children could have been buried in any 'sewage tank' and repeatedly focused on the use of the word 'dumped' in some media reports.

The article, in Ireland's paper of record, had an instant and massive impact. It led to the *New York Times* 'clarifying' its initial report and headline, which was quickly followed by one Catholic newspaper in the US declaring the story a 'hoax'. Pro-Church news organisations – primarily in the UK and USA – seized on this 'clarification' and produced many hundreds of news stories proclaiming that the Tuam mass grave story had been disproven, with most saying there was no mass grave on the site. None of these pieces focused on the fact that the bodies of 796 children were still unaccounted for.

Eamon Fingleton of *Forbes* magazine published an article entitled, 'Why that story about Irish Babies "dumped in a septic tank" is a hoax'. In it, he claimed that 'An image was created of satanic depravity: wicked-witch nuns shoveling tiny human forms into a maelstrom of excrement and urine. In reality the odds that anything like this happened are vanishingly small. The image of nuns consciously dumping babies in a septic tank is one of the most irresponsible press hoaxes of modern times.'

In 2014, French film-maker Saskia Weber requested an interview with the Bon Secours order. She received a written reply, via email, from their spokesperson, Terry Prone – probably Ireland's best-known PR expert – for which she later apologised on *The Late Late Show*.

Your letter was sent on to me by the Provincial of the Irish Bon Secours congregation with instructions that I should help you. I'm not sure how I can.

Let me explain. When the 'O My God – mass grave in West of Ireland' broke in an English-owned paper (the *Mail*) it surprised the hell out of everybody, not least the Sisters of Bon Secours in Ireland, none of whom had ever worked in Tuam and most of whom had never heard of it.

If you come here, you'll find no mass grave, no evidence that children were ever so buried, and a local police force casting their eyes to heaven and saying 'Yeah, a few bones were found – but this was an area where Famine victims were buried. So?'

Several international TV stations have aborted their plans to make documentaries, because essentially all that can be said is 'Ireland in the first half of the twentieth century was a moralistic, inward-looking, anti-feminist country of exaggerated religiosity'. Which most of us knew already.

The overwhelming majority of the surviving Sisters of Bon Secours in Ireland are over eighty. The handful (literally) still in active ministry are in their seventies. None of them is an historian or sociologist or theologian and so wouldn't have the competence to be good on your programme.

If you'd like me to point you at a few reputable historians who might be good, I'll certainly do that.

Terry Prone (Ms)

Chairman

The Communications Clinic

At another time in Irish history, the story of Tuam may have ended there – killed off by powerful voices and without the support of anyone within the Irish establishment. But this was now the Digital Age, and the campaign to delegitimise both Catherine Corless's research and the collective knowledge of Anna Corrigan and other families of children who had died in the Home, as well as the survivors, found itself facing an equally vigorous campaign on social media. The historical details relied on to discredit the story were subjected to rigorous and comprehensive cross-checking by a number of bloggers and social media users, not least by Catherine Corless's daughter Adrienne, who wrote a powerful and critical blog about the *Irish Times* article.

For Anna Corrigan and other campaigners, who had no experience of the nature of the media, the backlash was both painful and hard to understand. To many of them, it felt like a personal attack – even when the points were made in a considered and respectful manner. Most of the sceptical commentary focused on the existence, or otherwise, of a 'septic tank', rather than on the unaccounted-for remains of up to 796 children. To Anna and others who were desperate to learn more about their lost relatives, the narrow focus on the existence of a septic tank, and not on the 796 death certificates, seemed heartless and cruel. They simply could not understand how the disappearance of the remains of 796 children was being lost in a debate about what constituted a septic tank. It did not matter to them if their family's remains had been left in a septic tank, a concrete bunker or an underground cave – it was the fact that they were left unaccounted for and were not given a dignified burial that mattered.

For most of the survivors, the use of the word 'dumped' had never been controversial; instead, it was viewed as an apt and accurate description. For them, the stark contrast between the expensive and elaborate burial plots in Knock, County Mayo, which were given to the nuns who worked there after they were exhumed and reinterred following the nuns' departure from Tuam, and the unloved children's remains, which were left behind, tells its own story. Claims by certain commentators that the children's bodies were 'interred' in a 'crypt-like' structure have never held weight with the Tuam campaigners – particularly as none of the nuns' remains received the same treatment.

On the morning of the announcement by Minister Zappone, one of the first things Anna said was, 'At least, we will never have to read the words "hoax" and "Tuam" in the same sentence again. It will just be about those poor children from now on in.'

This has not proved to be the case, however.

On 11 November 2017, one of Ireland's best-known journalists, John Waters, gave a speech at the University of Notre Dame in the USA under the title, 'When Evil Becomes Virtual: Cyberspace, Failing Media and the Hoax of the Holocaust of Tuam'. Waters is a former columnist with *The Irish Times* and *Irish Independent*, among others, and has in the past defended the role of the Catholic Church and written extensively about the perceived negative impacts of feminism in Irish society. During this speech he said he didn't object to the work of Catherine Corless, but he did take issue with how some media outlets had reported the story by calling it a 'hoax'.

He said: 'Of course there's a story of Ireland, of these women and of these children. It's just not a story of slaughter and murder. That's my point.' He claimed the story would not have received the international attention it did if the media had not claimed the children's remains were in a septic tank. 'I want to stop this story from doing the rounds as it has been doing,' he said, adding that the hoax 'resides on the word "journalism" which used to be associated with truth and facts and has now become a byword for the poisonous propaganda'.

Addressing the audience, Waters said that at least two newspapers had used the word 'Holocaust' while reporting on the deaths. He said this was not merited:

> There was no Holocaust in Tuam. Nothing happened in Tuam that remotely invites the description Holocaust … No section of the population of people was targeted by another or by anyone for the purposes of extermination.
>
> No criminal acts are known to have been perpetrated. Nothing resembling a slaughter took place. There is no evidence that a single human being was killed either unlawfully or otherwise.

John Waters is not the first person to criticise the coverage of the Tuam Mother and Baby Home. The president of the Catholic League in the USA, Bill Donoghue, denounced the scandal as 'fake news'. Despite 'significant quantities' of human remains discovered at the site of the former Home in County Galway, Donoghue – a Fox News favourite – claimed there was 'no evidence of a mass grave'. Writing on Catholicleague.org he stated:

> It was a lie in 2014 and it is a lie in 2017. The hoax is now back again, and an obliging media are running with the story as if it were

true. Any objective and independent reporter would be able to report what I am about to say, but unfortunately there are too many lazy and incompetent reporters prepared to swallow the latest moonshine about the Catholic Church.

If there was a Pulitzer for fake news, the competition would be fierce. Mass graves. Sexually assaulted women. Children stolen. It is all a lie.

On 7 August 2017 Sr Goretti Butler, head of the Daughters of Charity order, which ran the country's largest Home, St Patrick's on the Navan Road in Dublin, told the *Irish Daily Mail* that the nuns there 'did the best they could. It was a crisis, and this was the response to unmarried mothers at the time. My own belief is that the people who were working there, they did the best they could with the amount they had to work with at the time. You judge on today, but that was a different time.'

In 2015 a row also broke out between the families of children buried in a mass grave in Tuam and residents living beside the site. In a letter printed in the *Tuam Herald* in September 2015, the families of the deceased were told 'you are not welcome to this area'.

The site is in the centre of a housing estate and the Bon Secours nuns who once ran the home have all moved away, leaving the grave behind.

In the letter, a Tuam resident writing to the *Tuam Herald's* letters page on behalf of the Athenry Road Tubberjarlath Residents Association complained about the coverage of the former Mother and Baby Home. She claimed there was 'no mass grave in the area' but then went on to say the 'burial site has been tended with loving care for over 40 years'. She wrote: 'It is now time to close the chapter and let our dead rest and stop degrading the families who suffered enough during those harrowing times. It was the times, and mistakes were made, but it's all part of our history of the times. It's happening on a large scale in Syria and surrounding countries.'

Professor Thomas Garavan, who believes he has family in the grave, at the time said: 'It is highly offensive to members of our group who believe they have family buried in this plot. It is our view that an excavation is necessary in order to establish that our relatives are or aren't buried at this site.'

The ideas articulated by Mr Waters, Mr Donoghue and Sr Goretti encapsulate the main criticisms of the Tuam Home revelations. Broadly, these critiques can be summarised into three main points. The first is that the story is exaggerated and told in a hysterical, irrational and emotive manner. The second is that there is a lack of proof or verification for the horror stories that have subsequently emerged. The third point, made by Sr Goretti in this case, is that judging the actions of people half a century or more ago by the standards of today is unreasonable.

Undoubtedly, this third point is the hardest to dismiss. There can be no doubt that the values of the average Irish person in the 1950s or 1960s differ vastly from those held by most people today. For the first half of the twentieth century, Ireland was a small, poor and closed country, in many ways unrecognisable from the state that exists today. At the time, there was no access to alternative views on a range of issues, such as homosexuality, divorce, race and women's rights. These things were simply not discussed in the public sphere. There was not the steady stream of contrary opinions, examples and discussion available from a range of sources that we experience today. To expect nuns to step outside of this mono-culture is, indeed, not reasonable. Just as it holds true for people throughout history, we are all a product of the political, social and religious culture in which we were raised and in which we matured.

Could anyone truly say how they would have viewed single women who fell pregnant out of wedlock if they had been alive at that time? Is it not reasonable to believe that the nuns, as Sr Goretti says, did the best they could?

For Anna, and many others, the search for the truth is not just about exposing the individual misdeeds of the nuns and the Church. There has always been an implicit understanding that the nuns, as well as the families of the women sent to these institutions, should be understood within the context of their times. Instead, campaigners have always sought to highlight society's treatment of 'sinful' women at the time, and by extension the treatment of their 'shameful' children. However, allowing the nuns, and others, the compassion to be understood within the context of their time is not the same as withdrawing all judgement on the impact of their actions. Despite the brutal experiences many women suffered in the Mother and Baby Homes, almost without exception, survivors also have stories of kindness and compassion they experienced from some of the nuns who worked there. Sadism and brutality existed but, undoubtedly, were only part of the story. Many nuns spent their lives working tirelessly to help make a grim situation as painless as possible. They were also pawns in a cruel system that dehumanised women who fell pregnant outside marriage.

Nor can the Church be held solely responsible for the cruelty that occurred in the Mother and Baby Homes. From the early days of the foundation of the state, report after report highlighted inadequacies and excessive mortality rates to the government, all to no avail. The state failed the women just as much as the Church did, and families were terrified of both.

It must also be noted that the Mother and Baby Homes existed during a time of widespread poverty in Ireland. The resources invested in social programmes, of all types, were minimal and the homes were no different. However, the mortality rates within these homes were still shockingly high – despite the fact that the government paid a relatively large stipend for each woman 'looked after' by the nuns. In 1938, the headage payment was £1.62 per child, per week. In today's money, that would amount to roughly €110 per child, per week. The children's allowance is currently €32.30 per week. It's worth noting, too, that the Bon Secours order benefitted from what survivors say was slave labour after they were incarcerated in the Tuam Home.

The figures also show us that mortality rates at the Tuam Mother and Baby Home were almost double the rate of other such institutions around the country. Figures from the National Archives show that 31.6% of children under the age of one died over a 12-month period in the Tuam Home.

Anna and other campaigners have called for the truth to be placed before the public. Understanding the actions of previous generations does not mean the past should be ignored or kept quiet. This is no less true for Ireland than it is for any other country. Within months of the findings of the ground scan in Tuam being made public, the US was also gripped with the fevered debate about whether having statues to figures like slave-owning president Thomas Jefferson were appropriate in the modern era. The death of Sinn Féin's Martin McGuinness, at around the same time, also saw a public debate about how to assess the impact of a man who was both a peacemaker and an IRA leader. Just as with Tuam, there are no easy answers to these complex issues, but the debate is necessary.

The claim that the broad thrust of the Tuam story is not factual is much more easily disproved. The story of the children who died in the Home is not a lie; the fact that they are buried in an unmarked septic tank is also not a lie Since the story first emerged in 2014, it has been based on clear documentary evidence. Catherine Corless only went public when she had amassed a wealth of documentary evidence to show that the remains of up to 796 children were unaccounted for. The evidence was literally presented in black and white: 796 death certs with no corresponding burial certs. This was the stark fact of Tuam that none of the 'sceptics' ever fully sought to engage with.

The idea of children's remains being dumped in a grave quite naturally gives rise to an emotional reaction. It also cannot be denied that these dead children were left in an unmarked grave because of the circumstances of their birth. They were disposed of in this manner because they were 'children of sin'. If they had been born to parents within wedlock, this would not have been their fate. This inspires horror in people because it is horrific, unjust and targets the most vulnerable of people. It is rightly seen as a shameful part of Ireland's past.

However, John Waters is correct that it is not comparable to the Holocaust, which saw six million Jewish people murdered by the Nazis. But was this a comparison that was widely made and accepted? Even a quick glance through the thousands of articles written about Tuam tells that this was not a common comparison in the media reports. In fact, it appears in only a fraction of 1 per cent of the articles written. And even in those articles, the two things are not directly equated. In reality, there have been as many articles written in defence of the Church's role in Tuam as there have been in condemnation of it. Similarly, on social media – where debate on any issue tends to be more extreme – there are as many people dismissing the story as defending it. In totality, like any other issue of major public controversy, the media – both traditional and social media – have given space to a wide range of views, with most of them expressed calmly and in a considered manner. There are intemperate views on both sides of the debate, but they are in the minority and confined to small corners of social media sites.

In writing this book and working with Anna and other survivors, more than anything I have come to realise how the impact of the Mother and Baby Homes is not a matter of history. While the institutions themselves, and even the moral values that allowed them to thrive, may be a thing of the past, their impact is still a live issue. The consequences of what happened have crossed generations and remain unhealed today. For Anna, the realisation that her mother's experiences had an impact on her and on her own family – despite the fact she never knew the truth during her mother's life – has come as hard-won knowledge. It has led her to question the truths that were the basis of her understanding of herself. For Anna and many others, the shattering of families decades ago – mostly in the name of 'respectability' – continues to be felt by thousands of people all over the world. Anna's teenage grandchildren are aware of what happened to their great-grandmother – will they tell their grandchildren this story? Probably.

This book tells Anna's story and her brave and tireless search for truth. But for Anna, the truth can never be completely known because her mother will never be there to tell it to her in her own words. This is a pain that can never be healed. Instead, it must be lived with and accepted. To end the story of Bridget Dolan, below is a letter to her mother written by Anna at Christmas 2017. Like the knowledge of what happened to her two brothers, Anna knows her questions to her mother will never be answered.

Dear Ma,

This has been the worst few years of my life. I have had nothing but troubles. I had work and health issues, I have had domestic and personal issues but do you want to know what has been the worst of them all? I have family issues. Ma, in 2012 I found out that I had two brothers. Two brothers that I never knew about and you never told me about! I was an only child but now I am a third child. God only knows how that feels. I used to think I was special, 'enfant unique', but that too has changed. Ma, why did you never tell me? I know our relationship was strained at the best of times, but this? I have never felt so sad and hurt and lost and betrayed, I could go on.

Ma, when I was young I know that you did your best for me, your very best, but I still grew up to be Anna. I was wild and you worried. The more you gave out, the further we pushed apart until eventually our relationship fractured. I still needed you, I brought you out, I brought you to stay in my home with the kids, but still the tension was always there. We fought like I'm sure most mothers and daughters do, maybe even a little more, but I have no yardstick. Looking back I know you loved me, but you never said it and now I know why. I have read what your life was like. I have seen and felt your losses. I cannot even begin to understand how damaged you were, but like me you always showed your tougher self. Did you teach me that? I remember you talked, you smiled, you enjoyed yourself, you were never bitter and the best thing I admire was your kindness and generosity. I hope that I have some of those traits, I try. You cared for everybody. You never spoke bad of anybody. You always kept your faith. Even now anybody who knew you only remembers you with fondness.

Ma, I am so sorry for what happened to you. I wish I could turn back time and put my arms around you and tell you. I wish that when you were alive that I could have done something to right the wrongs you endured. How did you feel being away from your family, ostracised from your village and giving birth to your children alone? Losing them and being alone and unloved. When you met my father, did he bring the joy into your life that was missing? Did he help heal you and you him? Are you with him now? Where are you, Ma?

Ma, I sit and talk to people who were in the Home the same time as John and William. I listen to what their lives were like. I listen to their stories of how they found their mothers. I try to fill in the gaps. I feel so protective towards them. I cry a lot when nobody sees.

Ma, I know you are in heaven and you looking down on us and I'm sure up there you know the true picture of what happened to your children and all the others. Help me find my brothers, Ma. I beg you send me a sign, help me, help us all. What is happening here can only be resolved by divine intervention. Send us your love, ask the other mothers to help, ask the children to help us find them, please do something because there is so much hurt and pain and so many fractured families. I don't know how long more I can go on.

I'm so, so sorry. I love you so much.

Anna

# Postscript,
# February 2018

During the writing of this book, and as part of her own research, Anna lodged an FOI Request to Forensic Science Ireland (FSI) regarding its involvement in the exhumation and DNA profiling of the Tuam Babies. This exhumation and examination process had been carried out over a period of months between late 2016 and 2017. The response to Anna's FOI request is shocking and definitive. It marks a new watershed in the story of the Tuam Babies.

Anna received detailed notes, in February 2018, about how bones were found both inside and outside an 'old septic tank'. The FOI disproves, again, in clear black and white, the well-repeated claim from some apologists that the children's remains were not found in a septic tank. There can be no further debate or query on this matter. The Forensic team found remains in 'an old septic tank'. That is now a matter of fact. It is indisputable.

However, the FOI also explains the challenges facing scientists in attempting to identify the remains found on the Tuam site. Sadly, this could mean that the most cherished hope of many of the affected families – that their relatives' remains be identified and reburied in a dignified manner – is now at risk. This is because, as the FSI memo explains, the children's bodies were 'stacked' on top of each other, which meant that over time they became merged as they decomposed. The FSI also highlighted the fact that it would be very difficult to extract DNA samples from some of the remains of young children and that, even if they could be extracted, they might struggle to get samples from the mothers to compare them against.

This is all set out in the notes of a meeting held on 12 July 2017 between Dr Dorothy Ramsbottom of FSI and Forensic Archaeologist Niamh McCullagh:

Most of the remains were in an old septic tank but some located outside the tank. Bodies had been stacked on top of one another and therefore over time had decomposed down on top of one another so it was difficult to separate individual bodies. DR explained the different DNA techniques and when to use them. Autosomal DNA profiling and Y- DNA profiling done at FSI while mitochondrial DNA profiling done in the UK. DR advised NMcC that we may or may not be able to obtain DNA from the skeletal remains given the fact the remains were between 35 week gestation and 2–3 years of age. We would have to test some of the bones to see if it was possible. In addition DR identified other difficulties. i. At most we could make mother to child identification but without the father's DNA sample the strength of the evidence would be weak. ii. Very few mothers were still alive. iii. Very little we could do statistically if we were asked to compare remains with putative siblings, this is because genetically and in turn statistically we could never be sure that putative siblings have the same father. It was agreed that we would test a few samples to see if we could generate a DNA profile from the remains. These samples were to be sent from the coroner in Tuam, through An Garda Síochána to me for analysis.

In an email from Mr James Martin, Assistant Secretary, Department of Justice & Equality to Dr Sheila Willis, Director-General, FSI, on 16 May 2017, the Department's position was clearly described:

The current position of the Department is that there is no indication of any crime or suspicious death (there seems to be death certs for all those who passed away in the Tuam Mother and Baby Home) so there is no role for an investigation by the Gardaí or Coroner and the Department of Justice does not see any significant role for itself. While the Minister has a role in ordering exhumations in the case of a request by the Gardaí and Coroner, this does not apply in the case of Tuam and decisions on exhumation fall to the local authority and its parent Department. While we would question whether any decision should be made that might be seen as prejudging/prejudicing the final report of the Mother and Baby Home Commission or implying offences or wrongdoing had been committed by a person or body that is a matter for the DCYA to determine. As regards expertise, it looks like the relevant expertise sought from this Department will relate to DNA sampling and identification and the FSI have some expertise in that area. The State Pathologist was approached before by the Commission and gave them some informal advice but did not have any official involvement and she did not see any role for her office.

In a second email, this time from Ms Niamh McCullagh to Dr Dorothy Ramsbottom, on 5 July 2017 it was explained that:

One of the issues we have been asked to explore is DNA options. We have Dr Tim Clayton whom is providing advice on paper as it were, in relation to what is possible. He has suggested that running test samples is a starting point to answering these questions. I am not a DNA scientist so forgive my rough use of language in relation to this. I would like to discuss issues such as would FSI be in a position to run test samples to see if it is even possible to extract DNA profiles from bone that has been interred in specific context. I am aware there are a great number of complicating issues around this but I think it pertinent to speak to the specialists in Ireland. I would also like to discuss based on the results of the sampling, if it was hypothetically possible for FSI to get involved down the road if this was an option that government decided to choose. At the moment all the discussions we are having are based on hypothetical scenarios in order that we can establish what would be required and what would be the outcome of any options on site.

One of the many queries Anna had during the exhumation process was: where were those remains that were exhumed removed to for examination? The answer to this was clarified in an email from Niamh McCullagh to Dr Ramsbottom on 13 July 2017: 'Dear Dorothy, The Coroner has directed that samples from the collection in Whitehall, Dublin, be sent to your lab for DNA analysis. He has requested that we select 3 samples to send to you via his agents. Could you please advise as to what types of bone you would prefer so we may assist him.'

In her reply on 13 July 2017, Dr Ramsbottom confirmed that 'we would take 6 samples, 3 from outside the tank and 3 from inside the tank. Can I suggest samples from the femur. We will be using a shard of bone in the extraction procedure which should fit in a 1.5ml eppendorf tube. Therefore a sample of about 1 inch long would be sufficient.' While the Minister for Children said she was not able to give detailed information on the number of children's remains found during the excavation by the Commission, a Freedom of Information request by Anna uncovered precisely what happened during those test examinations.

In a report written by the State Pathologist Dr Marie Cassidy on 6 July 2016 to the Galway Coroner, Dr Val Costello in Headford Health Centre, in charge of the Tuam grave, Dr Cassidy gave an account of her visit to the grave on 5 October 2016.

The information in this report, which has never before been published, showed just how accurate the verbal accounts given by children from Tuam who had stumbled upon the mass grave in the 1970s had been. Dr Cassidy's report uses the term 'septic tank' to describe the final resting place of the children's remains and also describes how the bones were not placed in shrouds or coffins. This report effectively dismisses claims that the dead children were carefully wrapped in shrouds and left respectfully in a tomb-like structure.

Dr Cassidy described what she had seen during a visit to the Tuam grave in her account of 5 October 2016: 'The excavation was well advanced at this stage and a sewage drainage system thought to be original to the site of the home and a more recent brick built structure had been identified. … I was informed that bones, believed to be infant remains, had been found out with the original septic tank during the excavation.'

Dr Cassidy's report notes how the remains did not appear to have been carefully laid out, and had been deposited unceremoniously in the tank: 'The bones were in a haphazard arrangement with no indication of having been encoffined or laid out. There were identifiable skulls and long bones. The bones were disarticulated, dark coloured and fragmented. The depth of the chamber, from the opening to the floor, was almost six feet. Excavation of the outside of the structure would suggest that there was a considerable depth of debris in the bottom of both chambers.'

Despite the fact that the children were not placed in coffins before being put in the septic tank, money was available from Galway County Council for burials and was regularly accessed by the nuns in the County Home.

According to the ledgers, which are currently available in the Galway County Council Archives, between 1925 and 1944 the nuns requested payment for residents on a yearly basis.

For accounts for the half year ended in September 1927, it shows that £19.15.6 was granted for burials (figures are written as pounds, shillings, pence). The following year in 1928, records show £45.0.7 was granted for burials, while in 1935 the money for burials at the County Home was reduced to £26.11.5. In 1944 £236.7.6 was granted for burials.

However, it is not known if the nuns were granted payment for the burial of any of the children whose remains have been found in the septic tank as none of the bones have been dated. After 1944 there are no ledgers available for public viewing, making it impossible to know if the nuns were paid for children's burials after this point.

The 1944 ledger also shows there was £15 for 'County Home Burials, value of Coffins and Shrouding of hands', but it is not clear if there were any finances provided for the children's burials at the Tuam grave.

Money was also granted in the same years for the registration of births, deaths, marriages and vaccinations. In 1944 the ledger shows £751.12.4 was granted for these registrations.

The ledgers also note how Thomas B. Costello, who was the Medical Officer in the Tuam Home, was paid £90 each year until 1944 when his salary was increased to £160 per year. The Rev. Cannon. J.S. Walsh, the Chaplain in the children's home, received a salary of £120 each year. The ledgers show no increase from 1925 to 1944.

An ad in the *Connacht Tribune* also shows adverts placed by the children's home for tenders for coffins. An advertisement from 25 August 1928 reads:

> The Committee invite Tenders for the supply of Coffins, plain and mounted in three sizes, to the Children's Home, Tuam from 1st October 1928 to 21st March 1929.
>
> Plain Coffins must be one inch thick, wd. strained, in large medium and small sizes. Mounted Coffins must be of similar make and sizes but mounted with electrobrassed grips, breastplate and crucifix.
>
> Tenders must be lodged with the undersigned before 12 o'clock noon, on Monday 3rd September 1928.
>
> By Order,
>
> J.J. Hanafin, Secretary
>
> Secretary's Office
>
> County Home, Loughrea
>
> 9th August 1928

While the state of the bodies is a cause of further grief for the families, this is nonetheless a huge step forward towards the truth and towards closure for the families. Anna's FOI request has provided the indisputable proof that the remains are there, that the nuns did bury the children who died in a septic tank at the site of the Home. The fact that those remains might now be indistinguishable is a blow to the families, but it is a definitive statement about the burial place, and this in itself is a welcome development.

For Anna, the next step is to prevent the fate of the burial place being decided by public vote, as has been put forward by Galway County Council. There is also the final report yet to come from the Commission, which will hopefully shed even more light on the nature of the burials and the possibility of exhumation and reinterment. On 5 February 2018, the Chairperson of the Commission, Judge Yvonne Murphy, invited the Tuam Babies Family Group to meet with her. Anna notified the Group, but she herself has chosen not to accept the invite. Her reasoning is: 'Why now? A whole three years has passed since this story broke, the Commission are aware of me, I sent them the HSE inspection reports by Declan McKeown as well as the Tuam inspection report on my brother, and nothing ever became of it. I'm happy to work on my own and with the Group, but I don't want to meet the Commission at this late stage.'

On 5 March 2018, Anna decided to meet with some of the members of the Expert Technical Group after an 'information-facilitated consultation on the finding of human remains in the Tuam septic tank' was scheduled in both Dublin and Galway.

Anna went along to the Ashling Hotel Dublin where Tim Clayton (DNA expert), Adrian Harte, Linda Lynch, Brian Farrell (Coroner) and Michael Owens (Director of Services with Galway County Council) were the experts in attendance.

To Anna's surprise, or maybe it was the fact that the country had come to a standstill during Storm Emma, she was the only member of the public who turned up.

I had to say I expected more people to be there and maybe it worked out for the best that I had a full two hours to tell everyone who was involved with the grave at an expert level how I felt, and to share my own knowledge and facts with them.

I wasn't going to go initially and then I realised we are not getting a voice and we are being side-lined. We have family in the grave, so I said even though I had objected to it … there was nothing left to do but go and meet them all face-to-face. Then it turned out that I was the only person there. They went to Galway a few days later but at that meeting, it was just me.

All of the experts were there so I told them everything … and asked them to go through the files in Tusla because there have to be answers in there. I told them William cannot be the only child marked as 'dead' in the ledgers; they can access them so they should go and count them all. The Tuam grave is a jigsaw and it needs to be put together.

Anna did send in a submission to the council on behalf of the Tuam Babies Family Group and she consoled herself later that week when she met Barbara O'Meara, who organised a stunning patchwork blanket with 796 squares to represent all of the babies, which was knitted by women all over Ireland in their memory. Barbara agreed to a special square for William so that he would 'represent all of the babies who are missing like him'.

Anna said the blanket is dedicated to the Tuam Babies and will be brought to the Tuam site in September where the women will cover the grave in a symbolic gesture of 'the covering up' of the Tuam Babies scandal.

It was such a difficult week dealing with the future of the Tuam grave and trying to have our voices heard, that this beautiful gesture by these women made things easier because I know so many people care about what happened to them.

There is still much to be said and done about the Tuam Mother and Baby Home, but this, then, is the state of play in February 2018, as the writing of this book comes to a close. The Commission's final report has been delayed until 2019, but Anna continues to work away, solidly and quietly, uncovering, unravelling, inching her way towards those buried babies so that she can, in some way, free them of their pasts. And she, like so many others, needs to be liberated from the dark aspects of her own past, too. This is a collective move towards the light of justice, and Anna, the families and the survivors carry on in hope.

*To be continued …*

# Appendix

## Death Records – Tuam Mother and Baby Home

| SURNAME | FORENAME | DOD | AGE |
| --- | --- | --- | --- |
| Derrane | Patrick | 22/08/1925 | 5 months |
| Blake | Mary | 23/09/1925 | 3 ½ months |
| Griffin | Matthew | 18/10/1925 | 3 months |
| Kelly | Mary | 06/12/1925 | 6 months |
| Lally | Peter | 25/12/1925 | 11 months |
| Hynes | Julia | 26/12/1925 | 1 year |
| Murray | James | 04/11/1925 | 4 weeks |
| McWilliam | Joseph | 05/03/1926 | 6 months |
| Mullen | John | 09/03/1926 | 2 ½ months |
| Wade | Mary | 05/04/1926 | 3 years 3 months |
| McTigue | Maud | 08/04/1926 | 6 years 6 months |
| Lynch | Bernard | 15/04/1926 | 3 years |
| Glynn | Bridget | 17/04/1926 | 1 year |
| Shaughnessy | Martin | 18/04/1926 | 1 year 6 months |
| Glynn | Margaret | 19/04/1926 | 1 year |
| Gorham | Patrick | 20/04/1926 | 1 year 9 months |
| O'Connell | Patrick | 21/04/1926 | 1 year |

| SURNAME | FORENAME | DOD | AGE |
|---|---|---|---|
| Carty | John | 22/04/1926 | 1 year 9 months |
| Bernard | Madeline | 22/04/1926 | 2 years 6 months |
| Kenny | Maureen | 22/04/1926 | 8 years |
| Donohue | Kathleen | 24/04/1926 | 1 year |
| Donelan | Thomas | 26/04/1926 | 2 years 3 months |
| Quilan | Mary | 26/04/1926 | 2 years 6 months |
| King | Mary | 26/04/1926 | 9 months |
| Warde | Mary | 27/04/1926 | 1 year 9 months |
| Coyne | George | 27/04/1926 | 2 years 6 months |
| Cummins | Julia | 29/04/1926 | 1 year 6 months |
| Folan or Wallace | Barbara | 30/04/1926 | 9 months |
| Carter | Pauline | 30/04/1926 | 11 months |
| Walsh | Mary | 30/04/1926 | 1 year |
| Stankard | Annie | 30/04/1926 | 10 months |
| Connelly | John | 01/05/1926 | 9 months |
| Cooke | Anthony | 01/05/1926 | 1 month |
| Casey | Michael | 10/05/1926 | 2 years 9 months |
| McCarron | Annie | 10/05/1926 | 2 years 3 months |
| Dunne | Patricia | 16/05/1926 | 2 months |
| Carty | John | 23/08/1926 | 3 months |

| SURNAME | FORENAME | DOD | AGE |
|---------|----------|-----|-----|
| Shaughnessy | Mary | 25/08/1926 | 4 ½ months |
| McNamara | Peter | 26/08/1926 | 7 weeks |
| Murphy | Mary | 01/09/1926 | 2 months |
| Coen | Joseph | 08/09/1926 | 5 months |
| Kelly | Patrick | 21/10/1926 | 2 ½ months |
| Rabbitte | Martin | 22/10/1926 | 6 weeks |
| Quinn | Kathleen | 08/11/1926 | 7 months |
| Halpin | Patrick | 10/12/1926 | 2 months |
| McGuinness | Martin | 31/12/1926 | 6 months |
| Connell | Mary Kate | 05/01/1927 | 3 ½ months |
| Canavan | Agnes | 08/03/1927 | 1 year 6 months |
| Lynch | Christina | 10/03/1927 | 1 year 3 months |
| O' Loughlin | Mary | 10/03/1927 | 6 months |
| Raftery | Patrick | 20/03/1927 | 7 months |
| Paterson | Patrick | 22/03/1927 | 5 months |
| Murray | James | 22/03/1927 | 1 ½ months |
| O' Loughlin | Colman | 31/03/1927 | 5 ½ months |
| O' Connor | Annie | 19/04/1927 | 1 year 3 months |
| Greally | John | 09/05/1927 | 11 months |
| Fenigan | Joseph | 24/05/1927 | 3 years 9 months |

| SURNAME | FORENAME | DOD | AGE |
|---------|----------|-----|-----|
| Connolly | Mary | 11/08/1927 | 2 months |
| Muldoon | James | 07/09/1927 | 4 months |
| Madden | Joseph | 18/10/1927 | 3 months |
| Devaney | Mary | 18/11/1927 | 1 year 6 months |
| Gannon | Michael | 18/01/1928 | 6 ½ months |
| Cunningham | Bridget | 22/01/1928 | 2 months |
| Conneely | Margaret | 20/02/1928 | 1 year 6 months |
| Warren | Patrick | 25/02/1928 | 8 ¼ months |
| Mulryan | James | 10/04/1928 | 1 month |
| Mahon | Mary | 11/04/1928 | 1 ¼ months |
| Fahey | Mary Kate | 04/05/1928 | 3 years |
| Flanagan | Martin | 25/05/1928 | 1 month |
| Forde | Mary | 19/07/1928 | 4 months |
| Hannon | Patrick | 02/09/1928 | 1 year 8 months |
| Donellan | Michael | 11/10/1928 | 6 months |
| Ward | Joseph | 24/11/1928 | 7 months |
| Jordan | Walter | 17/12/1928 | 3 years |
| Mullins | Mary | 18/12/1928 | 35 days |
| Christian | Peter | 26/01/1929 | 7 months |
| Cunningham | Mary | 29/01/1929 | 5 months |

| SURNAME | FORENAME | DOD | AGE |
|---------|----------|-----|-----|
| Ryan | James | 01/02/1929 | 9 months |
| O'Donnell | Patrick | 13/02/1929 | 9 months |
| Monaghan | Mary | 20/02/1929 | 4 years |
| O' Malley | Patrick | 12/03/1929 | 1 year |
| Healy | Philomena | 05/05/1929 | 11 months |
| Ryan | Michael | 20/05/1929 | 1 year |
| Curran | Patrick J | 08/07/1929 | 6 months |
| Fahy | Patrick | 27/07/1929 | 2 ½ months |
| Molloy | Laurence | 16/09/1929 | 5 months |
| Lynskey | Patrick | 07/10/1929 | 6 months |
| Nally | Vincent | 08/11/1929 | 1 year 9 months |
| Grady | Mary | 12/11/1929 | 1 year 6 months |
| Gould | Martin | 22/11/1929 | 1 year 9 months |
| Kelly | Patrick | 27/12/1929 | 2 ½ months |
| Quinn | Bridget | 02/03/1930 | 1 year |
| Reilly | William | 08/03/1930 | 9 months |
| Lestrange | George | 09/03/1930 | 7 months |
| Walsh | Christy | 03/05/1930 | 1 year 3 months |
| Gagen | Margaret Mary | 10/05/1930 | 1 year |
| Moran | Patrick | 25/06/1930 | 3 ½ months |

| SURNAME | FORENAME | DOD | AGE |
|---------|----------|-----|-----|
| Healy | Celia | 27/06/1930 | 4 ¾ months |
| Quinn | James | 26/11/1930 | 3 year 6 months |
| Walsh | Bridget | 04/12/1930 | 1 year 3 months |
| Shiels | Patrick | 27/01/1931 | 4 months |
| Drury | Mary Teresa | 03/02/1931 | 1 year |
| O'Brien | Peter | 10/02/1931 | 1 year 6 months |
| Malone | Peter | 20/02/1931 | 1 year 6 months |
| Burke | Mary | 26/02/1931 | 10 months |
| Moylan | Carmel | 03/03/1931 | 8 months |
| Garvey | Mary Josephine | 25/03/1931 | 4 ½ months |
| Warde | Mary | 11/04/1931 | 10 months |
| Howley | Catherine | 10/06/1931 | 8 ½ months |
| McKenna | Michael Patrick | 14/08/1931 | 3 months |
| Raftery | Richard | 24/12/1931 | 2 ½ months |
| Doorhy | Margaret | 25/01/1932 | 8 months |
| McDonagh | Mary | 02/02/1932 | 1 year |
| Leonard | Patrick | 06/02/1932 | 9 months |
| Coyne | Mary | 07/02/1932 | 1 year |
| Walsh | Mary Kate | 09/02/1932 | 2 years |
| Burke | Christina | 11/02/1932 | 1 year |

| SURNAME | FORENAME | DOD | AGE |
|---|---|---|---|
| Jordan | Mary Margaret | 14/02/1932 | 1 year 6 months |
| Sullivan | Annie | 15/02/1932 | 8 months |
| McCann | John Joseph | 16/02/1932 | 8 months |
| McMullan | Teresa | 17/02/1932 | 1 year |
| Gavin | George | 26/02/1932 | 1 year |
| Niland | Margaret | 26/02/1932 | 2 Years 6 months |
| O'Boyle | Joseph | 13/03/1932 | 2 months |
| Nash | Peter | 13/03/1932 | 1 year |
| Galvin | Bridget | 14/03/1932 | 3 months |
| Quinn | Christina | 22/03/1932 | 3 months |
| Cloran | Kathleen | 27/03/1932 | 9 years 6 months |
| Judge | Patricia | 07/05/1932 | 1 year |
| Birmingham | Mary | 09/05/1932 | 9 months |
| Hill | Laurence | 10/06/1932 | 11 months |
| Pender | Brendan Patrick | 18/06/1932 | 1 month |
| Fitzmaurice | Kate | 23/06/1932 | 4 months |
| Mulkerrins | None | 07/07/1932 | 5 days |
| Madden | Angela | 01/08/1932 | 3 months |
| Shaughnessy | Mary Christina | 05/01/1933 | 36 days |
| Moloney | Mary | 09/02/1933 | 11 months |

| SURNAME | FORENAME | DOD | AGE |
| --- | --- | --- | --- |
| Brennan | Patrick Joseph | 01/04/1933 | 5 weeks |
| O'Toole | Anthony | 04/04/1933 | 2 months |
| Cloherty | Mary | 08/04/1933 | 9 days |
| Fahy | Joseph | 29/04/1933 | 10 months |
| Cassidy | Martin | 17/05/1933 | 5 months |
| Walsh | Francis | 24/05/1933 | 2 ½ months |
| Cunniffe | Mary Finola | 05/06/1933 | 6 months |
| Garvey | Mary | 21/06/1933 | 4 months |
| Gilchrist | Kathleen | 01/07/1933 | 8 months |
| Walsh | Mary Kate | 14/07/1933 | 6 weeks |
| Fallon | Eileen | 10/08/1933 | 1 year 6 months |
| Leonard | Harry | 11/08/1933 | 3 months |
| Guilfoyle | Mary Kate | 14/08/1933 | 3 months |
| Callinan | John | 21/08/1933 | 3 months |
| Kilmartin | John | 22/08/1933 | 2 months |
| Shaughnessy | Julia | 31/08/1933 | 3 months |
| Ryan | Bridgid | 03/09/1933 | 9 months |
| Prendergast | Patrick | 06/09/1933 | 6 months |
| Fahy | Margaret Mary | 07/09/1933 | 1 year 6 months |
| Holland | Bridgid | 09/09/1933 | 2 months |

| SURNAME | FORENAME | DOD | AGE |
|---------|----------|-----|-----|
| Moran | Bridgid | 09/09/1933 | 1 year 4 months |
| Flattery | John | 20/09/1933 | 2 years 2 months |
| Brennan | Mary | 28/09/1933 | 4 months |
| Conole | Mary | 29/09/1933 | 1 month |
| Donohue | Margaret | 10/10/1933 | 10 months |
| Dunn | Joseph | 19/10/1933 | 3 years |
| Lenane | Owen | 06/11/1933 | 2 ½ months |
| Steed | Josephine | 09/11/1933 | 4 months |
| Meeneghan | Mary | 09/11/1933 | 4 months |
| McIntyre | James | 14/11/1933 | 3 months |
| Tuohy | Sheila | 07/01/1934 | 9 years |
| O'Gara | Margaret Mary | 08/01/1934 | 2 months |
| Murphy | John Joseph | 11/01/1934 | 4 months |
| Butler | Eileen | 16/01/1934 | 2 months |
| Molloy | Thomas | 22/01/1934 | 2 months |
| Bodkin | James Joseph | 24/01/1934 | 6 months |
| Kelly | John | 28/01/1934 | 2 ½ months |
| Walsh | Mary | 30/01/1934 | 6 months |
| Colohan | Mary Josephine | 17/02/1934 | 4 months |
| Conneely | Florence | 20/02/1934 | 7 months |

| SURNAME | FORENAME | DOD | AGE |
|---------|----------|-----|-----|
| McCann | Norah | 01/03/1934 | 6 weeks |
| Kelly | Mary | 02/03/1934 | 9 months |
| O'Dowd | Rose | 19/03/1934 | 6 months |
| Egan | Mary | 06/04/1934 | 4 months |
| Concannon | Michael | 09/04/1934 | 4 months |
| Joyce | Paul | 26/04/1934 | 10 months |
| Kennedy | Mary Christina | 07/05/1934 | 4 months |
| Finnegan | Bridget | 23/05/1934 | 2 ½ months |
| Flaherty | Mary | 21/06/1934 | 3 months |
| McDonagh | Thomas | 27/07/1934 | 4 months |
| Hoey | Joseph | 22/09/1934 | 1 year 1 month |
| Cunniffe | Teresa | 04/10/1934 | 1 year 1 month |
| Clohessy | Joseph | 20/10/1934 | 2 months |
| Kiely | Mary | 09/11/1934 | 4 months |
| Cloran | Thomas | 18/11/1934 | 6 months |
| Burke | Mary | 26/11/1934 | 3 months |
| Flaherty | Mary Margaret | 17/12/1934 | 4 months |
| Keane | John | 20/12/1934 | 17 days |
| Ward | Luke | 23/12/1934 | 1 year 3 months |
| O'Reilly | Mary | 24/12/1934 | 5 months |

| SURNAME | FORENAME | DOD | AGE |
|---|---|---|---|
| Mountgomery | Ellen | 22/01/1935 | 1 year 6 months |
| Lydon | Mary Elizabeth | 10/02/1935 | 4 months |
| Nealon | Mary | 14/02/1935 | 7 months |
| Murphy | Mary Margaret | 18/02/1935 | 4 months |
| Madden | Brigid | 20/02/1935 | 4 months |
| Linnane | Stephen | 27/02/1935 | 3 ½ months |
| Walsh | Josephine | 04/03/1935 | 1 year |
| Cunningham | Kate | 09/03/1935 | 2 months |
| Hibbett | Mary Bernadette | 12/03/1935 | 1 month |
| Linnane | Thomas | 28/03/1935 | 3 ½ months |
| Linnane | Michael | 28/04/1935 | 1 year 3 months |
| Glenane | Bridget | 29/05/1935 | 5 weeks |
| Lane | Patrick | 06/06/1935 | 3 months |
| Conway | Mary Anne | 07/06/1935 | 2 months |
| Kane | James | 19/09/1935 | 8 months |
| Leech | Christopher | 27/10/1935 | 3 months |
| McCann | Elizabeth Ann | 20/12/1935 | 5 months |
| Coen | Margaret Mary | 27/12/1935 | 2 months |
| O'Toole | John | 04/01/1936 | 7 months |
| Creshal | John | 15/01/1936 | 3 ½ months |

| SURNAME | FORENAME | DOD | AGE |
|---------|----------|-----|-----|
| Egan | Mary Teresa | 27/01/1936 | 3 months |
| Boyle | Michael | 28/01/1936 | 3 months |
| Ridge | Peter | 04/02/1936 | 4 months |
| Mannion | Anthony | 12/02/1936 | 6 weeks |
| Dowd | Donald | 27/02/1936 | 5 months |
| Collins | Eileen | 26/03/1936 | 2 months |
| Brennan | Mary | 28/03/1936 | 2 months |
| Fahy | James | 04/05/1936 | 5 months |
| Geraghty | Bridget | 10/04/1936 | 11 days |
| Hynes | Patrick Joseph | 16/05/1936 | 4 months |
| Hannon | Martin | 02/06/1936 | 6 months |
| Coyne | Martin | 09/06/1936 | 7 months |
| Leech | Mary Nuala | 15/06/1936 | 1 year |
| Monaghan | Michael | 30/06/1936 | 3 ½ months |
| O'Donnell | Patrick Aiden | 07/07/1936 | 2 months |
| Baker | Martin | 03/09/1936 | 3 months |
| Browne | Mary | 17/09/1936 | 4 months |
| Daly | Angela | 10/10/1936 | 1 year |
| Joyce | Mary Teresa | 10/10/1936 | 5 months |
| Coy | Francis | 16/10/1936 | 6 months |

| SURNAME | FORENAME | DOD | AGE |
|---|---|---|---|
| McLoughlin | Margret Rose | 20/11/1936 | 4 months |
| Walsh | Mary Philomena | 27/11/1936 | 7 months |
| Gleeson | Joan | 29/11/1936 | 1 year 2 months |
| Fahy | Michael Joseph | 29/11/1936 | 1 year 5 months |
| Walsh | Michael John | 02/12/1936 | 7 months |
| Corcoran | Annie | 02/12/1936 | 11 months |
| Mee | Michael | 04/12/1936 | 1 year 1 month |
| Hynes | Kathleen | 05/12/1936 | 10 months |
| Coyne | John | 05/12/1936 | 1 year 4 months |
| O'Toole | Michael | 06/12/1936 | 1 year 5 months |
| Feeney | Michael Edward | 07/12/1936 | 1 year 1 month |
| Conroy | Alfred | 07/12/1936 | 1 year 8 months |
| Ryan | Margaret | 07/12/1936 | 1 year 10 months |
| O'Reilly | Mary Kate | 09/12/1936 | 1 year |
| Joyce | Patrick | 09/12/1936 | 1 year 1 month |
| Munnelly | Edward | 10/12/1936 | 7 months |
| Leech | Bernadette | 13/12/1936 | 1 year 6 months |
| Flaherty | Thomas | 20/12/1936 | 3 years |
| Cummins | Teresa | 20/12/1936 | 3 weeks |
| Kilbane | Edward Desmond | 21/12/1936 | 2 years 6 month |

| SURNAME | FORENAME | DOD | AGE |
|---------|----------|-----|-----|
| Scanlon | Margaret | 22/12/1936 | 3 years 6 months |
| Larkin | Mary Bridget | 22/12/1936 | 8 months |
| O'Malley | Brian | 23/12/1936 | 4 months |
| Madden | Michael | 24/12/1936 | 6 months |
| Cahill | Mary Kate | 15/01/1937 | 2 weeks |
| Lydon | Mary Margaret | 20/01/1937 | 3 months |
| Sullivan | Festus | 21/01/1937 | 1 month |
| Curley | Annie | 16/03/1937 | 3 weeks |
| Lydon | Nuala | 11/04/1937 | 5 months |
| Collins | Bridget | 21/04/1937 | 5 weeks |
| Coleman | Patrick Joseph | 23/04/1937 | 1 month |
| Hannon | Joseph | 06/05/1937 | 6 weeks |
| Monaghan | Henry | 14/05/1937 | 3 weeks |
| Shiels | Michael Joseph | 17/05/1937 | 7 weeks |
| Sheridan | Martin | 18/05/1937 | 5 weeks |
| Loftus | John Patrick | 30/05/1937 | 10 months |
| Murphy | Patrick Joseph | 05/06/1937 | 3 months |
| McHugh | Catherine | 07/06/1937 | 4 months |
| Togher | Mary Patricia | 14/06/1937 | 3 ½ months |
| Sheridan | Mary Kate | 05/08/1937 | 4 months |

| SURNAME | FORENAME | DOD | AGE |
|---------|----------|-----|-----|
| Flaherty | Mary | 13/08/1937 | 1 year 7 months |
| Conroy | Eileen | 15/09/1937 | 1 year |
| Walsh | Mary Anne | 16/09/1937 | 1 year 2 months |
| Quinn | Eileen | 23/09/1937 | 2 years 6 months |
| Burke | Patrick | 25/09/1937 | 9 months |
| Holland | Margaret | 30/09/1937 | 2 days |
| Langan | Joseph | 03/12/1937 | 6 months |
| O'Grady | Sabina Pauline | 13/12/1937 | 6 months |
| Qualter | Patrick | 13/12/1937 | 3 years 9 months |
| King | Mary | 18/12/1937 | 5 months |
| Nee | Mary | 04/01/1938 | 4 months |
| Lydon | Charles | 09/01/1938 | 9 months |
| Larkin | Martin Andrew | 13/01/1938 | 1 year 2 months |
| Keane | Mary | 14/01/1938 | 3 weeks |
| Cuffe | Kathleen Veronica | 21/01/1938 | 5 ½ months |
| Linnane | Margaret | 23/01/1938 | 3 ½ months |
| Heneghan | Teresa | 23/01/1938 | 3 months |
| Neary | John | 25/01/1938 | 7 months |
| Madden | Patrick | 25/01/1938 | 4 months |
| Cafferty | Mary | 08/03/1938 | 2 months |

| SURNAME | FORENAME | DOD | AGE |
|---|---|---|---|
| Keane | Mary Kate | 12/03/1938 | 3 months |
| Hynes | Patrick | 30/03/1938 | 3 weeks |
| Solan | Annie | 10/04/1938 | 2 months |
| Mullins | Margaret | 23/04/1938 | 6 ½ months |
| Mulligan | Mary | 22/05/1938 | 2 months |
| Lally | Anthony | 03/06/1938 | 5 months |
| Spelman | Joseph | 06/06/1938 | 6 weeks |
| Begley | Annie | 07/06/1938 | 3 months |
| Egan | Vincent | 10/06/1938 | 9 days |
| Garvey | Patrick | 17/06/1938 | 6 months |
| Murphy | Nora | 01/07/1938 | 5 months |
| Burke | Patricia | 06/07/1938 | 4 months |
| Barret | Winifred | 07/08/1938 | 2 years 6 months |
| Marron | Agnes | 22/09/1938 | 3 months |
| Kennedy | Christopher | 12/12/1938 | 4 ½ months |
| Harrington | Patrick | 19/12/1938 | 7 days |
| Devine | Kathleen | 10/01/1939 | 2 years |
| Garaghan | Vincent | 18/01/1939 | 22 days |
| Gibbons | Ellen | 23/01/1939 | 6 months |
| McGrath | Michael | 29/01/1939 | 4 months |

| SURNAME | FORENAME | DOD | AGE |
|---|---|---|---|
| Fraser | Edward | 30/01/1939 | 3 months |
| McLoughlin | Patrick | 08/02/1939 | 4 ½ months |
| Lally | Bridget | 08/03/1939 | 1 year |
| Duffy | Nora | 13/03/1939 | 3 months |
| Healy | Martin | 18/03/1939 | 4 months |
| Higgins | Margaret | 17/04/1939 | 5 days |
| Egan | Patrick | 21/04/1939 | 6 months |
| Farragher | Vincent | 05/05/1939 | 11 months |
| Jordan | Patrick Joseph | 06/05/1939 | 3 months |
| Hanley | Michael | 19/05/1939 | 21 days |
| Gilmore | Catherine | 24/05/1939 | 3 months |
| Carney | Unknown (boy) | 08/06/1939 | 7 ½ hours |
| Coyne | Annie | 13/06/1939 | 3 months |
| Cosgrave | Helena | 05/07/1939 | 5 months |
| Walsh | Thomas | 11/07/1939 | 2 months |
| Walsh | Unknown (boy) | 25/07/1939 | 10 minutes |
| Hession | Kathleen | 02/10/1939 | 3 ½ months |
| Hurley | Brigid | 12/10/1939 | 10 ½ months |
| Beegan | Ellen | 27/12/1939 | 2 months |
| Keogh | Mary | 29/12/1939 | 1 year |

| SURNAME | FORENAME | DOD | AGE |
|---------|----------|-----|-----|
| Burke | Bridget | 30/12/1939 | 2 ½ months |
| Reilly | Martin | 08/01/1940 | 9 months |
| Hughes | Martin | 24/01/1940 | 11 months |
| Connolly | Mary | 24/01/1940 | 1 month |
| Ruane | Mary Kate | 27/01/1940 | 41 days |
| Mulchrone | Joseph | 28/01/1940 | 3 ½ months |
| Williams | Michael | 05/02/1940 | 1 year 2 months |
| Moran | Martin | 22/02/1940 | 7 weeks |
| Henry | James | 11/03/1940 | 5 weeks |
| Mahoney | Josephine | 07/04/1940 | 2 months |
| Staunton | Bridget | 03/06/1940 | 5 months |
| Creaven | John | 05/06/1940 | 13 days |
| Lydon | Peter | 01/07/1940 | 6 weeks |
| Ruane | Patrick Joseph | 10/07/1940 | 3 ½ months |
| Quinn | Michael | 10/07/1940 | 7 ½ months |
| Coen | Julia | 15/07/1940 | 6 days |
| McAndrew | Annie | 20/07/1940 | 5 months |
| Walsh | John | 23/07/1940 | 3 months |
| Flaherty | Patrick | 24/07/1940 | 6 months |
| Purcell | Bernadette | 05/08/1940 | 2 years 6 months |

| SURNAME | FORENAME | DOD | AGE |
|---|---|---|---|
| Macklin | Joseph | 20/08/1940 | 33 hours |
| Duffy | Thomas | 24/08/1940 | 2 days |
| Fahy | Elizabeth | 29/08/1940 | 3 ½ months |
| Kelly | James | 02/09/1940 | 2 months |
| Gallagher | Nora | 10/09/1940 | 3 ½ months |
| Cannon | Kathleen | 13/09/1940 | 4 months |
| Tighe | Winifred | 29/10/1940 | 8 months |
| Williams | Christopher | 31/10/1940 | 1 year |
| Lynch | Joseph | 31/10/1940 | 1 year |
| McHugh | Andrew | 02/11/1940 | 1 year 3 months |
| Glennan | William | 03/11/1940 | 1 year 6 months |
| Kelly | Michael J | 10/11/1940 | 5 months |
| Gallagher | Patrick | 28/11/1940 | 3 months |
| Keane | Michael Gerard | 13/12/1940 | 2 months |
| Lawless | Ellen | 27/12/1940 | 5 ½ months |
| Finn | Mary | 12/01/1941 | 2 ½ months |
| Timlin | Martin | 13/01/1941 | 3 months |
| McLoughlin | Mary | 22/01/1941 | 20 days |
| Brennan | Mary | 02/02/1941 | 5 months |
| Egan | Patrick Dominick | 20/02/1941 | 1 month |

| SURNAME | FORENAME | DOD | AGE |
|---------|----------|-----|-----|
| Thornton | Nora | 22/02/1941 | 1 year 5 months |
| Joyce | Anne | 22/02/1941 | 1 year |
| Kelly | Catherine | 02/03/1941 | 10 months |
| Monaghan | Michael | 13/03/1941 | 8 months |
| Hargraves | Simon John | 28/03/1941 | 6 months |
| Forde | Unknown (girl) | 09/04/1941 | 7 hours |
| Byrne | Joseph | 09/04/1941 | 2 months |
| Hegarty | Patrick | 11/04/1941 | 4 months |
| Corcoran | Patrick | 11/04/1941 | 1 month |
| Leonard | James | 25/04/1941 | 16 days |
| Gormley | Jane | 03/06/1941 | 22 days |
| Ruane | Anne | 05/06/1941 | 11 days |
| Munnelly | Patrick | 06/06/1941 | 3 months |
| Lavelle | John | 06/06/1941 | 6 weeks |
| Ruane | Patrick | 18/06/1941 | 24 days |
| Quinn | Patrick Joseph | 25/06/1941 | 3 months |
| Kennelly | Joseph | 05/07/1941 | 15 days |
| Monaghan | Kathleen | 12/07/1941 | 3 months |
| Quinn | Unknown (girl) | 13/07/1941 | 2 days |
| Roche | Anthony | 17/07/1941 | 3 ½ months |

| SURNAME | FORENAME | DOD | AGE |
|---------|----------|-----|-----|
| Roughneen | Annie | 29/07/1941 | 3 weeks |
| O'Hara | Anne Kate | 25/08/1941 | 3 ¾ months |
| Nevin | Patrick Joseph | 09/09/1941 | 3 months |
| Hopkins | John Joseph | 19/09/1941 | 3 months |
| Gibbons | Thomas | 18/11/1941 | 1 month |
| McTigue | Winifred | 22/11/1941 | 6 ½ months |
| Begley | Thomas Joseph | 24/11/1941 | 1 ½ months |
| Heneghan | Kathleen | 01/01/1942 | 25 days |
| Murphy | Elizabeth | 24/01/1942 | 4 months |
| Farnan | Nora | 28/01/1942 | 1 month |
| Tarpey | Teresa | 04/02/1942 | 1 month |
| Carey | Margaret | 05/02/1942 | 11 months |
| Garvey | John | 14/02/1942 | 6 weeks |
| Goldrick | Bridget | 16/02/1942 | 3 ½ months |
| White | Bridget | 20/02/1942 | 2 ½ months |
| Slattery | Noel | 21/02/1942 | 1 month |
| Connaughton | Mary Teresa | 27/02/1942 | 3 ½ months |
| McCormack | Nora | 03/03/1942 | 6 weeks |
| Hefferon | Joseph | 17/03/1942 | 5 months |
| Higgins | Mary | 20/03/1942 | 9 days |

| SURNAME | FORENAME | DOD | AGE |
|---------|----------|-----|-----|
| Farrell | Mary | 23/03/1942 | 21 days |
| McDonnell | Mary | 12/04/1942 | 1 month |
| Cunniffe | Geraldine | 13/04/1942 | 11 weeks |
| Mannion | Michael | 14/04/1942 | 3 months |
| McHugh | Bridget | 18/04/1942 | 7 months |
| McEvady | Mary | 19/04/1942 | 1 year 6 months |
| Walsh | Helena | 21/04/1942 | 2 ½ months |
| McDoell | William | 01/05/1942 | 2 days |
| Finn | Michael | 09/05/1942 | 1 year 2 months |
| Murphy | Mary | 12/05/1942 | 10 months |
| Glynn | Gertrude | 19/05/1942 | 6 months |
| Flaherty | Joseph | 05/06/1942 | 7 weeks |
| O'Malley | Mary | 20/06/1942 | 4 years 6 months |
| Callanan | John Patrick | 23/06/1942 | 13 days |
| McDonnell | Unknown (girl) | 28/06/1942 | ½ hour |
| McDonnell | Unknown (girl) | 28/06/1942 | ½ hour |
| Burke | Christopher | 29/06/1942 | 9 months |
| Connolly | Stephen | 12/08/1942 | 7 ½ months |
| Atkinson | Mary | 16/08/1942 | 6 months |
| Richardson | Francis | 10/10/1942 | 1 year 3 months |

| SURNAME | FORENAME | DOD | AGE |
|---------|----------|-----|-----|
| Rice | Michael John | 10/10/1942 | 6 months |
| Carr | Nora | 12/10/1942 | 3 ½ months |
| Walsh | William | 14/10/1942 | 1 year 4 months |
| Cunnane | Vincent | 15/10/1942 | 1 year 2 months |
| Coady | Eileen | 16/10/1942 | 10 months |
| Roache | Unknown (girl) | 19/10/1942 | 23 hours |
| Roache | Unknown (boy) | 19/10/1942 | 23 hours |
| Flannery | Patrick | 01/11/1942 | 2 months |
| Spelman | Margaret | 26/11/1942 | 3 ½ months |
| Dermody | John | 02/12/1942 | 3 months |
| Finn | Vincent | 02/12/1942 | 8 ½ months |
| Nally | Austin | 10/12/1942 | 3 months |
| Dolan | Margaret | 12/12/1942 | 2 ½ months |
| Grogan | Bridget | 23/12/1942 | 6 months |
| Cloran | Thomas Patrick | 07/01/1943 | 9 weeks |
| Devere | Catherine | 02/02/1943 | 1 month |
| Glynn | Mary Josephine | 03/02/1943 | 1 day |
| Connolly | Annie | 04/02/1943 | 9 months |
| Cosgrove | Martin | 06/02/1943 | 7 weeks |
| Cunningham | Catherine | 08/02/1943 | 2 years 6 months |

| SURNAME | FORENAME | DOD | AGE |
|---------|----------|-----|-----|
| Hardiman | Bridget | 08/02/1943 | 1 ½ months |
| Grier | Mary | 11/02/1943 | 4 ½ months |
| McCormick | Mary Patricia | 11/02/1943 | 2 months |
| Muldoon | Brendan | 13/02/1943 | 5 weeks |
| Moran | Nora | 15/02/1943 | 7 months |
| Maher | Joseph | 17/02/1943 | 20 days |
| Dooley | Teresa | 19/02/1943 | 3 months |
| Tully | Daniel | 23/02/1943 | 6 ½ months |
| Durkan | Brendan | 01/03/1943 | 28 days |
| O'Connor | Sheila | 03/03/1943 | 3 months |
| Coen | Annie | 12/03/1943 | 5 ½ months |
| Kennedy | Patrick Joseph | 23/03/1943 | 6 days |
| Walsh | Thomas | 28/03/1943 | 2 months |
| Rice | Patrick | 29/03/1943 | 11 ½ months |
| McGowan | Edward | 11/04/1943 | 10 ¾ months |
| Egan | Brendan | 12/04/1943 | 10 ½ months |
| McDonagh | Margaret | 14/04/1943 | 35 days |
| Donellan | Annie Josephine | 15/04/1943 | 10 months |
| Walsh | Thomas | 15/04/1943 | 14 days |
| Quinn | Bridget | 04/05/1943 | 5 ¾ months |

| SURNAME | FORENAME | DOD | AGE |
|---|---|---|---|
| Mulkerins | Mary | 12/05/1943 | 5 weeks |
| Parkinson | Kathleen | 17/05/1943 | 10 months |
| Flynn | Sheila Madeline | 26/05/1943 | 3 ½ months |
| Maloney | Patrick Joseph | 01/06/1943 | 2 months |
| Carney | Bridget | 04/06/1943 | 7 months |
| O'Connor | Mary Margaret | 09/06/1943 | 6 months |
| Geraghty | Joseph | 10/06/1943 | 3 months |
| Coen | Annie | 10/06/1943 | 10 months |
| Feeney | Martin Joseph | 13/06/1943 | 3 ½ months |
| Finnegan | Anthony | 15/06/1943 | 3 months |
| Coady | Patrick | 22/06/1943 | 3 months |
| Cunningham | Unknown (male) | 25/06/1943 | 1 ½ hours |
| Fahy | Annie | 28/06/1943 | 3 months |
| Byrne | Unknown (girl) | 16/07/1943 | 18 ½ hours |
| Mullaney | Patrick | 13/08/1943 | 1 year 6 months |
| Connelly | Thomas | 13/08/1943 | 2 ½ months |
| Larkin | Mary | 19/09/1943 | 2 months |
| Kelly | Margaret | 30/09/1943 | 3 ½ months |
| McDonagh | Barbara | 07/10/1943 | 4 months |
| O'Brien | Mary | 21/10/1943 | 3 ¼ months |

| SURNAME | FORENAME | DOD | AGE |
|---|---|---|---|
| Hennelly | Keiran | 04/11/1943 | 1 year 2 months |
| Folan | Annie | 17/11/1943 | 3 ½ months |
| McNamara | Unknown (girl) | 26/12/1943 | 12 hours |
| Murphy | Julia | 26/12/1943 | 2 ½ months |
| Rockford | John | 13/01/1944 | 4 months |
| Geraghty | Vincent | 14/01/1944 | 1 year |
| Deane | Anthony | 29/01/1944 | 2 days |
| O'Brien | Unknown (boy) | 24/02/1944 | 2 ¼ days |
| O'Brien | Mary Teresa | 06/03/1944 | 15 days |
| Connelly | John | 10/03/1944 | 2 ¼ months |
| Murphy | Bridget | 22/03/1944 | 2 ¼ months |
| Dunne | Patricia | 25/03/1944 | 2 months |
| Sweeney | Joseph | 25/03/1944 | 20 days |
| Kinahan | Francis | 28/03/1944 | 23 days |
| O'Hagan | Josephine | 29/03/1944 | 6 months |
| Lavin | Patrick | 30/03/1944 | 1 month |
| Glynn | Annie Maria | 30/03/1944 | 13 months |
| Moore | Kate Agnes | 09/04/1944 | 1 ¾ months |
| Kearns | Kevin | 12/04/1944 | 1 year 3 months |
| Doocey | Thomas | 12/04/1944 | 1 year 3 months |

| SURNAME | FORENAME | DOD | AGE |
| --- | --- | --- | --- |
| Conneely | William | 15/04/1944 | 8 months |
| Spelman | Margaret | 22/04/1944 | 1 year 3 months |
| Cullen | Mary Kate | 24/04/1944 | 1 year 10 months |
| Brown | Kathleen | 27/04/1944 | 3 years |
| Kelly | Julia | 30/04/1944 | 1 year 7 months |
| Connolly | Mary | 30/04/1944 | 7 years |
| Harrison | Catherine | 30/04/1944 | 2 year 3 months |
| Forde | Eileen | 07/05/1944 | 1 year 9 months |
| Monaghan | Michael | 27/05/1944 | 2 years |
| Lenihan | Mary Frances | 05/06/1944 | 3 days |
| Byrne | Anthony | 11/06/1944 | 6 months |
| Thornton | Jarlath | 15/06/1944 | 7 weeks |
| Kelly | John | 24/06/1944 | 6 days |
| O'Brien | Joseph | 25/06/1944 | 1 year 6 months |
| Hyland | Anthony | 30/07/1944 | 2 year 6 months |
| Murray | Unknown (boy) | 03/08/1944 | 8 hours |
| Murray | Unknown (girl) | 03/08/1944 | 10 hours |
| McDonnell | Joseph Francis | 05/08/1944 | 11 days |
| Walsh | Mary | 05/09/1944 | 1 year 3 months |
| Glynn | Unknown (boy) | 16/09/1944 | 16 hours |

| SURNAME | FORENAME | DOD | AGE |
|---------|----------|-----|-----|
| Gaughan | James | 25/10/1944 | 1 year 2 months |
| Walsh | Margaret | 30/10/1944 | 3 ½ months |
| Moran | Mary Philomena | 26/11/1944 | 9 days |
| Malone | John Francis | 03/12/1944 | 7 days |
| Dempsey | Michael Francis | 01/01/1945 | 7 weeks |
| Greally | Christina Martha | 12/01/1945 | 3 ½ months |
| Donnellan | Teresa | 23/01/1945 | 42 days |
| King | Rose Anne | 07/02/1945 | 5 weeks |
| Joyce | Christopher John | 13/02/1945 | 1 ¼ months |
| Mannion | James | 22/02/1945 | 7 ½ months |
| Sullivan | Mary Teresa | 05/03/1945 | 3 weeks |
| Holohan | Patrick | 09/03/1945 | 11 months |
| Keane | Michael Joseph | 24/03/1945 | 24 days |
| Keaney | Bridget | 07/04/1945 | 2 months |
| Flaherty | Joseph | 20/04/1945 | 8 days |
| Mahady | Unknown (boy) | 08/05/1945 | 3 days |
| Rogers | James | 12/05/1945 | 10 days |
| Taylor | Kathleen Frances | 16/06/1945 | 9 months |
| Hogan | Gerard Christopher | 09/07/1945 | 6 ½ months |
| Corrigan | Kathleen | 03/08/1945 | 2 months |

| SURNAME | FORENAME | DOD | AGE |
|---|---|---|---|
| Connolly | Mary | 10/08/1945 | 3 months |
| Farrell | Patrick Joseph | 21/08/1945 | 5 months |
| Grehan | John Joseph | 08/09/1945 | 2 years |
| Hynes | Fabian | 28/09/1945 | 8 months |
| O'Malley | Edward | 17/10/1945 | 2 ½ months |
| Fleming | Mary | 29/10/1945 | 5 ¾ months |
| McHugh | Bridget Frances | 02/11/1945 | 2 ½ months |
| Folan | Michael | 04/11/1945 | 1 year 6 months |
| Holland | Oliver | 12/11/1945 | 6 months |
| Nevin | Ellen | 21/11/1945 | 7 months |
| Horan | Margaret | 26/11/1945 | 6 months |
| O'Brien | Teresa Frances | 06/12/1945 | 3 ½ months |
| Mullarky | Peter | 09/12/1945 | 4 months |
| Laffey | Patrick | 11/12/1945 | 3 ¼ years |
| O'Brien | Mary Philomena | 13/12/1945 | 3 ¾ months |
| Kennedy | Mary | 15/12/1945 | 18 months |
| Carroll | Sara Ann | 23/12/1945 | 3 ½ months |
| Maye | Unknown (girl) | 24/12/1945 | 5 days |
| Devaney | Mary | 02/01/1946 | 21 days |
| McDonnell | Anthony | 09/01/1946 | 6 months |

| SURNAME | FORENAME | DOD | AGE |
|---------|----------|-----|-----|
| Molloy | Vincent | 21/01/1946 | 7 days |
| Lyons | John Patrick | 25/01/1946 | 5 months |
| Timlin | Gerald Aidan | 27/01/1946 | 3 days |
| Costelloe | Patrick | 29/01/1946 | 17 days |
| Henry | Martin Dermott | 02/02/1946 | 43 days |
| O'Grady | John Francis | 07/02/1946 | 1 month |
| Flaherty | Bridget Mary | 14/02/1946 | 12 days |
| Finnegan | Josephine | 15/02/1946 | 1 year 8 months |
| McGrath | Martin | 23/02/1946 | 3 days |
| Haugh | none | 10/03/1946 | 10 minutes |
| Frayne | James | 18/03/1946 | 1 month |
| Crealy | Mary Frances | 19/03/1946 | 14 days |
| Davey | Mary | 10/04/1946 | 2 months |
| Hoban | Patrick Joseph | 17/04/1946 | 11 days |
| Dolan | Angela | 19/04/1946 | 3 months |
| Laffey | Bernard | 24/04/1946 | 5 months |
| Waldron | Mary Ellen | 29/04/1946 | 8 months |
| O'Boyle | Terence | 11/05/1946 | 3 months |
| O'Hara | Mary Frances | 24/05/1946 | 1 month |
| Coneely | Bridget | 27/05/1946 | 4 months |

| SURNAME | FORENAME | DOD | AGE |
| --- | --- | --- | --- |
| Lyden | Mary | 29/05/1946 | 5 months |
| O'Toole | Austin | 01/06/1946 | 4 months |
| Devaney | Mary | 20/06/1946 | 3 months |
| Foley | Bridget | 26/06/1946 | 6 months |
| Kilkelly | Martin | 03/07/1946 | 40 days |
| Hehir | Thecla Monica | 15/07/1946 | 6 weeks |
| Mitchell | Patrick Anthony | 20/07/1946 | 3 months |
| Kearney | John | 24/08/1946 | 4 ¾ months |
| Kelly | John Joseph | 24/08/1946 | 3 months |
| Conneely | John | 03/09/1946 | 4 months |
| O'Toole | Stephen Laurence | 14/09/1946 | 2 months |
| Buckley | Thomas Alphonsus | 18/09/1946 | 5 weeks |
| Gilmore | Michael John | 21/09/1946 | 2 ½ months |
| Monaghan | Patrick Joseph | 09/11/1946 | 2 ½ months |
| Murray | Mary Teresa | 20/11/1946 | 2 months |
| McKeighe | Patrick | 25/11/1946 | 1 ½ months |
| Feeney | John Raymond | 28/11/1946 | 2 ½ months |
| Noone | Finbar | 01/12/1946 | 2 months |
| O'Brien | John | 08/12/1946 | 21 days |
| Keane | Beatrice | 08/12/1946 | 5 years |

| SURNAME | FORENAME | DOD | AGE |
|---|---|---|---|
| Veale | Mary Philomena | 09/12/1946 | 5 weeks |
| Gillespie | Winifred | 11/12/1946 | 1 year |
| Coen | Anthony | 13/12/1946 | 10 weeks |
| Sheridan | Michael Francis | 13/12/1946 | 3 months |
| Holden | Anne | 21/12/1946 | 3 months |
| O'Brien | Martin Joseph | 26/12/1946 | 7 weeks |
| Larkin | Winifred | 29/12/1946 | 1 month |
| Coen | Patrick Thomas | 07/01/1947 | 1 month |
| Joyce | Mary Bridget | 21/02/1947 | 8 months |
| Collins | Geraldine | 22/02/1947 | 1 year 1 month |
| Flaherty | Mary | 01/03/1947 | 5 days |
| Keogh | Vincent | 06/03/1947 | 5 months |
| Healy | John Francis | 09/03/1947 | 10 days |
| Kennelly | Martin Jarlath | 09/03/1947 | 24 days |
| Keaveney | Patrick | 17/03/1947 | 1 ½ months |
| Flynn | Philomena | 18/03/1947 | 2 months |
| Reilly | William | 20/03/1947 | 8 ½ months |
| Concannon | Margaret Nuala | 20/03/1947 | 1 year |
| Fitzpatrick | Patrick Joseph | 28/03/1947 | 14 days |
| Cunningham | Joseph | 13/04/1947 | 2 months |

| SURNAME | FORENAME | DOD | AGE |
|---|---|---|---|
| Flaherty | Mary Josephine | 16/04/1947 | 1 year 1 month |
| O'Connell | John | 20/05/1947 | 2 years 3 months |
| Murray | Kathleen | 22/05/1947 | 3 years |
| Hanley | Alphonsus | 25/05/1947 | 1 year 9 months |
| Muldoon | Bridget Pauline | 05/06/1947 | 11 months |
| Higgins | Patricia Christina | 07/06/1947 | 5 months |
| Kennedy | Catherine Bridget | 08/06/1947 | 1 ½ months |
| Dolan | John Desmond | 11/06/1947 | 1 year 3 months |
| Joynt | Stephen | 13/06/1947 | 2 years |
| Kearns | Catherine Teresa | 16/06/1947 | 2 years |
| Hurney | Margaret | 17/06/1947 | 2 years |
| Patton | John | 18/06/1947 | 2 years |
| Williams | Patrick Joseph | 18/06/1947 | 1 year 3 months |
| Hynes | Nora | 18/06/1947 | 8 months |
| Donohue | Anthony | 19/06/1947 | 2 years 6 months |
| McGreal | Brendan | 20/06/1947 | 1 year 1 month |
| Cafferky | Anthony | 01/07/1947 | 23 days |
| Ellesmere | Kenneth Anthony | 07/07/1947 | 1 day |
| Joyce | Mary Teresa | 10/07/1947 | 1 year 3 months |
| Conneely | Nora | 14/07/1947 | 1 year 1 month |

| SURNAME | FORENAME | DOD | AGE |
|---------|----------|-----|-----|
| Daly | Kathleen | 15/07/1947 | 1 year 6 months |
| Cullinane | Nora | 16/07/1947 | 2 years |
| Carroll | Mary Patricia | 30/07/1947 | 4 months |
| Collins | Thomas | 31/07/1947 | 1 year 5 months |
| Moloney | Margaret Mary | 07/08/1947 | 3 months |
| Tierney | Josephine | 08/08/1947 | 8 months |
| Deasy | Margaret Mary | 13/08/1947 | 3 months |
| Bane | Martin Francis | 15/08/1947 | 3 months |
| Kenny | Bridget Agatha | 23/08/1947 | 2 months |
| Kelly | Unknown (boy) | 06/09/1947 | 14 hours |
| Judge | Mary Teresa | 18/09/1947 | 1 year 3 months |
| Bennett | Paul Dominick | 18/09/1947 | 2 years 6 months |
| Giblin | Mary Bridget | 30/09/1947 | 1 year 1 month |
| Carroll | Sarah | 20/11/1947 | 8 months |
| Brehany | Francis | 02/12/1947 | 1 year |
| Conneely | Anne | 12/12/1947 | 6 weeks |
| Kelly | Patrick | 21/12/1947 | 2 years 6 months |
| McDonnell | James | 22/12/1947 | 4 months |
| Staunton | Josephine | 29/12/1947 | 5 days |
| Madden | Kathleen | 02/01/1948 | 2 months |

| SURNAME | FORENAME | DOD | AGE |
|---|---|---|---|
| Byrne | Mary Philomena | 05/01/1948 | 8 weeks |
| Byrce | Joseph | 20/02/1948 | 3 ¾ months |
| Byrne | Joseph | 21/02/1948 | 10 ½ months |
| Glynn | Kathleen | 22/02/1948 | 3 ½ months |
| Carr | John Joseph | 23/02/1948 | 3 weeks |
| Jordan | Augustine | 26/02/1948 | 9 months |
| Dwyer | Michael Francis | 04/03/1948 | 1 year 6 months |
| Murphy | Noel Christopher | 06/03/1948 | 1 year 2 months |
| McNamee | Margaret Mary | 11/03/1948 | 5 ½ months |
| Grealish | Patrick | 14/03/1948 | 6 weeks |
| O'Reilly | Bernadette | 23/03/1948 | 6 ½ months |
| Gardiner | Paul | 31/03/1948 | 10 months |
| Folan | Simon Thomas | 06/05/1948 | 9 weeks |
| Ferguson | Joseph | 25/07/1948 | 3 months |
| Heffernan | Peter Joseph | 30/07/1948 | 4 months |
| Killeen | Patrick Joseph | 01/08/1948 | 14 weeks |
| Halloran | Stephen | 07/08/1948 | 7 months |
| Grealish | Teresa | 19/08/1948 | 5 months |
| Finegan | Mary Anne | 20/08/1948 | 7 weeks |
| Joyce | Mary | 25/08/1948 | unknown |

| SURNAME | FORENAME | DOD | AGE |
|---|---|---|---|
| Keane | John | 06/10/1948 | 3 ½ months |
| Burke | Mary | 10/10/1948 | 8 ½ months |
| McTigue | Brigid | 22/11/1948 | 11 weeks |
| Broderick | Margaret Rose | 04/12/1948 | 8 months |
| Mannion | Martin | 05/12/1948 | 2 ¼ months |
| Riddell | Mary Margaret | 18/01/1949 | 8 months |
| Noonan | Thomas Joseph | 28/01/1949 | 7 weeks |
| Casey | Peter | 08/02/1949 | 10 months |
| Scully | Michael | 13/02/1949 | 3 months |
| Lyons | Unknown (boy) | 06/03/1949 | 5 days |
| Finnegan | Mary Margaret | 19/03/1949 | 3 months |
| McLoughlin | Hubert | 29/03/1949 | 4 months |
| Morley | Nicholas Patrick | 31/03/1949 | 3 months |
| Bane | Teresa | 03/04/1949 | 6 months |
| Forde | John | 06/04/1949 | 2 years |
| Kennedy | Patrick Joseph | 11/04/1949 | 5 weeks |
| Ryan | Michael Francis | 11/04/1949 | 3 days |
| Cunnane | Mary Patricia | 23/05/1949 | 2 ½ months |
| Sheridan | Margaret Patricia | 14/07/1949 | 3 ½ months |
| Nevin | Patrick Joseph | 20/09/1949 | 3 months |

| SURNAME | FORENAME | DOD | AGE |
|---------|----------|-----|-----|
| Nally | Joseph | 16/08/1949 | 4 ½ months |
| Burke | Christopher | 29/08/1949 | 3 months |
| Madden | Anne | 19/11/1949 | 7 weeks |
| Madden | Bridget Teresa | 22/11/1949 | 1 ¾ months |
| Murphy | Thomas | 24/11/1949 | 3 months |
| Carroll | Francis | 10/12/1949 | 1 ½ months |
| Linnan | Bridget Josephine | 17/12/1949 | 9 months |
| Staunton | Josephine | 25/12/1949 | 8 days |
| McKeigue | Mary Ellen | 28/12/1949 | 7 weeks |
| Mulchrone | Mary Josephine | 05/01/1950 | 2 ¼ months |
| Higgins | Catherine | 06/01/1950 | 4 years 3 months |
| Egan | Catherine Anne | 15/01/1950 | 2 ½ months |
| McQuaid | Thomas | 15/01/1950 | 3 ¼ months |
| Muldoon | Dermott | 16/02/1950 | 3 ¾ months |
| Hanley | Martin | 21/02/1950 | 9 weeks |
| Lally | John Joseph | 24/02/1950 | 3 months |
| Larkin | Brendan | 01/03/1950 | 4 ½ months |
| Bell | Unknown (boy) | 02/03/1950 | 3 hours |
| Larkin | Mary Josephine | 12/04/1950 | 6 ½ months |
| Fleming | Annie | 28/04/1950 | 8 ¾ months |

| SURNAME | FORENAME | DOD | AGE |
|---------|----------|-----|-----|
| McNulty | Colm Alphonsus | 13/05/1950 | 1 month |
| Flaherty | Walter | 27/07/1950 | 3 months |
| Burke | Sarah | 15/08/1950 | 15 days |
| Boyle | Mary Ann | 17/09/1950 | 5 months |
| Murphy | John Anthony | 25/09/1950 | 4 ½ months |
| Colohan | Joseph Augustine | 23/11/1950 | 3 ¾ months |
| Begley | Christopher Martin | 15/12/1950 | 18 days |
| Meehan | Catherine Ann | 09/01/1951 | 4 months |
| McLynskey | Martin | 11/01/1951 | 5 ½ months |
| Crehan | Mary Josephine | 16/01/1951 | 3 months |
| McDonagh | Mary Ann | 10/04/1951 | 2 months |
| Folan | Joseph | 13/04/1951 | 22 days |
| Barrett | Evelyn | 23/05/1951 | 4 months |
| Morris | Paul | 27/05/1951 | 4 months |
| Morris | Peter | 18/06/1951 | 4 ¾ months |
| Joyce | Mary Martyna | 20/09/1951 | 1 year 6 months |
| Lane | Mary Margaret | 03/10/1951 | 7 months |
| Noone | John | 10/02/1952 | 4 months |
| McDonnell | Anne Josephine | 31/03/1952 | 5 ½ months |
| Burke | Joseph Anthony | 17/04/1952 | 5 ½ months |

| SURNAME | FORENAME | DOD | AGE |
|---|---|---|---|
| Hardiman | Patrick | 30/04/1952 | 5 ½ months |
| Naughton | Patrick | 02/05/1952 | 12 days |
| Staunton | Josephine Teresa | 07/09/1952 | 2 days |
| Mills | John Joseph | 07/10/1952 | 4 ¾ months |
| Hastings | Unknown (boy) | 06/05/1953 | 3 hours |
| Donlon | Mary | 16/10/1953 | 4 months |
| Connolly | Nora | 01/12/1953 | 1 year 3 months |
| Heneghan | Anne | 23/01/1954 | 3 months |
| Keville | Mary | 21/01/1954 | 9 months |
| Murphy | Martin | 24/02/1954 | 5 months |
| McDonagh | Mary Barbara | 04/03/1954 | 5 months |
| Logue | Mary Philomena | 14/03/1954 | 5 months |
| Cooke | Margaret Elizabeth | 21/03/1954 | 6 months |
| Fahy | Anne Marian | 24/04/1954 | 3 ¾ months |
| Broderick | Mary Ann | 25/04/1954 | 1 year 2 months |
| Dillon | Anne | 31/05/1954 | 3 ½ months |
| Halloran | Imelda | 09/08/1954 | 2 years |
| Mulryan | Marian Brigid | 12/02/1955 | 10 months |
| Rafferty | Mary Christina | 29/03/1955 | 3 months |
| Gavin | Joseph | 24/05/1955 | 10 months |

| SURNAME | FORENAME | DOD | AGE |
|---|---|---|---|
| Howard | Nora Mary | 01/07/1955 | 3 ½ months |
| Heaney | Francis Martin | 25/07/1955 | 2 years 10 months |
| Dempsey | Joseph | 16/08/1955 | 3 months |
| Walsh | Patrick | 14/11/1955 | 3 weeks |
| Gavin | Dermot | 19/01/1956 | 2 weeks |
| Burke | Mary Christina | 14/05/1956 | 3 years 6 months |
| Burke | Patrick | 29/05/1956 | 1 year 11 days |
| Connaughton | Gerard | 03/09/1956 | 11 months |
| Nee | Paul Henry | 26/11/1956 | 4 ½ months |
| Murphy | Rose Marie | 01/12/1956 | 2 years 9 months |
| Folan | Peter | 29/12/1956 | 4 months |
| Reilly | Oliver | 30/12/1956 | 4 months |
| Browne | Stephen Noel | 02/01/1957 | 2 years |
| Connaire | Margaret | 09/01/1957 | 3 ½ months |
| Fallon | Baby (boy) | 30/05/1957 | 4 days |
| O'Malley | Geraldine | 26/05/1958 | 6 months |
| Conneely | Dolores | 10/04/1959 | 7 months |
| Maloney | Mary | 23/08/1959 | 3 ½ months |
| Carty | Mary | 15/01/1960 | 4 ½ months |